ALEXANDER BROTT

My Lives in Music

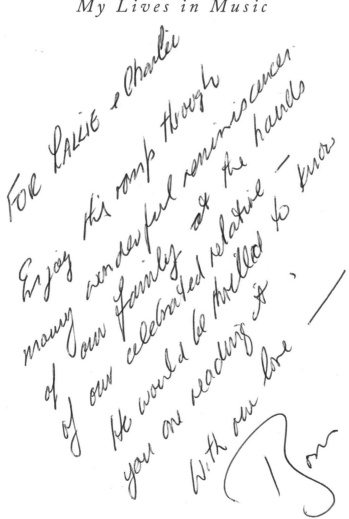

For Lallie & Charlie

Enjoy this romp through
many wonderful reminiscences
of our family at the hands
of our celebrated relative — I know
He would be thrilled to know
you are reading it

With our love

Alexander Brott

ALEXANDER BROTT

My Lives in Music

Alexander Brott & Betty Nygaard king

mosaic press

Library and Archives Canada Cataloguing in Publication

Brott, Alexander, 1915-
Alexander Brott : my lives in music / Alexander Brott
and Betty Nygaard King.

Autobiography.
ISBN 0-88962-854-8

1. Brott, Alexander, 1915-. 2. Conductors (Music)--Canada--
Biography.
3. Composers--Canada--Biography. 4. Violinists--Canada--Biography.
I. King, Betty Nygaard, 1955- II. Title. III. Title: My lives in music.

ML422.B874 2005   784.2'092   C2005-900865-2

Published by Mosaic Press, offices and warehouse at 1252 Speers Road, Units 1 and 2, Oakville, Ontario, L6L 5N9, Canada and Mosaic Press, PMB 145, 4500 Witmer Industrial Estates, Niagara Falls, NY, 14305-1386, U.S.A.

Mosaic Press acknowledges the assistance of the Canada Council and the Department of Canadian Heritage, Government of Canada through the Book Publishing Industry Development Program (BPIDP) for their support of our publishing activities.

Copyright © 2005, Alexander Brott & Betty Nygaard King
Designed by Keith Daniel
Printed and Bound in Canada.
ISBN 0-88962-854-8

**Canada Council
for the Arts**   **Conseil des Arts
du Canada**

Mosaic Press in Canada:
1252 Speers Road, Units 1 & 2
Oakville, Ontario
L6L 5N9
Phone/Fax: 905-825-2130
mosaicpress@on.aibn.com   www.mosaic-press.com

Mosaic Press in U.S.A.:
4500 Witmer Industrial Estates
PMB 145, Niagara Falls, NY
14305-1386
Phone/Fax: 1-800-387-8992
mosaicpress@on.aibn.com

Contents

A Note

As a violinist, Alexander Brott was concertmaster of the Montreal Orchestra, *Les Concerts Symphoniques* and *Orchestre Symphonique de Montréal*. He also toured Europe and North America as a solo violinist.

As a conductor, Alexander Brott guest-conducted most Canadian symphony orchestras, including the CBC Symphony Orchestra, Toronto Symphony, Montreal Symphony and Edmonton Symphony. He founded the McGill String Quartet and its successor, the McGill Chamber Orchestra, now celebrating its 65th season and also the Montreal Young Virtosi.

As a composer, his work number over 100 compositions which have been performed across Europe and North America by leading composers, including Sir Thomas Beecham, Pierre Monteux, Leopold Stokowski, Sir Malcolm Sargent, Sir Ernest MacMillan, Charles Munch and others.

As a teacher and educator, Alexander Brott was Professor of Music at McGill University, Head of the String Department and Composition Professor.

Among his numerous awards are the Bronze Medal for Composition at the Olympiads of London in 1948 and Helsinki in 1952, Fellow of the Royal Society of Arts of London, the Pro Mundi Beneficio Medal of the Brazilian Academy of Human Sciences, 1975, the Canadian Music Council Medal, 1976, Member of the Order of Canada, 1979, Knight of Malta of the Order of St. John of Jerusalem, 1985, *Chevalier de l'Ordre national de Quebec*, 1987, the Association of Canadian Orchestras Award, 1990, *Grand Montrealais*, 1993, Canada 125 and Queen's Jubilee Medals.

Preface

These memoirs were compiled from a variety of sources. Alexander Brott provided his memories of events and personalities during personal interviews, telephone conversations, and letters. Boris, Denis and Stephen Brott contributed many valuable family memories and anecdotes. The Brott family archives - an extensive collection of scrapbooks, newspaper and magazine clippings, concert programs, photographs, certificates, correspondence, other memorabilia, and recordings – were a rich source of material. The authors have endeavoured wherever possible to check facts, dates, and details against this archival material. Standard musical reference works, such as the New Grove Dictionary of Music and Musicians and the Encyclopedia of Music in Canada, various databases, and the files of the National Library of Canada Music Division, provided additional background information and confirmation of details.

The 75 year span of Alexander Brott's illustrious musical career posed challenges in terms of how to accurately reconstruct long-past events, while being true to Dr. Brott's memories and opinions, yet respectful of the feelings of others. After the passage of so many decades, some details, names and dates have faded. The individual impressions and memories that remain are what are important and these have been recounted on these pages. Some readers will, no doubt, have different memories or opinions of the events or personalities presented here, such is the richness of human experience. This volume is a personal memoir, not an academic history of the Montreal music scene.

We have tried to include a sketch, at least, of all significant aspects of Alexander Brott's life, but clearly, every aspect of his complex career could not be treated in detail. All of Dr. Brott's many colleagues who do not find their roles sufficiently acknowledged in these pages may be assured that their contribution has been deeply appreciated.

Bettry Nygaard King, January 2005

Lotte Brott in 16th century costume

Acknowledgements

I would like first to express my gratitude to:

Betty Nygaard King my co-author, for the countless hours of interview, the reading of my texts and the translation of my prose into an everyman's language. She has been a partner in every sense of the word in writing this book.

Howard Aster and Keith Daniel of Mosaic Press, my publisher. Without their confidence and commitment in accepting the book, detailed editing, invaluable suggestions and guidance the book would never have been realized.

My wife and life's partner Lotte, who is the inspiration of this book. Without her meticulous scrapbooks and record keeping Betty, Boris and I would never have been able to do the research which makes this book a valuable record of the achievements of almost a century of Montreal's music. And Talosa Timmins for her part in helping Lotte keep early records.

My son Boris for hundreds of hours of consultation, research, writing and re-writing, editing, seeking and finding of a publisher, selection of photographs, recollection of past incidents, helping me unlock my sentiments and being my true partner in the writing of this book. I also want to thank his wife Ardyth and their children Alexandra, David and Benjamin for giving me so much of Boris' time, as well as their advice and counsel. My Daughter-in-Law, Ardyth for extensive editing of the final proofs of the book.

My son Denis, for reading the text, providing insightful suggestions, checking references, helping research, writing one of the forewords and being there for me in my hours of need. I also want to thank his wife Julie and their children Talia, Aleta, Vanessa and Joshua.

My brother Steve for his many suggestions and recollections of our early youth.

Gisele Sherman for assistance in the preliminary edit of the first draft of the book. My secretary Lise Charette who worked with Lotte and me during over a quarter century and provided much guidance in research and assisted in typing so much of this book.

Alexander and Lotte

My housekeeper Luisa Mignogna who, like Madame Charette, shared the past fifteen years with Lotte and me. Louise provided recollection of events, documents for research and the physical task of finding and bringing scrapbooks and documents to me from our basement archives during the three years it took to write this book. Malou Alea ably assisted her in this.

McGill Chamber Orchestra Executive Director Susan McKinnon Bell for helping edit. Steven Kondaks, my esteemed musical colleague and member of the McGill String Quartet and later McGill Chamber Orchestra, who provided many recollections of our past lives.

Neil Chotem, my esteemed pianist/conductor/composer colleague, who awakened my memory to the days when we shared engagements under the aegis of CBC Drama Producer Rupert Kaplan. In addition other CBC producers with who I had the privilege of working: Kit Kinnaired, Pierre Mercure, Ted Farrant and Gilles Potvin.

Dr. Alexander McKay and John Peter Lee Roberts for reading early versions of the texts and providing invaluable input. Harry Pollack, colleague, fellow musician in the MSO and the sculptor of my bust which is displayed in the Salle Maisonneuve at Place des Arts, for his advice.

The Estate of the late Yousef Karsh, Jerry Fiedler Curator, for the use of his portrait of me, Jean Francois Berube for the use of his photo of me, and the Estate of the late Jack Markow for the use of his photographs.

Mildred Goodman for her assistance in recalling incidents in our youth and Tania Plaw for her advice and recollections of incidents during her forty year Presidency of the McGill Chamber Orchestra and her personal friendship.

Yaela Hertz for her advice and recollection of incidents during her long standing service as Concertmaster of the McGill Chamber Orchestra and personal friendship.

The Archives of the City of Montreal for their assistance in the research of Montreal Orchestras.

Arthur Kaptainis, Critic of the *Montreal Gazette*, for his assistance in researching files of the *Gazette* relating to my career and others with whom I worked.

Alexander Brott, January 2005

Foreword
by Denis Brott

Resilient, single-minded, proud, defiant, uncompromising – my father is a man who gives credence to the belief that in order to succeed in life, you must have a goal greater than your self.

It appears to have worked for him. At 89, he has yet to undergo a general anesthetic. He has defied illness that would have stopped many dead in their tracks. He has responded to medical treatment in almost miraculous ways. Anyone seeking a definition of the word "survivor" would do well to examine Alexander Brott's life story for inspiration.

My father, as this book outlines, has achieved numerous international successes and musical "firsts." Yet fate has not dealt kindly with him. It imposed hardships and illnesses that would have overcome many would-be heroes. Despite all this, Alexander Brott has never lost his flame, never failed to find ways to follow his muse. He allowed his work to be his inspiration and his savior. Still an active composer and conductor, he continues to find reasons to stare down life's onslaught and win. Now he has cracked his silence to share his perspectives on how he lived his life and from where springs his eternal flame, his raison d'être. It is truly a remarkable story.

Checkered throughout my many recollections of life with my dad, is one of his favorite sayings: "The more I know people, the more I like my dog!" Well, as of the fall of 2002, this octogenarian has undertaken yet another challenge - housebreaking a Shih Tzu puppy, appropriately and musically named Piccolo.

May he continue to love his dog and, through this autobiography, inspire us all with his zest for life. L'Chaim!

Foreword
by Boris Brott

Few men get a chance to really know their fathers. This is particularly true of fathers with dynamic careers and protective wives and mothers. Throughout the writing of this book, I was able to share in the unfolding story of my father, Alexander Brott, and in the process to know him and myself better. I have, as will you in the reading, relived the fascinating life of an ultimate survivor. In the process, I've learned something about the alchemy of living life to the full, yet with dignity, and of pursuing dreams and living fantasies.

This book is not just a catalogue of Alexander Brott's considerable achievements in classical music. It is a roller-coaster ride through World War II, the Great Depression, fabulous international successes and debilitating illnesses; it is a road-map to the enjoyment of great victories and survival of defeats by finding ways to re-invent yourself.

In these pages you will find motivation, inspiration, joy, sadness, and above all, the spirit of survival. Survival in style! I don't mean just by living well, but by giving something back to the world. Alexander Brott's ethic of survival can be seen in his creation of musical compositions with the breadth and vision of *War and Peace* or *From Sea to Sea*, or in his nurturing of performance organizations that bring great music-making into the lives of ordinary people. It is also present in his bringing up of two musical sons to continue his legacy, and in his fanciful lapidary creations, which make new fashions and liberate us from conventions.

Alexander Brott is an original. In this book, he not only tells us about his life, but encourages our own originality, our own courage to believe that in this life everything is possible - if you have the will to survive with substance.

Part 1

The Early Days of the McGill String Quartet

(1939–1950)

"Somebody help me with this goddamned door!" the recording engineer screamed.

I regained consciousness, painfully raised myself on my elbow, and looked around me in a daze. A huge crater appeared where the CBC studio floor had just been.

I then heard my wife's panicky voice shouting, "Alec, Alec, where are you?"

I peered through the fallen plaster, dust and smoke and was relieved to see she was safe. Only her silk scarf was ripped to shreds. I was amazed at how composed she looked – possibly in shock, as we all were. She clutched her unharmed cello in her hand.

And my precious violin?

Lotte's first words to me were, "Don't worry about your Rogeri."

It had been saved by the piano. The explosion had broken off one leg of the massive Steinway causing it to tilt toward the floor. The violin had slid unscathed into the cavity created there.

Lemieux shouted again. Just a minute ago I had called him out from his control booth to ask, "Are you sure you're getting your balance between the second violin and the viola?" The furnace had exploded at the very moment he came out of the booth, which saved him from falling into the deadly boiler room.

Now it was his turn to save our lives. The door he was pushing was the emergency escape to a lane that opened onto Ste Catherine Street.

Through the tangle of firetrucks, policemen, and crowds outside, a taxi pulled up. My mother and Boris ran out. They had heard about the explosion over the radio. Mother was terrified. Five year old Boris thought only of the drama and exclaimed, "Too bad I missed it!"

Despite our son's enthusiasm, Lotte and I recognized we were lucky to be alive. The janitor was killed that day. Fortunately there was no permanent damage to the members of the quartet or to our instruments and we were able to continue performing in and around Montreal.

But the incident changed us. Knowing how capricious fate could be, we relaxed. It helped us shake off the setbacks and difficulties we encountered over the years. And we realized we were survivors. It made Lotte and I redouble our efforts to succeed in Montreal's music scene.

The year was 1948. Our main contribution to that scene up until then was the McGill String Quartet, Montreal's first permanent and successful chamber music ensemble.

Let me take you back to the beginning – 1939.

What a year to begin! Our world was crashing towards war. But I was twenty-four years old, an accomplished violinist, recently graduated from New York's Juilliard School of Music with diplomas in composition, orchestration, and interpretation. I had just returned to Montreal and was hungry for a job in music. I went to see my first composition teacher, Douglas Clarke, Dean of Music at the McGill Conservatorium from where I had graduated in 1932. He offered me a job to teach orchestration and violin and to coach chamber-music upon my return.

I happily accepted Clarke's offer. Regular musical employment was scarce and the opportunity to teach at a university with an international reputation like McGill was a great honour. Besides with the onset of war, I felt a duty to my mother and brother Steve to stay in Montreal, although I couldn't help thinking of what I had left behind in New York. Juilliard had provided many opportunities to exchange information with the world's finest musicians and perform great chamber music repertoire. These opportunities weren't available to students and faculty at McGill. So I asked Clarke if I could include string quartets in the concerted music section of the syllabus. He liked the idea and the rest of the staff agreed.

We formed a professional string quartet made up of faculty members and called it the McGill String Quartet. I felt it would be best for us to form a student string quartet too. Clarke and my faculty colleagues welcomed that idea as well.

I believed chamber music could flourish in Montreal and we could find the formula to build a subscription audience and provide an employment base for Montreal musicians. During the late 1930s, the Montreal Symphony could not fully employ our city's finest musicians, so in order to earn a decent salary we had to teach, play in vaudeville theatres, and find other freelance work. I was convinced that if we could set high performance standards, program a mix of old and new, European and Canadian compositions, and engage the best guest artists from Canada, America and Europe, we could make chamber music take root here. I'm as devoted to that belief today as I was over sixty years ago.

The first members of the McGill String Quartet were Edwin Sherrard, second violin; Stephen Kondaks, viola; Jean Belland, cello; and I was first violin. I was particularly touched that Clarke, a fine pianist as well as pedagogue, agreed to be featured as guest pianist in the great piano quartets and quintets. He loved Brahms, whom we often played.

Our first objectives were accuracy and brilliance. We were always conscientious about detail, the prerequisite to success. We didn't necessarily want to sound like the European string quartets. The European style was different – precise, integrated, perhaps understated. Our approach was to be more direct and more virtuosic.

The first performances of the McGill String Quartet were sponsored by Madame Antonia David, a great musical philanthropist and the wife of Senator Athanase David. We played in Moyse Hall, the Arts Building auditorium at McGill, which then served as the Quartet's home venue for years. We first enlarged the quartet when we invited other McGill faculty members to play the additional wind and string parts in order to perform Schubert's *Octet* and Beethoven's *Septet*.

I enjoyed the stimulation of creating new musical points of departure for the McGill Conservatory and my colleagues at the faculty were also eager to participate. All that was needed was a catalyst to conceive the ideas and implement them. I took on that task with relish. I had great dreams and the will to fulfill them.

In my library hangs a photograph of the first formation of the McGill String Quartet rehearsing in a barn. It may appear a bit strange, but it was certainly very Canadian! Culturally speaking, Canada was in its infancy. Montreal didn't even have a proper concert hall for music – the Montreal Symphony played at a high school auditorium, L'ecole du Plateau.

Quartet playing is a very intimate medium. It is by far the most challenging of ensemble playing, requiring the players to be intuitive about each other's interpretation to the point of mind reading. Someone, who shall remain nameless, described it as a "marriage between four people without benefit of sex." "A string quartet is a very refined idiom," I told the members of the quartet. "We need to practise regularly *together* towards uniformity," and we set up a schedule for several rehearsals every week.

The second violinist, Edwin Sherrard, whose father was the president of the Manufacturers' Association of Canada, made an offer. "My dad has a barn in Lac Manitou. Why don't we go live there and we can rehearse every day?" We all thought it was a good idea. Since we were on holiday from our regular work, we took the one hour train ride to the Laurentians, lived in the small house next to the barn, and played there throughout the summer. Living and working together all summer was an ideal way for everyone to get to know one another and become sensitized to each other. Thus the McGill String Quartet was able to achieve a unanimity of style.

Sherrard's dad had a raised stage built especially for us where we practised daily and performed concerts every two weeks. Our advertising consisted of a loudspeaker system on an old truck which would drive around announcing the concerts. Many people who lived in the area surrounding Lac Manitou were interested in music. Well educated, keen, and appreciative of our efforts, they became the base of a new and devoted audience. In this way we worked up the repertoire for our first regular winter season of concerts in Moyse Hall in Montreal.

The members of the audience brought their own kitchen and dining room chairs. We wore smart dark jackets and pressed white slacks and dressed up the back of the stage with a large Union Jack. Although the barn was all cleaned up, the odor of cows permeated the walls. The building was all wood – no synthetic concrete and metal – so its acoustics were what we call 'live', meaning reverberant but with not too much of an echo. Since string instruments are also made of wood – a natural substance which resonates – they sounded wonderful in the ambiance of the old cattle barn.

In these circumstances our quartet developed accuracy, precision, a freedom for virtuosity, and a uniformity of playing. Each of us leaned on and learned from the others. Consequently we developed an unanimity of sonority which pleased the audiences. The reviews were mostly flattering. Once we had the barn rehearsal hall and an audience, the McGill String Quartet simply took off.

We performed a series of six concerts each winter and began to make side trips to nearby towns. For example, on February 15, 1945, we filled in for a Belgian quartet at the Chateau Laurier Hotel in Ottawa when passport difficulties forced them to cancel their engagement. Our program included works by Turina, Glazounow, Haydn and Dvorak's *American Quartet in F Major, Op. 96*. It was sponsored by the Morning Music Club. The Ottawa reviewer remarked on our precision, our well-conceived interpretations and our excellent balance, noting that we played together with ease and smoothness.

The McGill String Quartet began to enjoy modest success, but that meant financial sacrifice for some of our members since we were paid only for the performances, not our weekly rehearsals. Jean Belland, our very fine cellist who had studied in France said, "I can't do this so often. I'm giving up paying freelance engagements and I can't afford to lose the employment." I couldn't blame him at all as he had a family to support. String quartets being democratic, we decided that Belland should be consulted in finding his replacement and we announced public auditions.

Lotte Goetzel, a young and dark-haired beauty recently arrived from Switzerland, presented herself for audition. I already knew her as a McGill student who had attracted my notice. She had a warm cello sound and a consummate technique. I admired her verve and her piercing blue eyes. Belland chose Lotte to replace him and I didn't object. She became the permanent cellist of the McGill String Quartet and three years later, she became my wife.

The method of choosing a replacement for Belland worked out well. As leader of the Quartet, and in other leadership capacities which included being Assistant Conductor for the Montreal Symphony Orchestra, I was learning how to get along with fellow musicians. I found that conductors and leaders need to employ diplomacy to encourage improvement without insult. To attain a certain objective, a quality of sound, a characteristic, you must be able to suggest what you want without causing hurt feelings, irritation or argument. This is the hallmark of leadership.

Classical music has a very long history. Interpreting it requires an understanding of history and performance practice since each period interpreted music in a different way. For example a work written in the Romantic Period (from Beethoven to the early 20th century) expects greater liberty in the interpretation of dynamics and phrasing than a piece of music by Mozart or Haydn written in the Classical Period (from the 18th to the 19th century). So in leading performances of the latter, a conductor must insist on clarity, precision, and dynamic planes which are easily discernible.

There are many theories about the interpretation of Baroque music (from the 16th to early 17th century). Some performance practices suggest a complete detachment with no gradual gradations of dynamic, no crescendos and diminuendos and little vibrato, only planes of either loud or soft. I disagree. I believe the instruments of that time were capable of many gradations of colour and dynamic. Though this may not be the popular view of twenty-first century authorities, I point to books on performance practice written by masters of the time, such as Francesco Geminiani who clearly demonstrates in *Art of Playing The Violin*, (1740) that crescendos and diminuendos and vibrato were used during the period.

The quartet literature requires a certain attitude, a subtle balance of combined sound and articulation, because the four voices must be heard. One player may dominate at a given moment, but then must give way to another or all the others. It's like a discussion among four intellectuals, each allowing the other's voice to be heard. Constant domination by any one voice is unacceptable if not impolite. Every quartet must develop its own style. Of course I'm speaking of great subtlety of differences. Once they have decided what that style will be, it should be observed by each of the four musicians in turn, to make it uniform throughout the ensemble.

Musical expression and musical communication can't be taught, but are learned by observation. I began to develop these views into my credo: *music is the arch-communicator of the spirit.* It's not restricted by time, place or condition, yet embraces and describes them all. To me, music represents the great liberator. Music-making begins when you have exhausted words!

The McGill String Quartet was not the first, nor the only quartet in Canada at that time. Toronto had its famed Hart House String Quartet and the Conservatory String Quartet. The Montreal String Quartet already existed, but did not perform regularly with the same personnel. Through the late 1930s and 1940s, there was a growing appetite for music in Montreal. In time of war, music becomes an important inspiration and reflection and, perhaps, escape. Most importantly, the financial support existed with Clarke at the Conservatorium and the generosity of Madame David. It was the perfect time to establish a permanent string quartet to rehearse and perform together throughout the year.

I had observed that a major expansion in research and publication, as well as public performance of chamber music from Baroque to contemporary, was taking place world-wide. There were the Boyd Neel Ensemble performing in England, the I Musici in Italy, the Basel Chamber Orchestra in Switzerland conducted by Paul Sacher, and the Netherlands Chamber Orchestra conducted by Simon Goldberg. All of this chamber music activity helped to raise the profile of string quartet playing and chamber music generally, and made audiences more aware and eager.

Visiting string quartets from overseas helped draw audiences to the McGill String Quartet. John Pennington's London String Quartet played in Montreal as our guests at McGill in 1939. Pennington was a fine musician and a generous man. He was traveling with two Stradivari violins in a specially built case, and he lent me one of them to play, saying, "Here, you can't play on that fiddle you've got! Use this until I have to leave the continent."

The joy of playing this extraordinary instrument was only one of the many aspects of my musical life in 1939. I led the McGill String Quartet as first violin, taught at the university, and was also interested in conducting, while working hard to prove myself as composer.

In March 1939, I conducted the premiere of my own composition *Oracle*, with the Montreal Symphony Orchestra. An oracle is a prophecy. I was looking into my future. With *Oracle* I described those worrying years in Canada's history, including the doubts and fears we felt as the nation prepared itself for war. The recent 9/11 terrorist attacks provide a similar opportunity to compose works which portray the drama and emotion of the event in musical terms.

Oracle is a symphonic poem for full orchestra and piano and was picked up by several orchestras. Sir Ernest MacMillan led the Toronto Symphony when it performed it in 1942. A full five years after I wrote it, the Montreal Symphony performed it again in March 1944, under the baton of the great British conductor Sir Thomas Beecham. The solo piano part was played by the internationally renowned French pianist Severin Moisse. Sir Thomas explained to the audience that the piece was essentially Romantic in style, which is true of most of my early work.

I worked with Beecham on numerous other occasions. Madame Antonia David ran a series of concerts called the Montreal Festivals during the summer months. She would put on large choral-orchestral works and invite Beecham to conduct these choral extravaganzas.

Our chamber music offerings were as popular as those large orchestral efforts. While the war years dragged on, the McGill String Quartet thrived despite several changes in membership.

Unlike Belland's initial departure, these members left when they were called up for military service. It was unfortunate, even nightmarish. Things happened quickly. My brother was called up to the army, which he hated, until he found a way to get transferred to the RCAF. Steve Kondaks, a fine viola player from my days at Juilliard, was conscripted as well. His father, who owned a restaurant in Toronto, came here one day and begged, "Alec, you've got to help me. I don't want Steve to go off to fight in all those hellish places. What can you do to keep him at McGill?" I had already been excused from military service for medical reasons and tried to help Steve, but wasn't successful. We were sorry to lose him.

Edwin Sherrard, our second violinist who also played the viola, agreed to move to the viola position and we selected Mildred Goodman to replace him as second violin. The additional advantage clearly was that neither Mildred nor Lotte would be drafted. Steve Kondaks served a year and a half in the Black Watch as a soldier, then became sergeant-major and was assigned to entertain the troops in Belgium, Holland and France. After the war we felt blessed that he returned safely to the quartet and we enjoyed his talents with both the McGill String Quartet and later with the McGill Chamber Orchestra until his retirement in 1985. Steve made a tremendous contribution to both ensembles.

During the war years, the members of the McGill String Quartet gave concerts for the troops and for internees at military camps near Montreal, under the aegis of the Writers' Artists' and Broadcasters' War Council. We always had a good response from the troops, which proved to me that even though the soldiers came from many different backgrounds and most had never heard our kind of music, they were positively affected by the music and appreciated it. I am proud of the sterling silver medallion with Canada's coat of arms which I received in 1944 from the federal government for giving those war-time benefit concerts. It is inscribed:

ALEXANDER BROTT.

CANADA THANKS YOU FOR YOUR GENEROUS HELP.

1944.

Admission to a concert, at that time, was $1.25 for the general public and thirty-five cents for students and members of the armed forces.

At the request of the Canadian Government we played for the internees at a camp about forty miles outside Montreal. I was pleased to see these prisoners of war were well-treated and amazed at their cultural awareness. It didn't dawn on me that they were so familiar with our repertoire because they were from Europe, the seat of great classical music.

We were asked to mingle with the audience during the break. They spoke many languages including English and French and seemed wonderfully well-educated people. That surprised me. I guess it didn't occur to me that Germans from all walks of life were being drafted into military service the same way Canadians were. In retrospect I was a young and naïve twenty-five year old.

That same year I wrote another large piece somewhat along the same lines as *Oracle*. *War and Peace* is a symphonic poem scored for full orchestra, which takes about thirty minutes to perform. It suggests in music the transition from a state of war and destruction to a time of peace and construction. It uses barbaric piano rhythms intended to suggest ruthless modern mechanical warfare, includes mourning for the fate in store for the youth in combat, a horns and trumpets call to arms, and a musical expression of ideal peace, which reviewer Hector Charlesworth called "moments of singular beauty." It culminates in a massive chorale in which the forces of the orchestra are joined in triumph – a testament of hope and faith in the world to come. *War And Peace* won a gold medal for composition at the Olympics in London, England in 1948. I dedicated it to Sir Thomas Beecham, who had strongly encouraged me to complete it after seeing the first movement.

The McGill String Quartet continued to enjoy gratifying reviews of our performances and in 1947 we were given a vote of confidence in the form of financial support from the university and the newly-formed McGill Chamber Music Society. The *Montreal Gazette* headline read, "Chamber Music Saved – McGill University sponsors continuation of great musical art in Montreal." Lotte, the other musicians and I were overjoyed. We could finally earn a living.

Although this was almost sixty years ago, things haven't changed that much. Private support is still critical for orchestras and ensembles across the country. Other orchestras fold for lack of support, but we had it – audience, corporate, government and volunteer – and, thankfully, we were able to continue.

I think one element which contributed to the McGill String Quartet's, (and later the McGill Chamber Orchestra's,) success was the careful way we chose our repertoire. I tried to achieve a balance between well known works audiences already loved and an injection of lesser-known composition. We chose music by international as well as Canadian composers, such as Violet Archer, Andrew Twa, Claude Champagne, Jean Vallerand, and Jean Papineau-Couture.

In 1950 the expanded McGill String Quartet premiered my composition *Critic's Corner*. Since this piece also calls for percussion, Louis Charbonneau performed the added part. Douglas Clarke who often appeared with us as pianist, played the Brahms *Piano Quintet in F*, an often-ignored piece. Beethoven's *Quartet Op. 18 #5 in C Minor* rounded out our mix of familiar favourites, new music and neglected pieces – a little something for everyone. This was one of many occasions on which we departed from strict quartet playing.

Among the concerts in which we expanded our musical forces, our performance of the Beethoven *Septet,* to which I referred earlier, was a very important occasion. Moyse Hall was filled for the concert, even though the unusually warm spring weather outside was lovely. The newspaper reviewer and we musicians took it as a sign of the popularity of the *Septet.* For this special event we added four guests, all faculty members at McGill – Raphael and Joseph Masella, clarinet and french horn, Roland Gagné, oboe, and Charles Hardy, double bass.

During the early 1950s we realized that concerts where we augmented the quartet attracted a larger audience so we played more works with an expanded ensemble. The economics of it were simple – the more seats we filled, the longer we could keep our chamber ensemble alive. Although my primary expertise was as a musician, economics, especially when it related to feeding a family and running a household, was something I understood as well.

11

I had grown up during the Great Depression when money was scarce, particularly in our Montreal neighbourhood. I had had the experience of being a struggling student away from home in another country, scraping together my means of support. Now the prospect of leading a full chamber orchestra that was both financially and artistically successful and doing so in my own home city, began to be more than a dream. But I had to be careful.

Training for Three Lives in Music

(1915–1939)

My mother hummed and sang Russian-Hebrew folktunes while she nursed me and held me in her arms. I'm certain this developed my awareness of the effects of music. I never forgot those tunes and years later, when she died, I incorporated one of those melodies in my tribute to her entitled, *My Mother – My Memorial.*

My parents were humble refugees. My mother, Annie Fixman, came to Canada from Russia at age seventeen and my father, Samuel Brod, arrived from Latvia. We lived in Montreal, on Napoleon Street, off the Main. My father was a quiet man who whistled while he worked. Mother was strong-willed and devoted to her two sons. In a newspaper interview many years later, one of my neighbours described her as, "One hell of a handsome woman." Her waist-long auburn hair was always brushed to a gloss. For years she designed and sewed her own clothes. She didn't have much to eat, but she always dressed in high style thanks to her skill as a seamstress and a knack for creating fancy out of plain.

Mother encouraged my younger brother Steve and me to value the finer things in life. She often talked about her dream as a young girl, that she would have two sons, one would be a violinist, the other, a pianist. They would become famous musicians, enthusiastically acclaimed wherever in the world they performed. That dream influenced our lives.

When I was old enough, my mother enrolled me in Devonshire School, a short walk away from our house. The young teacher, newly-arrived from Scotland, asked my name. My mother spoke mainly Russian and Yiddish at the time. "His name is Yolik, or Yolickel as a term of endearment." The teacher was bewildered. "How do you spell it? Sounds Eskimo to me."

Now my mother was *really* confused. (In the Hebrew registration at birth, my given name was Joël, which translates into English as the Biblical character Joel. Luckily, she didn't mention that as it would have complicated the situation even more.) But no matter which way mother tried to pronounce it, the young lady could not say my name. Finally she asked, "Do you mind if I call him Alec?" And so I became Alec, spelled and pronounced the Scottish way.

My father, on his passport, spelled his surname Brod, but through various digressions and misusages (Bread, Broat, Bret,) we were finally called Brott. Years later, when I received my graduation degree *Licentiate of Music* from McGill, I changed my name to Alexander, after the historic conqueror Alexander the Great. It was a creation of fancy and folly. By then I was seventeen and so very modest!

Many of my classmates at school had similar name problems, though later in their lives. For example, Jack Wiseman, a gifted singer, became Jacques Jourdain; Samuel Tolchinsky, a talented humourist, went to Hollywood and became Mel Tolkin. At age seventeen, even my brother changed his Jewish name from Shloime, or Solly, to Steve, after New York Rabbi Stephen S. Wise, a man he admired. Despite his formidable pianistic talent he had decided, much to my mother's chagrin, to become a writer rather than a pianist and, like countless other Jews, he feared his given name would be an obstacle to success. I'm still waiting for his surname to become Brault!

Our neighbourhood spawned several names that became famous in Montreal and beyond. Mordecai Richler and Saul Bellow lived in the vicinity. As the children of mainly newly-arrived working-class immigrants from eastern Europe, we shared the same influences. The people in our area had a need for identity, a desire for mastery. The goal of every parent seemed to be to give the children a good education.

My father was a tailor. In the 1920s he used to bring home his work, and Mother's job was to sew the vests while he made the rest of the suits. There was that kind of co-operation. Years later I saw that again in my own family when Lotte and I and our sons organized our musical endeavours.

Steve and I were taught to help out with household chores. One evening we decided to bring hot tea to some guests after dinner. When the water had boiled we both reached for the kettle on the ancient iron stove. In our anxiety to do it right, we let the kettle slip through our fingers. It splashed scalding water and caused third degree blisters all over our legs. My left leg never quite healed. Whenever I removed the heavy 'boy scout' stockings I wore, they pulled off everything – blisters and skin too.

Despite our poverty then and later during the Great Depression, our mother managed to keep us tidily dressed and ready for our music lessons – Steve at the piano and me on the violin. My first violin was a half-sized instrument with very little tone, that my mother brought home when I was about five. Steve remembers a couple of burly men depositing a shiny new upright piano in our living room two years later and Mother telling him he was going to learn to play it. We were encouraged to practise our instruments twenty minutes here and there during the day.

My first violin teacher was Mr. Misha Kogan, a Russian engineer who played the violin as a hobby. Afterwards I went to Mr. Eugene Schneider, a professional musician who loved music and taught me well. Finally I found Monsieur Alfred DeSève, a retired senior violin professor at McGill who had studied under Sarasate and Vieuxtemps.

Neither of my parents had studied music or knew much about it, but they valued it highly. For Eastern European Jews, the musician held a position of respect and privilege. If there was a pogrom, a musician could move to a new community and begin to earn a living immediately. My parents surrounded me with music. They expected me to play and I responded. I had a natural and instinctive love for music and it became an important part of my home environment. By the time I was nine years old, I practised two to three hours a day, to make my lessons worthwhile. This was a task that I did not find oppressive. Mother and Father and Steve, who was more athletic than I, would often go for Sunday morning walks on Mount Royal. I thought they were a bore and stayed home to play my violin in peace.

Cultural appreciation was more important to us than material possessions and even sustenance. Someone once asked my mother, "Why don't you have the boys sell papers on a route each morning so you'll get a little more money?" That was the last thing she would ever do. Mother wanted us to concentrate on music. She preferred that we rehearse at home and play music together wherever we could. Steve and I performed at school concerts at Devonshire Public School and Baron Byng High School.

I loved to attend concerts, especially when the great artists such as the brilliant violinist Jascha Heifetz came to town. Seats at His Majesty's Theatre were expensive, so my parents would buy me the best ticket they could afford, drop me off at the theatre, and wait for me in a nearby restaurant until it was over. Steve by then preferred to read omnivorously and had begun to write poetry and short stories.

For me, music was the absolute and total outlet – a dream world into which I could escape from our impoverished life. Problems disappeared when I thought about music or concentrated on playing well.

I wrote my first 'commissioned' compositions at the request of my English teacher, who asked me to set the poems of Wordsworth and then Tennyson to music. I found the assignments so challenging and enjoyable that they inspired me to become a composer as well as a violinist. Since we were also expected to know each poem's form and meter, I could write vocal works with relative facility years later. To this day I value form highly – a work that is formless in music is not a structured composition.

Life at home in the 1920s was stringent. To meet expenses, my parents had to rent a room in our house to a suitable person, a common enough solution then. One day my father came home with a gentleman who was to affect our lives forever. They had met in one of the tea rooms my father and his men friends frequented. Abraham Lenson was engaged to demonstrate his craft as upholsterer in the window of Goodwins, a large department store on St. Catherine St. West. He accepted our accommodation, though he wasn't sure how long he'd stay. Little did he know it would become a lifetime commitment. Abe Lenson was keenly interested in music. He knew almost all the tenor arias from the Italian operas and he belonged to a synagogue choir.

Hard times and the lack of work continued to weigh heavily upon my father and in 1927, when I was twelve, he headed to New Jersey to work at his sister's hardware store. We never saw him again. I remember the winter gifts he sent my brother and me – two warm coats and his love. I missed my father and his whistling, but admired my mother's zest for life.

I was now the man of the household and we thought I could earn some money as a violinist. Those were the days of vaudeville and silent films. Musicians played the piano to accompany the movies and sometimes pit orchestras backed them. Between the movies, outstanding artists and some new talent performed live on stage for thirty-five to forty minutes. My mother took me to audition for the manager of the Imperial Theatre on Bleury Street. He hired me. Some of the co-artists were quite distinguished so I was kind of a prodigy exhibition. The job took priority over school and I missed some classes and sport activities, which was fine with me. I can still remember the works I played – *Praeludium and Allegro* by Pugnani-Kreisler and *From the Canebrake* by the American composer, Samuel Gardner, because the manager wanted something 'folksy'.

There were three performances a day and because the last showing was after ten at night, my mother came down to the theatre to take me home when the break came. It was my first real job as a violin soloist and the first engagement where I was paid properly – $100 per week – an awful lot in those days. I didn't particularly enjoy it, but it gave me an opportunity to appear before an audience.

Of course, I had other interests outside music. I loved my dog, a miniature black and tan fellow named Sparky. My mother raised yellow canaries and I also kept tanks of tropical fish (while they lasted.) I enjoyed some of the films at the Imperial Theatre too. The funny ones were my favourites and I still remember Charlie Chaplin in *Goldrush*.

I had many musical influences during this period. Abe Lenson took Steve and me to concerts. He invited the Italian singer Ardelli, who had sung at the Metropolitain Opera House in New York, to our house after a performance at the Imperial Theatre. Abe wanted to see my brother and me progress and in my father's absence, he helped my mother create a very conducive atmosphere in the house. It was a very correct one too. Eventually our former boarder became "Abie" to us and a surrogate father through our formative years. In the process our mother and Abie fell in love, though it was not until 1965 (and we had had no contact with my father for twenty seven years) that my mother applied to the religious and civil authorities for permission to remarry.

When I was twelve my teacher Alfred DeSève suggested I was ready to attend classes at McGill Conservatory. I auditioned, was accepted, and for four successive years received either the Peterson or the McDonald Memorial Scholarships. Consequently I came under the tutelage of Monsieur Maurice Onderet in violin and the Dean, Douglas Clarke, in theory and composition. My scholarships meant that not only would I receive free lessons, but I could perform at concerts. Shortly thereafter, the Dean established his Montreal Orchestra and engaged me amongst his second violins. I was thrilled to play and get paid for it.

The Montreal Orchestra was the brainchild of two men who visited our McGill classroom unannounced one day. For the students in attendance it was a noteworthy visit. Mr. Tupper, the secretary, knocked at the classroom door and said to Clarke, "Sir, two gentlemen wish to see you."

Since there were only three or four students in the class, Clarke acquiesced. "Send them in." So we lowly students overheard the whole historic transaction. One of the visitors was manager of personnel, Joseph Mastracollo.

They got right to the point with an attractive proposition. "We know you're aware that many musicians are out of work since these talkie movies have replaced silent pictures. The theatres don't need to hire orchestras any more. Even musicians who perform serious music have no place to perform. Because you have sway with the University we appeal to you to form an orchestra and become its conductor. We want to see a committee created that could give continuity to an orchestra, so our people don't go hungry."

Clarke said thoughtfully, "Well, that is a good proposition. I'll consider it." And he did just that, selecting the best musicians for his orchestra, concentrating on those who were used to playing serious music and weren't intimidated by the great Classical and Romantic repertoire instead of light-hearted accompaniments to silent films.

This incident and many marvellous personalities made my studies at McGill most fascinating. My Belgian violin teacher, Monsieur Onderet, wanted me to "cool down" and concentrate on precision and technique which was more the Belgian school. "Vot for you get so excited?" he would often rebuke me.

My composition professor, Dean Clarke, encouraged me to "warm up," to think of English poetry, of fantasy, imagery and abandon. Together they made a happy combination. They taught me that music had many styles and many means. I preferred my own style, "controlled involvement." I did not lack confidence.

At McGill I played recitals, wrote music, practised, studied and performed as soloist with the orchestra. Playing with the fledgling Montreal Orchestra, I thrilled to each work we rehearsed – Brahms, Sibelius, Vaughan Williams, Elgar, Holst, Wagner – all of the great Romantics. I benefited greatly from being a member of the Montreal Orchestra. Douglas Clarke was a sensitive musician with clear and intelligent demands. My studies of music history, form and analysis taught me not to do anything I couldn't explain. From watching some colleagues jostle for positions I learned that envy was a many-headed monster who would lie and betray. Self-discovery was the goal to reach for – and I did.

After five years of studying music at The McGill Conservatory, I graduated in May 1932 with a *Licentiate in Music* Diploma in violin. I was seventeen years old. It was a happy occasion with family celebration and graduation photos. The next year I received my laureate from the Quebec Academy because DeSévre wanted me to study in Quebec City too.

There were many distinguished visiting artists who performed in Montreal. Maestro Georges Enesco, the famous composer, conductor and solo violinist had come to play Beethoven's *Violin Concerto*. Perceiving that Enesco was the type of multi-faceted musician I aimed to become, I decided to ask him to listen to and advise me.

We rehearsed on the ninth floor of the Mount Royal Hotel. Enesco was quiet, almost humble, pointing the head of his violin gently to the orchestral instruments carrying the themes. The nature of his tone, romantic and flexible, was almost gypsy-like, on the very border of licentiousness. The coda of the first movement, a thin filament of sound, was remote, played *pp senza vibrato*. Enesco took it into space and beyond.

At the concert the audience was transfixed. Even after the first movement, when normally one would not expect it, they applauded wildly. I was tremendously moved by the sheer beauty of the concerto and I thought – what nerve do I, a seventeen year old, have to play this very movement to Enesco for his counsel? I had just heard him playing the same piece. But I was ambitious, so I took the liberty of asking him to listen to my playing for his expert opinion. He agreed and gave me his room number on the eighth floor.

I approached the room with trepidation. He opened the door and asked, "What are you going to play?"

"Maestro, may I play the first movement of the Beethoven *Violin Concerto*?"

To my relief he laughed, then sat down on the chair and directed me, "Well, play!"

I did. I marvelled at his ability to hum the orchestral accompaniment while I played the solo part. Afterwards, Enesco told me I was a very gifted player and I would benefit from a teacher who could help me stabilize my quieter emotions.

He recommended me to Louis Persinger (Yehudi Menuhin's other teacher – Enesco had been one of his first) for an audition before the staff of string teachers at the Institute of Musical Arts in New York City. This school would soon become the world-famous Juilliard School. I was thrilled. My mother arranged all the practical matters and I concentrated on the audition. I chose two contrasting works, Bach's *D Minor Suite* and Saint-Saëns' *Concerto No. 3 in G minor*.

After the audition one of the members rose to say, "Thank you. You'll hear from the School." It was Sascha Jacobsen, a violinist whom I had esteemed through his records.

We waited. I kept practicing. My mother was confident I'd get in. I had to. There was nothing left for me to learn in Montreal. After a fortnight I received word that I was accepted, with a scholarship! I spent the next five years of enlightenment in New York.

The next and last time Maestro Georges Enesco came to conduct in Montreal, I had progressed up the ranks to the first violins and we played his famous *Rumanian Dances*. He left me his conductor's baton, a very generous gesture to a young man at the beginning of his career.

Getting admitted to Juilliard was a coup, but it was difficult financially. In order to survive in New York City I had to take on many menial duties. I coached youngsters, such as Israel Senitsky, Bernard Landsman, and Mildred Goodman. Mildred's father, who was a well-to-do manufacturer of men's clothing, asked me to recommend his talented daughter to my own teacher. Eventually she too was accepted at Juilliard. Mr. Goodman arranged for Mildred to take a room in my house and paid me to practise with her for one hour every day. I also earned money playing in the Richmond Virginia Symphony Orchestra periodically, though I had to pay for the long bus ride to rehearsals.

I lived in a room at the Morningside Residence Club at 122nd Street and Morningside Drive. We had a lot of space, with a rehearsal room in the basement and when my mother visited, I took her to the rooftop garden.

I played there in a trio with two young ladies. Imagining we were characters in a Greek tragedy one of them called me "Alexis" and I named her "Helena." Our cellist was "Miss Bacon II," because together, we brought home the bacon.

During the summer I performed on Canada Steamship boats, like the luxury vessel SS Richelieu which carried tourists up and down the Saguenay River to Arvida in Quebec. We played classical music from 4:00 p.m. until 5:00 p.m. to dowager ladies and bored gentlemen. The jazz band attracted the wilder, young crowd in the evenings. The captain, a friendly Dutchman named Master Carl Bodensieck, treated me kindly and I was fascinated to observe the passengers – posh society, famous Americans and film crews in the rapidly developing field of movies. I enjoyed steaming along the beautiful Saguenay River, always followed by baby seals. I loved to see their little heads bobbing in the water behind us.

Periodically I returned to Montreal to visit my family and perform. I played the Glazounov *Violin Concerto in A Minor* with the Montreal Orchestra at Her Majesty's Theatre, which no longer exists. My mother used to send me telegrams and letters with newspaper clippings of reviews of these performances. "Letter following with splendid reviews from the *Gazette* and *Star*. Love, Mother." Having worked diligently to launch my career, she maintained the keenest interest in my activities while I was living in New York.

During my Juilliard days many people and events pushed my career forward or broadened my approach. Dean Douglas Clarke was one of them. I once wrote to him, "It is very difficult for me, not only from the lack of time, but it is very hard being away from home and having inadequate means to function." I mentioned thoughts of dropping the composition course because I had too much on my plate. I was studying 16th century counterpoint with Dr. Madley Richardson, Folk Idiom with Professor Howard Brockway, as well as the Baroque and early classic styles. Now I'm grateful that I did not drop them since they all stood me in good stead later. But at the time it all seemed too much. There was still my violin and conducting, the extra jobs, and hours of practice which I squeezed into every spare moment I had.

I couldn't expect sympathy from Clarke. He replied with a letter of encouragement and a cheque. He wrote, "Remember that violinists are legion, composers, rare."

I was shocked because I suddenly felt, God, I *cannot* give up those classes, I have to continue with composition as well. That quote has remained with me to this day.

I don't know if I should describe Dean Douglas Clarke as my mentor, but I do think he was pleased with my work in New York. He had heard that I played with the Juilliard Symphony Orchestra and that my teachers were impressed with my compositions.

In retrospect, I realize Juilliard was trying to civilize us by obliging us to attend a variety of courses at Columbia University. We had excellent professors, wonderful experiences and exciting courses which probed the mind and its functions. In Child Psychology we even learned to describe the muscular movements involved in teaching a youngster how to "think" a flying staccato.

Sascha Jacobsen became my violin teacher at Juilliard. My chamber music coach was Willem Willeke and Albert Stoessel taught me conducting for five years. These men inspired and guided me to realize my potential to the fullest.

Willeke was also the symphony orchestra conductor and he frequently brought exciting soloists to play with us. One time he told us he had invited a 'young' pianist who was six feet tall and as straight as a ramrod, to rehearse two Liszt concerti. Alexander Siloti turned out to be in his early eighties. He introduced himself by saying, "I am illegitimate son of von Franz Liszt. Kom play *E flat Concerto*." He was incredible. The verve, the style, the double octaves, were awesome.

That night it seemed as though all the pianists in New York were in the audience – Joseph Levine, Ernest Hutchison, Rudolf Serkin and Arthur Rubenstein. We had just played *Les Préludes* as an overture and were expecting Alexander Siloti to appear in the wings, but no soloist appeared. The conductor stepped down from the podium and asked me, as concertmaster, to see if there was anything wrong. I left the stage and knocked at the soloist's door. No reply. I called for the caretaker, Felix, who had the key. He opened the door.

There Siloti was seated before the triple mirror, head in hands. "*Je ne peux pas, l'esprit de Liszt m'a quitté!*" ("I can't, the spirit of Liszt has left me.")

I whispered to Felix, "Tell him...no play, no pay." It took twenty minutes for that spirit to come back, but when it did, it was sensational.

Sascha Jacobsen was also the first violinist of The Musical Art Quartet. Alongside Sascha were Paul Bernard, William Hymanson and Marie Rosanoff. The Quartet frequently performed in Town Hall, New York City, but occasionally played larger works on tour. I well remember Sascha asking me to join the group in Washington, at the luxurious Dumbarton Oaks Estate, for which Igor Stravinsky wrote an exotic string and wind suite.

The concert was to be attended by various dignitaries, including Hans Kindler, conductor of the Washington Symphony and a cellist of renown. When I mentioned that I had no tuxedo, Sascha gave me money to rent one. After I was paid for my services and returned the tuxedo, I blew my pay on a flamboyant 'horsey jacket' (a sort of brilliant plaid sports jacket like the Dumbarton Oaks crowd wore to the racetrack), plus a yellow silk shirt and brown suede shoes, which I wore at my next lesson. In those days you didn't appear that way in the classroom – it was disrespectful. But I had a peculiar streak – I wanted to identify myself as being able to do what I wanted to do. Sascha was livid. I can still see him. "So that's what you do with your money!" He slapped his broad hand against my back and almost sent me reeling across the room. Years later, my wife Lotte located that jacket in a closet and remade it into a jacket for herself.

Nevertheless, I was engaged to play again with the Musical Art Quartet at the Stradivari Bicentennial concert at Carnegie Hall in 1937, which was the two hundredth anniversary of Antonio Stradivari's birth. The concert was the brainchild of Emil Herrman, the famous dealer in rare instruments who had offices in London, Berlin and New York. Herrman engaged Walter Damrosch to conduct and arranged a string orchestra consisting of some of the foremost players in New York, each using a famous Strad. The invaluable collection was transported to and from Carnegie Hall by Brinks Express. Efrem Zimbalist and Sascha Jacobsen appeared as soloists and I played on the Rochester Strad of 1720. It was in a perfect state of preservation, a joy to hold and an even greater joy to play. I have very fond memories of it.

An amusing incident during my student days concerned Professor Carl Friedberg's wife. Friedberg was giving a concert with his most gifted piano students (mostly female), and many people were waiting to enter the concert hall. I had often been coached by Friedberg, but had never met his wife. As I stood in line with one of the secretaries, someone whispered, "There goes Mrs. Friedberg." I couldn't see because the lady directly in front of me was wearing an enormous hat. I whispered to my companion, "Which one is Mrs. Friedberg?"

The lady wearing the hat turned, looked at me haughtily and replied, "We're all Madame Friedberg." I avoided that hat all evening.

Many of my contemporaries during my years at Juilliard went on to make their mark. I recall the beautiful blonde Miss Drake, who tried to teach me ballroom dancing. Juilliard wanted you to be a complete gentleman or lady when you left their program. I had never had much time to be with girls and I certainly had never met one like Miss Drake – a gorgeous creature with the grace of someone unreal. I was very taken with her, but dared not get too close. I have equally vivid memories of many others, Joseph Visca, Emanuel Vardi (who used to boast, "I can play it faster."), Maro and Anahid Ajemian, Charles Jones (who became assistant to Darius Milhaud), Frances Breed, Steve Kondaks, Miss Mary McKenzie (Senior Secretary), Zvi Zeitlin (the youngest of Jacobsen's brood), Mildred Goodman (my house maiden), William Masselos (who played the Schumann and Brahms quintets to victory with my quartet at school), and Gisella Erenworth (known for her playing of the Glazounov Concerto). And I remember Rose Bampton, the future wife of Wilfrid Pelletier, who later sang my vocal composition, *Songs of Contemplation*, in a CBC broadcast.

I'll never forget the concerts of the Juilliard Symphony Orchestra. Being concertmaster and violin soloist enabled me to broaden my repertoire and learn a good many virtuoso works for solo violin, such as pieces by Spohr, Paganini, and Ernst, all of which extended my technique to the virtuoso level. Among the first important opportunities I had in the United States was that solo performance of the Beethoven *Violin Concerto* at Dumbarton Oaks. Sascha wrote later to tell me people had given him enthusiastic reports of the concert. On other occasions with the Juilliard Symphony Orchestra, I played violin concerti by Brahms and Prokofiev, all part of the rigorous but rewarding training I received.

In preparation for such challenges, Juilliard held Saturday afternoon recitals that we would either attend or take part in. Chamber music competitions were another method of transforming us into professional musicians. During one such contest we waited our turn backstage, watching and listening while it got down to the final three string quartets. We were still in the running. The remaining contestants promised each other that whoever won would use the prize money to host a party for the others. Our quartet won and I'm embarrassed to admit, the party we put on took up most of our winnings.

My time in New York was a tough period but I'm grateful for every moment. I found, as I had at McGill, that if musicians see someone is musical and trying hard, they will take you under their wing, just as Sascha Jacobsen had done for me.

In 1936, I received my first violin diploma from Juilliard. Then on May 28, 1937, I graduated with three additional diplomas – orchestration, composition, and a two year post-graduate diploma in violin. While at Juilliard, I was honoured to receive the Loeb Memorial Award for chamber music performance two years running and the Elizabeth Sprague Coolidge prize for orchestral composition for a piece entitled, *Two Symphonic Movements*. The following year I wrote *Oracle*. Upon graduation I received an invitation to work in New Zealand but this was not to be.

It was obvious to everyone that we were approaching a war and my mother wanted me to return home to Canada. So did the Canadian military authorities! I presented myself for active service. However, because of the injury to my leg sustained in my childhood, I was deemed unfit for regular duty and received a medical discharge. I was able to serve my country by using my musical abilities to entertain the troops and teach.

In truth it was indeed time to return home. I was anxious to get somewhere professionally after all those years of study. Other Canadian musicians studying abroad felt a similar pull toward home, as Canada prepared to fight and the United States maintained its isolationist stance. So I returned to Montreal to be of use to my country and begin my professional career in music.

Building an Orchestra
and a Marriage
(1939–1989)

It was good to be back home with my family. My mother had maintained all my pets – the tropical fish, my turtles, and my dog. But if I was to achieve my goal of making a living as a musician in my home town I had much to do. I was grateful Dean Douglas Clarke had hired me as a violin instructor and teacher of orchestration at McGill and offered his priceless encouragement. I also played with the Montreal Orchestra which Clarke conducted, but my income from both these part-time positions was not enough to support us.

I heard that Wilfrid Pelletier had ambitions to expand his activities in Montreal. I contacted him. He already held an influential position at the New York Metropolitan Opera as Director of French Opera and was both well-regarded and highly successful. In Montreal he became Director of the *Conservatoire de Musique* which included educational concerts among his responsibilities. Occasionally he asked me to conduct those and the first English one was held at Montreal High School. As I got into the swing of my Montreal career, I also served Douglas Clarke as assistant conductor of the Montreal Orchestra.

So two of my goals – violinist and conductor – were covered. Since I knew that my association with both McGill and the Montreal Orchestra, (later the Montreal Symphony), would provide me the venues for performance of my own compositions, I tried to find time to write as well.

Maurice Onderet, principal violin teacher at the McGill Conservatory, decided to return to Belgium and I was asked to replace him, a position I maintained until my retirement forty-five years later.

In this world there are people who are afraid to take up an opportunity and those eager to accept the challenge. In my career I have found this willingness to take a bold step, to try, makes all the difference. You must believe you are worth something. It requires a special character – it takes need and the desire to do well for yourself. These were certainly the values my immigrant parents taught me. I think one of the problems with the education system today is that it doesn't allow some people to feel they have an identity until after age thirty. They don't know who they are or what field they should be working in. But in music, if you have talent, you have an identity at once. This is where I got my audacity. I knew I had the support of those around me.

My functions at McGill soon included an appointment to the Faculty of Music and expanded to include chamber music classes as well as orchestral conducting classes. I also taught courses in adult music appreciation, in general, for which the McGill String Quartet gave demonstrations. Eventually, I was appointed Chairman of the Instrumental Department and had to revise the syllabus, which entailed deciding what courses were assigned and what was expected for a degree. I made it my mission to bring the curriculum up to date, and to feature some more contemporary works. Coaching the university symphony orchestra became my responsibility, and eventually, McGill named me conductor-in-residence. I especially enjoyed my association with Douglas Clarke because he really loved music and thought much like I did, that music was more than just a question of science and technique.

One of my goals as a professor at McGill was to provide qualified musicians to join the Montreal Orchestra. A number of my students went on to distinguished professional music careers: Blair Milton became a worthy member of the Chicago Symphony Orchestra, Eddy Kudlak has played for years in the Vienna Philharmonic, William Lunn is violist with the Montreal Symphony Orchestra, and Eugene Husaruk served the MSO as violinist and assistant concertmaster from 1977 to 1982.

Teaching gave me tremendous pleasure. I like to see things grow and change. When I shared my knowledge and technique with the students in a logical and clear manner and suddenly saw that magic 'click' of understanding, I felt great. It's the same when you conduct an orchestra and make suggestions and immediately see an improvement.

One day a young enthusiastic cellist, Lotte Goetzel, showed up at a rehearsal of the McGill Student Orchestra. I was impressed by her deportment, as well as by her playing. She had piercing blue eyes. During the interval I asked her about herself and she replied she had come from Switzerland and studied under Emanuel Feuermann. I tried to think of a way to get closer to her. Boldly I suggested, "I'm writing a work for two cellos. Would you like to try it out?" She was wary of me. Lotte was beautiful and statuesque, full of vitality and good spirits, the perfect complement to my serious scholastic personality.

We were both as busy as only young performers can be and didn't have much time for socializing. But after some two years and many absences, Lotte Goetzel still did not leave my mind. I continued to see her even after she left Montreal to study with Zara Nelsova in Toronto and I would go there expressly to visit her. Seven years younger than I, she was most refreshing for an aging (twenty-eight year old) professor.

When Lotte returned to Montreal, she auditioned for Désiré Defauw and was accepted into the Montreal Symphony Orchestra. She was already a member of the McGill String Quartet. Since Désiré Defauw had appointed me assistant conductor of the Montreal Symphony, Lotte and I got to see each other more often. The first play I took her to was *Othello*, with Paul Robeson, at His Majesty's Theatre. We spent a good deal of the night discussing Shakespeare's intent. I brought her home to meet my mother who as I told you earlier was central to my life to that point. She not only approved of Lotte – who, to my mother, appeared a healthy outgoing person full of vitality and energy and seemed to care for me – but encouraged me to think of "settling down" as she called it.

Until then I had not considered myself the marrying type, but after serious consideration – how would I afford my own household? – I asked Lotte to marry me. We planned how we wanted to manage our home and our future without offending anyone, especially her parents who opposed our marriage. They were successful international brokers – merchants of Cuban cigars and coffee – and had expected their daughter to follow a career in business. But in March 1942, we got married, and Lotte became mine forever. Her parents disapproved totally. Not only was I a mere musician but I was also Jewish. They were of Jewish background themselves but after a narrow escape from Nazi Germany in 1939, they had vowed to, "erase the stain of our Jewish background from future generations of our descendants," and joined the Unitarian Church. You can well understand why they were so upset at her choosing me.

Her parents' objections seemed to make it more exciting for Lotte. Truth to tell, we were really two old-fashioned young people who believed in the noble virtues of love, trust, allegiance, devotion, and we both had a burning desire to achieve.

As it turned out, not only did we have family opposition to deal with, but we also blundered into a legal stumbling block. We had married in Montreal's City Hall, hoping that by avoiding a religious ceremony we might bring Lotte's parents more on side and then, like all newlyweds, we happily went away on our honeymoon.

It was early spring and the Laurentians were still snowbound. I wore a heavy furlined coat since I have always been susceptible to chills. Upon entering our room at the Edelweis Hotel (Lotte chose it because of her affection for Switzerland) I saw only one hook over the bed so I hung my coat on it. When we returned several hours later we were surprised to find the fire department hook and ladder truck outside the hotel entrance. I had unwittingly hung my coat on the sprinkler system and the weight had set off the system and drenched the hotel!

Lotte was an avid alpine skier but I had never been on skis since my mother was afraid I might injure my hands. We decided that I should give cross-country skiing a try. We set off with great enthusiasm, Lotte leading and shouting, "Yahoo Switzerland!" at the top of her lungs. We were crossing the railway tracks, Lotte up ahead, when we heard the whistle of an oncoming train. I froze with fear – unfortunately with my skis right across the tracks.

Lotte scurried back and pushed me aside seconds before the train sped by. It was an exciting honeymoon!

A few days after our return, the notary, who was drawing up our marriage contract, phoned Lotte. "Miss Goetzel, when are you planning to have your wedding ceremony?"

She quickly corrected him. "I'm Mrs. Brott now. We were married in a civil ceremony two weeks ago."

Then the notary corrected her: "Oh no, you're not! The province of Quebec requires a religious ceremony and, until you have one, the marriage is not recognized."

The news came as a shock and we rushed to arrange a religious ceremony, so that the world could call my new wife "Mrs. Brott." Our second wedding ceremony was held in my family's residence, complete with canopy, broken glass, the Rabbi and witnesses. We even went together to purchase Lotte's favourite yellow roses for the ceremony. She looked absolutely radiant. Lotte's parents not only refused to attend but sent her belongings to my parents' apartment in an old leather steamer trunk, cut up in pieces. We did not hear from them again until Denis was born eight years later.

My mother supported our decision to marry. Her Eastern European philosophy regarding the marriage was, "You should live here together, but alone." Lotte didn't quite understand that. Neither did I. We weren't alone at all, because for the first few years we lived with my mother and step-father, Abe Lenson, in their apartment on Maplewood Avenue across from the Université of Montréal. Before long, we knew another Brott would be joining us there. Lotte was pregnant. She insisted on practicing and playing in all of the orchestra's rehearsals and I insisted on doing all the performances. (Boris was later to remark when studying the violin, playing quartets and studying orchestral scores that he knew the cello parts of these works from memory having heard them in the womb during the last trimester of Lotte's pregnancy carrying him. He claims to have had an "in at the womb.") My mother was there for us when we had to be out working, and young Boris grew up in the one room the three of us occupied. We came to understand my mother's words seven years later when Denis arrived.

Lotte was a precious, revitalizing force in my life. We shared everything and she took over the total management of my affairs and the McGill String Quartet. Her business acumen, probably inherited from her parents, was astounding. She obtained sponsorships, arranged properly-timed publicity, judiciously invited dignitaries, and wisely asked our lawyer to register the McGill Chamber Orchestra as a non-profit organization. Naturally she did all this with the knowledge and approval of the university and Douglas Clarke. Lotte spoke several languages and was charming in all of them. Her tone was suave, her patter international, and she had abilities which were of distinct value to an artistic career. For musical, business, social and personal needs, Lotte was marvelous.

For several years the McGill String Quartet was content to perform during the regular season for sizeable audiences at McGill's Moyse Hall. Even from the earliest days, our group didn't limit itself to strict quartet playing. For example, Dean Clarke often performed with us as a guest artist, playing the piano parts of the Schumann *Quintet*, the Brahms *Quintet* and the Brahms *Piano Quartet* in one of our early series at the Bell Telephone Building Assembly Hall on Beaver Hall Hill.

Chamber orchestra literature was enjoying a period of revival. Many chamber orchestras had been started in England, Holland and France. I showed Clarke the statistics and asked if we could speak to the Faculty of Music about forming a committee to support chamber music. He concurred.

For the 1945-46 season I conducted the first Montreal performance of the complete *Brandenburg concerti* with an orchestra the same size as the one Bach wrote it for. Some of the additional players came from the McGill faculty and the MSO. John Newmark played with us with style and good taste and he shone. It was a big event for us to play the *Brandenburg concerti* at Moyse Hall and we received a good deal of press coverage and support. It was a learning experience, too. The violinist took sick at the last minute and I had to call Pierre Iosch quickly and persuade him to substitute.

Given the type of support our ideas received, I challenged myself to come up with new ones. When the 25th anniversary of the

McGill Faculty of Music rolled around in 1945, people wanted to make a special splash of a program. I had a bolder suggestion. "Another performance in string quartet or quintet would be nice, but wouldn't it be better if we expanded it to start a chamber orchestra?"

Madame Antonia David, who was president of *Les Festivals de Montréal*, welcomed my suggestion that the expanded ensemble should give a series of one-composer evenings under the aegis of *Les Festivals*. To broaden our base outside the university, The Prince of Wales Salon at the Windsor Hotel became our new venue for these concerts. We called the expanded version of the McGill String Quartet, the McGill Chamber Orchestra and played an all-Corelli evening, an all-Vivaldi program, as well as all-Bach and all-Handel concerts. We performed the complete *concerti grossi* of Handel in four concerts. Aiming for authenticity, we used the instrumentation and size of orchestra the composer himself did. This series was a huge success. Although it may seem commonplace now, at that time, it was a pioneering achievement. Up to then, Montrealers had only heard these *concerti grossi* individually, or in orchestral arrangements because the authentic works had never been performed as a complete unit here. To mark the occasion the audience attended in top hats and décolleté gowns.

The McGill Chamber Orchestra committee had approved the alteration of our regular repertoire just for this special series. But when they realized that the new McGill Chamber Orchestra drew a larger audience, they suggested we throw ourselves fully into the more liberating chamber orchestra repertoire. As the founder of the quartet, I was consulted. I agreed absolutely and began to select additional players. This was the birth of the McGill Chamber Orchestra, as we still know it today!

For the additional members for the Chamber Orchestra I had many choices. Members of the faculty from McGill, the *Conservatoire de Montréal* and the *Université de Montréal* were good because, as teaching staff, they could play in the proper style. We could also draw from the tremendous influx of players who came from the United States to avoid being drafted by the army and, of course, the musicians who had escaped war-torn Europe.

There were wonderful people, including Walter Joachim, Otto Joachim, Yaëla Hertz, Arthur Garami, Robert Verebes and others, who augmented the quality and quantity of our orchestra.

Our goal for the new McGill Chamber Orchestra was to continue to select programming with the best artists we could afford and who could draw an audience. My secondary goal was to present lesser-known works of living composers to the public. We introduced the works of Canadian composers such as Jean Coulthard and Pierre Mercure, England's Benjamin Britten and Sir Arnold Bax, and the American Samuel Barber. We made plans to attract younger audiences with more accessible concerts that presented the Baroque and Classical repertoire in a more relaxed or casual setting.

Lotte and I were well placed to manage the new chamber orchestra. Since we were both members of the Montreal Symphony Orchestra, we were personally acquainted with local and international musicians and we could persuade them to accommodate our needs.

Through these early years with the string quartet and the chamber orchestra, our domestic life also flourished. On 14 March 1944, my 29th birthday, Lotte had given birth to our first child. We named him Boris, simply because he was 'good enough.' (This was our private joke on the name of the Mussorgsky opera *Boris Godunov*).

With awe and delight we watched this little bundle turn human. "Look, Lotte, he smiles!" "Look, Lotte, he crawls." "Look, Lotte, he walks!" "Listen, Lotte, he's ready to talk. Where's the record player?" I decided, to my wife's amusement, that it was time to expose our baby to music. I played Bach and Brahms to him, beseeching our little one, "Listen to the violins; listen to the oboe solo."

Finally Boris spoke his first word. "Oso-bolo."

My wife was astounded.

"Now get it straight," I said. "Oboe solo!" Bravo, we were off.

Baby Boris grew up surrounded by music at home. We brought him to rehearsals where he listened to us practice for concerts as he played with his toys. He and, later, his brother Denis were raised amid the hurly-burly of two multifaceted music careers in progress.

Around 1947, we began to discuss presenting the chamber orchestra's concerts as a regular series. We had been performing in the larger chamber orchestra form for five or six years and drawn larger audiences than with the smaller Quartet. It was obvious that Montreal had both ample musical resources and audience support for our chamber orchestra. The musicians agreed provided we did not make the orchestra a full-time job with concerts every week. Talented players often don't like that because repeating the same repertoire every night is not sufficiently creative or challenging. Secondly, most of our members held teaching positions or posts in other ensembles and simply did not have time for the many rehearsals, performances and preparations that a full-time cham-ber-music venture requires. What appealed to them was that with a main body of only fifteen players, the chamber orchestra was not so large a group that you got lost in the crowd. As an individual musician you knew for whom you were playing and why. You were playing for yourself.

The solution began to take shape. What if we were to establish a regular concert series of eight concerts a year, about one every six weeks during the season, and always hold them in the same hall? In that way the McGill Chamber Orchestra could become a semi-permanent contender on Montreal's arts scene providing audiences with the music they wanted to hear, and (equally im-portant from our point of view) ensuring a secure income for the musicians.

We hoped to offer additional concerts with pre-eminent guest soloists too. One of the first musicians we invited was Lili Kraus, the pianist and Mozart specialist. Over and above other Canadian cities and orchestras, we were fortunate to attract the highest-cali-ber soloists and conductors in the world, Victoria de los Angeles, Mstislav Rostropovich, Jean-Pierre Rampal, Yehudi Menuhin, David Oistrakh and more.

It was a busy time. We still lived with my mother and step-father. When we were away on tours or at rehearsals or concerts, they took care of everything, especially young Boris. Lotte became pregnant again. Just as she had the first time, Lotte continued working with both orchestras – nothing could have stopped her playing the cello. She continued playing so late into the pregnancy that I feared she would one day deliver more than music at a rehearsal. We debated whether it would be a girl or a boy and what we would name the infant. Secretly, I bought a framed French graphic imprinted, *C'est un Fils Monsieur*. Imagine Lotte's surprise when, after midnight on 9 December 1950, our second son, Denis made his entry in full voice, full of energy. Lotte and I were delighted and seven year old Boris was fascinated with both his infant brother and his hobby horse.

It became apparent that our living quarters would become far too crowded. Four in one room was entirely too much. As it was my orchestral scores were stored underneath our coffee table, the only remaining space available. In 1951 we moved into larger accommodations, an apartment at 5565 Trans Island. (Most of the other apartments there were occupied by the families of Montreal's hockey greats. Elmer Lach was our next door neighbour and Maurice Richard a frequent visitor. Every child carried a hockey stick.)

For the first time we were alone. At last, we had space. But we lost my mother's help and the boys, particularly Boris who had spent seven years in the almost constant companionship with my mother and stepfather Abe, missed playing with Abe who was to them their grandfather. In spite of hiring someone for the children, Lotte and I found it impossible to do as much as we needed to in our musical careers. So within three years we bought a duplex jointly with my parents, who lived in the upper flat. This arrangement worked well and that house on Earnscliffe is still my home, office and the office of the McGill Chamber Orchestra today.

By 1953, with all its exciting developments and success, the larger and newly-evolved McGill Chamber Orchestra superseded the McGill String Quartet, which formally ceased to exist. Montreal's Little Symphony also disbanded around that time, leaving room for the McGill Chamber Orchestra to step up to fill the musical void.

The first annual concert series of the McGill Chamber Orchestra had begun a little earlier, in the autumn of 1951. For the next several years we alternated between Moyse and Redpath Halls, at McGill University, the ballroom of the Mount Royal Hotel, and, later, the Port Royal Theatre, as the venues for the concert series, depending on cost and availability. We presented specially-chosen programs in keeping with our goal to bring neglected music to the Canadian public. It was gratifying that our efforts were appreciated. For example, there are still people who remember our 1954 North American premiere performance of fellow Canadian Leonard Isaacs' arrangement of Bach's *Art of the Fugue*. I had met Isaacs two years earlier in England, while I was conducting the BBC Orchestra. He had given me copies of the parts which I eagerly studied. We performed that work as part of the Montreal Festival. Again, we were proud to present the complete work which had only been done in Montreal once before and even then, not by an orchestra.

Pleased with that success, I put together a 1957 Christmas program of pieces by Giuseppe Torelli and Alessandro Scarlatti, among others. The *Montreal Gazette* complimented us. "It was a program which emphasized in more ways than one the fine work the Society is doing to bring us out-of-the-way music in its authentic setting and with intelligence and thought behind it. These people mix the salt of scholarship with the sugar of making you enjoy it." This type of review was so encouraging.

Occasionally, we varied our routine of regular concerts and special concerts with guest artists. One such variation was the series Lotte and I organized for Madame Athanase David at the Windsor Hotel Salon. These were fashionable events at which the audience could enjoy cocktails first and go off for a marvelous meal afterwards, all within the hotel. Sadly, this type of evening has largely disappeared now.

By the time the larger Place des Arts was built in Montreal in June 1966, the McGill Chamber Orchestra was well established. During the construction, there was much talk about who would open it. Someone suggested we go have a look. We discovered the sound was excellent, but the final touches had yet to be completed. Sheala Seigerman, a member of our orchestral committee, made us an offer. "Most of your repertoire was written or performed during the time Marie Antoinette was queen of France. I have a wonderful graphic of her music salon at Versailles. I would like to donate the same decor to a performance hall here that would be exclusively for the McGill Chamber Orchestra." Mrs. Seigerman was a McGill graduate, an excellent violin player, the wife of an influential stockbroker, and a person of good taste. She reproduced every detail of Marie Antoinette's music salon for us, right down to the candles. We were doing well by that time, so it seemed natural to not only accept the invitation, but to transfer our stage setting for our entire concert series.

So the McGill Chamber Orchestra regular concert series at the Place des Arts came into being. The day after our first concert there, the newspaper article declared, "Filling a real need and the house: There can hardly be any doubt that concerts given by the McGill Chamber Orchestra fill the real need of a substantial public." We performed on our specially-designed stage for over thirty years.

As additional proof that our dream had taken root, our concert series was usually sold out, thanks to brilliant management by Lotte. By augmenting the McGill Chamber Orchestra, we even performed the *9th Symphony* of Beethoven. From the beginning, the McGill staff and our sponsors wanted to make the concerts, 'evenings out on the town.' The audiences appeared in formal dress. Someone would host a reception before the concert and afterwards, as well.

Although the McGill Chamber Orchestra was usually sold-out, we still could not survive without additional financial support. We were grateful for the annual grant approved by the McGill University Board of Governors for the McGill Chamber Orchestra. The wording of the official documents stated, "the Orchestra has brought distinction and recognition in Canada and abroad to the university whose name it bears." Prior to the grant, there had been talk, just as there often is now about various orchestras, whether chamber music was a paying proposition. The sponsorship from McGill helped us mount not only our various concert series, but also other outreach activities.

Lotte and I continued to attend to the many duties involved in leading and managing the orchestra. I chose repertoire, studied scores, researched, led rehearsals and conducted the performances. Until around 1960, I still played the violin with the chamber orchestra, especially if there was a guest conductor. In addition to her roles as cellist and a mother, Lotte devoted herself to management, obtaining corporate sponsorships, organizing social occasions during which we could promote the orchestra, and handling the administrative side, budgeting and paperwork. And the more success the McGill Chamber Orchestra enjoyed, the more quickly the years flew by!

Our family life and musical careers progressed side by side throughout the 1950s and soon the 1960s were upon us. Listening to the radio one Saturday afternoon Lotte was inspired by the Texaco Metropolitan Opera Broadcast. "They have gas stations in Montreal! It will be excellent public relations for them to sponsor our concerts," she exclaimed. She picked up the telephone and somehow got through to the President of Texaco Canada himself. In her elegant, lightly European accent she convinced him to sponsor the concerts on Montreal's chalet atop Mount Royal. Thus she eased the financial burden of operating the chamber orchestra, ensured that all the musicians would be properly paid, and basically helped the McGill Chamber Orchestra survive. We didn't know it then but this was the first commercial sponsorship of an orchestra concert in Canada.

Lotte's technique was to phrase everything in the positive. Our concerts were a "prestigious privilege" with which sponsors would naturally want to be associated. She was never the supplicant. Instead she was offering them something of value and they had better accept quickly lest she give the opportunity to a lucky someone else. The sponsors she seduced in this way never had cause for regret.

We continued to bring in famous artists, headliners like Julian Bream and Philippe Entrement, to perform with the chamber orchestra. We planned evenings of the national music of various nations, to which Lotte drew the attention of the respective embassies in Ottawa. Much like our all-Corelli and all-Bach concerts, we were rehearsing and performing concerts of all-British and all-Scandinavian music. Foreign commentary was laudatory and McGill University benefited as well. Later these activities and Lotte's organizational gifts aided enormously in obtaining invitations to travel to the countries involved.

Lotte and I planned tours, for me as soloist and conductor, as well as for the McGill Chamber Orchestra. We spared no effort to create the venues for these opportunities. We would contact the ambassador or mayor of the next place we were to visit and invite that official to attend one of our concerts in Montreal. He or she would invariably give a reception and one thing meshed into the next. It was a conscious effort on our part to keep our music careers flourishing. My wife was quadrilingual and had been well-educated in Switzerland. She had the ability to contact many dignitaries in Ottawa and the personality and talent to entertain them graciously. Just to watch her employ her incredible technique was a pleasure for me. When they attended our concerts in Montreal, we would invite them to lunch at our house. Ambassadors and diplomats from the Soviet Union and Europe sat at our humble table and always enjoyed themselves.

So we created liaisons and, of course, our guests wanted to return the favour. Lotte knew these diplomats were always looking for an opportunity to send a report to their government about their activities, so any interaction they had with us solidified their position. She was very, very polished and had a remarkable gift for achieving results without irritating anybody. You don't see her kind of ability and insight very often.

We branched out briefly into other cultural areas such as the concert series at the Museum of Fine Arts in 1961. The museum was showing a large collection of French paintings and our six concerts attempted to recreate the musical atmosphere from the time of painters such as Watteau and Poussin. We included in the programs such works as the French composer Couperin's *Pieces en Concert*, with a beautiful solo by Lotte. But, this type of concert is difficult to keep profitable, so we didn't pursue it for long.

Although the McGill Chamber Orchestra was well-known locally for its highly successful live concerts, we tried making recordings in an effort to reach people outside Montreal. We had some success in this arena, too. In fact, in 1969 we won a Grand

Prix du Disque for a recording of my composition, *Paraphrase in Polyphony*, on the RCA label. Our recording, on the Select label, of *The Young Prometheus* was chosen as "Record of the Month." For the McGill Chamber Orchestra's twenty-fifth anniversary, one of our favourite guests, Jean-Pierre Rampal, teamed up with us to do two recordings. They helped us broaden the audience's music repertoire, as well.*

Centennial Year, 1967, provided us with other welcome opportunities, as festivities and even new festive venues seemed to crop up almost weekly. We gave the five opening concerts at Expo 67's Canadian Pavilion and, for good measure, we inaugurated a hall at Bishop's University. We often appeared in the United States, such as an engagement at New York's Town Hall for Canada Week. By that time, the McGill Chamber Orchestra had become a successful, vibrant mix of musicians – Asian and Nordic, Germanic and Italian, husbands and wives, and lovers. Some of our best performances included our beautiful concert mistress from Israel (Yaëla Hertz), a Greek violist (Steve Kondaks), a German cellist (Walter Joachim), a Hungarian first violinist (Arthur Garami), and an American bass player (Michael Leiter). They were all loyal to their craft and sufficiently flexible to merge their individual idiosyncrasies towards the common goal of our discernable style.

I engaged Yaëla Hertz just after she had won the third international violinist's prize in Prague, awarded by a jury composed of highly respected people like David Oistrakh. She came to this continent to study at Juilliard and was a student of Mischa Mischakoff, who preceded me as concertmaster of the Juilliard Orchestra (he became Toscanini's concertmaster). Whenever I was in New York, I would phone him. One day he said, "Alec, you've got to come to my house and hear this girl play." It meant travelling to the farthest of New York's five boroughs, but I went. There she was in Israeli uniform (girls were obliged to serve in the Israeli army), and she played like an absolute angel.

Back home, I suggested to Lotte that we give Yaëla the oppor-

---

* The details of these and other recordings are found in the discography at the end of this book.

tunity to play Beethoven's *Violin Concerto* at a concert coming up in Sherbrooke. Yaëla was thrilled to accept our offer. So she came to Montreal where she played for a good many years as assistant to Garami.

But eventually they became unhappy working together. I didn't want to be preoccupied with this, so I advised him, "Listen Arthur, if it bothers you too much, really you don't have to come." He replied, "I'm glad you're telling me that," and he left our orchestra.

These painful situations can happen as any orchestra develops. But I considered Yaëla a brilliant violinist and wrote a challenging violin concerto for her – *Cupid's Quandary* – which described both her personality and her capability. She performed it beautifully in Halifax and Montreal. Yaëla's talent is the kind that sticks in the minds of those who have heard her play. She was a match for the best. In February 1972, she met up again with her former examiner David Oistrakh in one of our concerts, performing a double concerto that is still remembered for its fiery brilliance thirty years later.

Many times in connection with Yaëla, I have thought of Sir Thomas Beecham's (today rather outrageous) remark after the Berlin Philharmonic decided to accept a woman. "If they are good they will distract the men; if they are pretty, they would distract me." Obviously Yaëla did much better than distract, for she held the position of concertmistress with the Orchestra for some forty years, until she retired.

Yaëla was at the helm throughout the golden period of the McGill Chamber Orchestra's most notable national and international successes. For our fortieth anniversary in 1979, four of our number reprised Leonard Isaacs' version of the *Art of the Fugue*. Lotte, Steve Kondaks, John Newmark and Mario Duschenes had played the same piece at the first performance in 1954. No other version pays so much attention to the original text. For me the work was a pure pleasure to conduct on both occasions. It represents something almost holy. During the same anniversary, the Canada Council sponsored the orchestra's tour of Ontario and Eastern Canada. Our regular concert series was sold out, a fact which speaks to the quality of our soloists and to the good taste of Montreal audiences.

Many of our events sold out, or nearly so. After thirty-five years, the orchestra still operated in the black and there were very few clouds on the horizon. Of course, we had some minor unpleasantness, as must occur in any field. Sometimes our dealings with the Montreal Symphony Orchestra were awkward. Since many of our personnel also played with the MSO, we had to arrange rehearsals and concerts carefully to avoid scheduling conflicts. However, both groups dealt tactfully with any difficulties and with each new challenge the McGill Chamber Orchestra grew in strength.

By 1989, our original plan for the orchestra had served us well over five decades of operation. Just as we had envisioned, the appeal of the Chamber Orchestra still derived from two main factors – consistent excellence of our musical product and the performances of international star soloists. On the fiftieth anniversary of the Chamber Orchestra, reviewer Eric McLean wrote what we were too modest to say. "From its tentative beginnings the McGill Chamber Orchestra has moved from strength to strength until it is now one of the foundation stones of Montreal's musical season."

In a country where foreign-born musicians are often more valued than Canadian musicians, where we still are too modest about our own accomplishments, and where the twin challenges of the economy and language tensions sometimes stand in the way of talent, the longevity of our orchestra is, indeed, a feat of which we can be proud. It has been my privilege to devote my career to performing classical music in my hometown.

The arts scene in Montreal has changed dramatically since I first played the violin for vaudeville on the stages of now-defunct movie houses, three-quarters of a century ago. Yet, the joy of performing the best and most challenging works with talented colleagues remains the same for me now as it was in my youth when I set out to earn a living as a professional violinist during the Great Depression.

My First Life – Violinist and Concertmaster
(1920–1960)

For the first two decades of my life the violin was my means of musical expression. I had trained as a violinist from early childhood, in part, because it had been my mother's dream that one of her sons would become a first-class violinist, the other a first-class pianist. She ensured that by giving us the proper musical training and encouraging Steve and I to perform wherever we were asked – school, synagogue, churches. Our repertoire consisted of a variety of works from the classical literature with appropriate encores to suit the occasion. A program might begin with the *Preludium and Allegro* by Pugnani-Kreisler, and a Mozart or Beethoven sonata. After the intermission, generally lighter music would follow, such as arrangements of Brahms's *Hungarian Dances*, Massenet's *Thaïs*, Ravel's *Habanera,* works by de Falla and Prokofiev, or *From the Canebrake* by Samuel Gardner (who later became my chamber-music coach at Juilliard), and my own *Chassidic Dance*. Since most concerts were in the evening, my mother always accompanied us and took us home.

From age eleven I worked hard to ear money as a musician – first at Montreal's Imperial Theatre, then by giving various recitals, then amongst the second violins in the Montreal Orchestra. I performed with numerous freelance orchestras in the Montreal area with conductors Edmond Trudel and Jean Deslauriers. While barely out of my teens I traveled as soloist to Ottawa, Toronto and Halifax and prepared to commit myself to a career as a solo violinist.

Behind every solo artist I know works a devoted conscientious mother like mine, who zealously dedicates herself to her offspring's profession. My mother made every effort and devoted much time supporting our musical careers. When we were young, she would attend every music lesson with us to observe and find out what we had to accomplish. She would make sure we practiced. She often did without so that we could afford those lessons and instruments.

She was thrilled when I was offered a job as a second violinist with the Montreal Orchestra. My Musicians Union registration shows that I was fifteen. I stayed in that position while continuing my schooling from 1930 to 1934. We gave symphony concerts at Royal Victoria College and every Sunday afternoon at His Majesty's Theatre. We gave educational concerts at the Montreal High School on University Street. In fact, I played in the first concert the Montreal Orchestra ever gave.

All of these venues provided many memorable learning experiences. The early movie theatres put on vaudeville-style entertainment, something for everyone, featuring live performers in addition to a silent feature film. I played my violin on the same bill as a dancing act, Harry White and Alice Manning, the comedy team of Del Chain and Art Conroy, or the Polar Pastimes, a group of acrobats dressed as polar bears. While I was a student at McGill, my brother Steve, or Mina Weinstein, and I sometimes performed at the Baron Byng Choral Concerts or at the musicales The Women's Club put on at Montreal's Victoria Hall. For a time, in the early 1930s when I was interested in chamber music, I was a member of the Montreal Trio with Edmond Trudel and Jean Belland. Edmond and I played on radio as early as 1931. For two or three summers during my Juilliard days I was part of a trio with cellist Jack Cantor and pianist Severin Moisse, entertaining on board passenger ships of the Canada Steamship Lines.

I played as guest concertmaster for visiting orchestras, some of which were quite notable, such as the orchestra of the *Ballets Russes de Monte Carlo*, with Antal Dorati, the Hungarian-American conductor. I used to come to rehearsal an hour early just to gaze at the beautiful ballerinas. One particular dancer, Irina Baranova, was amazingly beautiful and poetic, one of the most arresting women I have ever met. My memory of Baranova doesn't fade. I was disappointed when she married Colonel de Basil, the director of the ballet company.

In 1934 I left Montreal for Juilliard where I eventually became concertmaster of the Juilliard Orchestra and made many American musician friends. I learned a good number of virtuoso works for solo violin, such as pieces by Spohr, Paganini, and Ernst, which extended my violin technique to the virtuoso level. Among the first opportunities I had in the United States was in chamber music when my teacher generously hired me to play with his Musical Art Quartet when programs such as the Mendelssohn *Octet* called for extra personnel and I also had periodic stints with the Richmond Virginia Symphony Orchestra.

During this New York period, I occasionally returned to Montreal to perform solo and had my first independent recital at the Ritz Carlton Hotel in October 1935. My pieces were a Bach *Chaconne*, the Tchaikovsky *Concerto in D*, the Pugnani-Kreisler *Prelude and Allegro* that my brother Steve and I used to play together, Ernest Bloch's *Nigun*, and De Falla's *La Vida Breve*. During that visit I managed a solo broadcast feat – performing the technically flashy and technically monstrous *Witches' Dance* by Paganini on a live CBC broadcast with the CBC Montreal Orchestra conducted by Real Chartier.

I still keep a copy of a really flattering review of my December 1935 performance as a guest artist with the Montreal Orchestra in Her Majesty's Theatre. Regrettably, my mother chopped off the newspaper name when she put it in my scrapbook. In part it said, "Mr. Brott, who played the solo part of the Glazounov *Violin Concerto in A Minor* received an ovation from the audience at its conclusion, an ovation he thoroughly deserved." Regardless of what some performers and orchestra managers may say, critical reviews do make a difference. They were always important to me. I was encouraged when they praised me and discouraged by even the slightest critical comment. (Perhaps that's why I later wrote a parody on musical criticism called *Critic's Corner*.)

In the same year, I began to travel around Canada. Toronto was a mecca for Canadian artists, so I played there several times, as well in Ottawa.

Several Hebrew organizations and synagogues assisted my career tremendously. They helped Steve, my mother and me, especially in our difficult years after my father left. At one point, my mother had to accept help from the *Malbisch Arumim*, a Hebrew foundation which provided meals and clothing for the poor. They invited me to play for them as soloist in Toronto and Halifax and also gave Steve and me many opportunities to perform piano and violin recitals together.

Years later Jean Belland, Mina Weinstein and I gave a program for Temple Emanuel in Montreal, to help their scholarship fund. At Hillel House in 1951, I presented an illustrated lecture on Canadian music. I accepted such invitations whenever possible, partly because I was pleased to have the opportunity to play and mainly because it was a way to show my gratitude.

Another way I gave back to the synagogue was by regularly playing the violin for the Day of Atonement, which is part of the Jewish New Year observances. Cantorial singing of the *Kol Nidre* is an important part of this ceremony. From about 1930, I accompanied the *Kol Nidre* for Temple Emanuel on Sherbrooke Street West. Some time after Lotte and I married, I suggested that she do it instead. She happily played for the Temple observances until Denis began his cellist career and took over.

I never had a permanent manager until Lotte came along. Before that, Mrs. A.M. Russell often managed my violin recitals. She entertained Josef Szigeti in her home on Peel St. when he was invited to play all the unaccompanied Bach suites and partitas at Redpath Hall. He was a solitary figure on stage, but he always transfixed his capacity audience. Upon his departure, Szigeti gave me an authentic copy of the original Bach manuscript. The other local impresario was Mrs. Russell Smith, president of the Ladies Musical Club, who engaged me to play a recital with Judith Caranov, an excellent pianist from my Juilliard days.

Usually I received offers to play from people I knew or through word-of-mouth referrals. Sir Ernest MacMillan of the Toronto Symphony Orchestra, who periodically came to Montreal to conduct the MSO and knew me as their concertmaster, sometimes suggested certain engagements. The frequent exchanges between

Toronto and Montreal musicians, especially the CBC orchestras, were healthy for everyone and raised the calibre of music performance in Eastern Canada.

Those were the days when Canada's music infrastructure was first being built, so opportunities existed across the country. Canadian cities were opening their own conservatories and the Royal Conservatory of Music, although based in Toronto, was starting up branches and sending out examiners. Since 1909, McGill, too, had set up fifty-six examination centres across Canada. The CBC was expanding. They required orchestras for live radio broadcasts in Vancouver, Winnipeg, Toronto, Montreal and Halifax. At that time music was performed live to air or to tape. I played in the CBC radio orchestras under J.J. Gagnier, Eugene Chartier and Jean Deslauriers and for the CBC drama department. Those of us who took part in these developments were really musical pioneers. I'm so glad I was there to participate.

Geoffrey Waddington, a talented musician born in England, conductor of the CBC Symphony in Toronto, and general music director for CBC English Radio in the 1950s, often invited me to play as soloist. Other CBC producers and executives who encouraged me and commissioned my works and to whom I owe a debt of gratitude include John Peter Roberts, Jean-Marie Beaudet, Pierre Mercure and Kit Kinnaird.

The CBC expected an artist to include Canadian compositions written in that province, so when I performed with the CBC orchestra in Winnipeg I played Sonia Eckhardt-Gramatté's violin concerto. With the CBC Toronto Orchestra, I played works by Harry Freedman, Harry Somers, John Weinzweig, and Oscar Morawetz.

Thanks to the CBC, I was frequently heard on national radio as well as on local programs. I have no doubt these performances led to other engagements for me – in Ontario, the Maritimes and across the country in British Columbia. Furthermore, the CBC via its short-wave broadcasts, enabled my violin solo performances to be heard throughout the United States, Mexico and Latin America.

During my final years at Juilliard, I began an earnest search for a quality violin. I had already had the good fortune to borrow some very fine instruments, but I wanted to own one myself. The best violins possess a human quality and make a great difference to the player and his performance. The inherent personality of each quality instrument is special and doesn't suit everyone. It takes a specific person to play a specific instrument – you are 'made for each other.' It has to belong to you in order to become part of your nature. Eventually, I found my violin at Emil Hermann's, the famous international dealer on 57th Street in New York City and it inspired me for several decades. It was a master instrument made by J.B. Rogeri in the year 1690. He was a pupil and protégé of Nicolo Amati and was held in great esteem. First, I fell in love with my Rogeri's looks, then the tone quality. I needed a sensitive instrument for my variegated musical practice – one that would adapt itself to solo as well as chamber music playing. My Rogeri suited me perfectly of course!

I owed the bank money for that Rogeri for many years and I only made the final payment shortly after Lotte and I got married.

Montreal benefited from the many European performers such as Georges Enesco, who visited here after the war. Another was pianist John Newmark, an inspiring musician with whom I enjoyed playing chamber music. Together we played the Beethoven and Brahms sonatas in CBC broadcasts. Newmark first fled Nazi Germany as a Jew, then was held prisoner in Canadian internment camps as a German. He finally cemented his reputation in Montreal as a pianist in 1945 when he played Bach's *Brandenburg Concerto in D, No. 5* with us. He also played with the McGill Chamber Orchestra the following year for all twelve of Handel's *concerti grossi*. Newmark was an excellent pianist and sensitive chamber musician. So with the first cellist, Roland Leduc, and me, we formed The CBC Trio for three seasons in the same manner that I had with Jean Belland and Edmond Trudel some years earlier.

We played all the Beethoven, Brahms and Mozart trios together mainly as radio series on various CBC stations and were the first to perform the complete Beethoven piano and violin trios on CBC radio. Newmark excelled as a vocal and musical coach as well. He knew where to breathe and what to stress, and as Maureen Forrester's long-time accompanist and coach, he contributed greatly to her artistic success as the greatest contralto of her time.

When the opportunity arose I played chamber music with other musicians as well. I recall performing Schoenberg's *Ode to Napoleon* with Bernard Diamant as reciter and John Newmark at the piano. Diamant was another refugee who became a great musical asset to Montreal as well as Maureen Forrester's best-known voice teacher. John's skill was always a Godsend to the musicians he worked with. There were many other excellent accompanists too, my brother Steve, Mina Weinstein, Edna-Marie Hawkin, Edmond Trudel, Claude de Ville, Judith Carenov, Charles Reiner, Severin Moisse, Mara Ajemian, William Masselos and more. They each provided valuable support and friendship whether we played concerts, radio broadcasts or recordings.

The CBC was a great boon to Canadian musicians. I performed many times on broadcasts of CBC Radio, in recitals on CKVL, CKAC, CFCF, and CJAD (at the time these commercial radio stations produced live recitals of classical music from their studios – alas not any longer) and got to know the radio producers. Each station required a different piece for a specific purpose so I would play one selection for one station, and something contrasting for the other. Sometimes their invitations became a series, with one program per week. On average the works I played for them took between twenty-five and twenty-seven minutes, so they fit perfectly into these half-hour programs. Once, producer Don McGill hired John Newmark, Roland Leduc and me to play the whole series of Beethoven and Brahms trios. Beethoven wrote ten violin sonatas and eleven trios, Brahms composed three violin sonatas and three quartets, as well as piano quartets, and of course the big *Quintet in F major*. They are amongst the best works written for this idiom.

For these broadcasts the producer would help the audience achieve a better understanding of each composer by playing all of the works in that idiom. He would ask the announcer or one of the players to speak about it so the programs were also educational. Occasionally we recorded the programs in advance, but generally we performed them live. With the changes in recording technology, that seldom happens nowadays.

Upon my return to Montreal in June of 1937 I got a lot of exposure as a violinist. I performed solo recitals, trios and chamber music, playing first violin in our McGill String Quartet, demonstrating to my students at McGill, and from 1939 playing in the first violin section of the Montreal Orchestra. I became its concertmaster in 1945 and served in that position until 1958, when I became chairman of the instrumental department at McGill.

A concertmaster ensures that the string players employ uniform bowings and work together with the conductor to help realize their interpretation. The concertmaster plays all the violin solos required in orchestral repertoire. Some of them have the complexity of concertos – works like Strauss' *Ein Heldenleben*, and *Bourgeois Gentilhomme*. Frequently solos include concertante parts in Baroque and Classical repertoire as well as works like Beethoven's *Triple Concerto*, Mozart's *Sinfonia Concertante* and Haydn's work of the same title which are often assigned to the orchestra's principal players. All this was part of my responsibilities as concertmaster, a job where the light frequently shone in my direction.

Additionally I played a great deal of chamber music. Chamber music requires give and take. Goethe accurately described it as, "intellectuals in interesting conversation." It is really the ultimate collaborative musical experience. Playing first violin in the McGill String Quartet gave me the opportunity to engage in that vast and challenging repertoire and to enjoy the social aspect of being part of an intimate group of professional peers.

Playing as a soloist with a full symphony orchestra accompanying is the ultimate in personal expression for a violinist. I immensely enjoyed the opportunities to perform as a soloist with the Montreal Symphony. A solo violinist must be able to cope with the limelight. You must know how and have the courage to assert yourself – a talent which is easy to lose. You have to play very well to assure yourself that you are deserving of it.

Playing well in an orchestra is demanding regardless of where you sit. Lotte used to say it takes five years of playing in an orchestra before you deserve to be there. Performers who play solo and chamber music often look down upon orchestral playing as beneath them. I enjoyed every opportunity to make music in the three practices, solo playing, chamber music, and orchestral playing. I believe that each contributes to one's sensitivity and sensibility to colleagues. There is a thrill to playing exceptional music in an orchestral team under an inspiring conductor.

Like other soloists, I found that I had to protect my own needs. When I first started playing freelance, I sometimes worried that I was wasting my time there, instead of staying home to practise. It came down to the question of earning money versus perfecting myself. Was it worthwhile to sacrifice a bit of income in order to keep my playing level at its best?

Rehearsal time for a soloist is very isolating – you can spend six hours a day in solitary practice. Composition is introverted – it's all done in your head. Public performance is a form of extroversion. The moment you accept an engagement to perform with others, it is a camaraderie for a common result.

People have asked me to describe my style of playing the violin. I have never really been able to describe it in words. Perhaps others recognize my playing by a particular trademark. I only know that music directs *me* in a certain way and I simply react to it. I am constantly searching for what I think the message is. As the debate between my teachers Clarke and Onderet used to go, I have always looked for more of the "warming up" and less of the "cooling down." If I had to define it, I would say I am more for passion provided it remains controlled passion.

As a soloist, I was interested in being detached enough to know what I sounded like. It always sounds differently when you hear it coming back at you. I had a few opportunities to make recordings as a violinist. They were mostly of my own compositions, like *Critic's Corner*, and my *Invocation and Dance*. I found it very satisfying to record my own works, because I could bring the piece to life in exactly the way I imagined. But there are many more recordings of works I conducted. These were mainly for the

CBC, which always played a huge role in encouraging Canadian musicians and composers.

In those earlier soloist years recording technology was not sufficiently advanced to allow us to record longer pieces. To record a half-hour concerto would have taken up several 78-rpm records. Long-playing technology – the LP – didn't become easily available until the late 1950s or early 1960s, so for classical artists, there were few recording opportunities then.

In our business, the curse of recording is the fact that it has to be perfect. You know the producer or someone will say, "That was not so perfect, play it again." But in being super-careful you may lose the momentum of uninhibited playing. You can become so cautious that you don't try half the things you'd normally do in a concert hall. Even the great soloists constantly struggle with this. The problem may be inconsequential, but it is there. I admired a player like Ysaye who would say, "Look, warts and all, this is how I play. I don't want to go back and correct one little piffling thing."

Many of my concerts and broadcasts with pianist John Newmark and cellist Roland Leduc were played at the same time as I had my teaching responsibilities at McGill. So it seemed efficient to dovetail the two and I would tell my students, "I'm playing such-and-such a piece two weeks from now. Why don't you learn it too and we can work together."

As a professor I made many professional liaisons and was sometimes invited to adjudicate at violinists' competitions. I was a jury member of the first Montreal International Violin Competition when the Russian Vladimir Spivakov won first prize. We immediately engaged him to play as soloist with the McGill Chamber Orchestra.

These professional liaisons led to my first trip to Europe just after World War II, where the British Arts Council arranged engagements for me as violinist and conductor. While I was rehearsing sonatas with Jon Oien (the pianist suggested by the British Arts Council) at Radio Hilversum in Holland, we took a few minutes to rest on a park bench in the beautiful garden. I marvelled aloud at how the Dutch could have everything so neat and lovely so soon after the devastation of the war. Jon was silent. I further asked how they could find top administrators in this specialized field, and who might they be? This time Jon clarified things for me. "They're the same directors who were there during the war. Don't forget to look at the microphones when we do the broadcast." I did and noticed that the microphones were still engraved with Nazi swastikas. There was no money to replace this equipment, or surely it would have been done already. The administrators obviously thought that music doesn't discriminate but once I noticed them, it bothered me to look at them while playing. We performed our best.

I assumed the dual roles of violinist and conductor during that European trip, the same roles as I had at home. After the McGill String Quartet metamorphosed into the McGill Chamber Orchestra in 1947, I did far more conducting. But there were certain works, such as the Bach *Double Concerto* or the Vivaldi *Double Concerto*, for which I would still play my violin. From time to time, I still played outside engagements, but my responsibilities in Montreal were demanding, so solo performances became rarer and rarer.

There was another reason why my solo violin engagements decreased. I have a secret or "skeleton in my closet" which I have never revealed until now. In 1957, I was, at age 43 enjoying the prime of my playing career. I began to feel a strange sensation in the little finger in my left hand while performing certain solo passages of the orchestral repertoire. I survived those concerts, but worried my way back home and was often up all night trying to make the little finger (in violinists' parlance, the fourth finger) behave in the way it always had for me.

I did every exercise I could invent, but to no avail. I tried using supports of rubber or plastic but the discomfort increased. Doctors diagnosed the problem as having to do with the synovial fluid. Soon I was unable to master control of my fourth finger at all. It would just slide under the neck of the violin. I could not will it to perform reliably and in control. I kept this a secret, but playing as concertmaster began to present me with problems – most orchestral works require solo playing of great virtuosity. I tried to refinger the complex passages but nothing could alleviate my discomfort. I was devastated!

Still, I was reluctant to be operated on. On my next visit to New York, I consulted a noted pedagogue, Dr. D. Charles Dounis, who devised various sequences of finger-extensions which I tried valiantly to practise, but as good as they were, they were not reliable. So on my next voyage to England, I went to see a renowned specialist and surgeon on London's Harley Street who told me there must be some sediment at the base of the fourth finger which might be cured by an operation. I left thinking that if I had to be operated on, it might as well be at home. The surgery was done in Montreal under local anesthetic, so I saw everything. The doctor sliced open my palm and bent the flesh forward to expose the faulty joint. He started scraping to remove the sediment he thought was there. When I saw beads of perspiration on his forehead, I despaired – "oh my God, he knows it's not good, he knows they can't do anything."

It's not unusual among musicians, just like athletes, to suffer a performance injury of some kind. I just didn't want it to be me. This was catastrophic. My entire series of scholarships, my career, my reputation, were based on my abilities as a violinist. My world had collapsed.

My ability to play the violin was never the same. I lacked my original freedom of articulation. So when I felt my playing was no longer at its best, I stopped performing. I gave my last performance as a violinist in 1960 playing Bach's *D Minor Double Concerto*, for the 20th anniversary of the McGill Chamber Orchestra with the orchestra's concertmistress Yaëla Hertz. I conducted from the violin as had been the Baroque performance practice in Bach's time.

That is the real story of why I gave up playing the violin. Although people have frequently asked me about it, I've never told it to a soul, outside my family.

At first I feared that I could no longer serve music to my satisfaction. But I soon told myself, I can do many other things.

I decided I would coach more chamber music and conduct more often. And I decided I would start composing more. Douglas Clarke's advice to me so many years before, "Violinists are legion, composers rare," stood me in good stead. I realized my life wasn't tied entirely to my instrument. Even if I was no longer the violinist I had originally studied to be, I had not lost my strong determination to serve music to the best of my ability and at the highest professional level.

Though my first love was the violin, I had always had a strong desire to pursue a multi-faceted career including chamber music, composition, and conducting. It was time to concentrate on the other talents.

As chairman of the orchestral instrument department at McGill since 1955, I also had a lot of administrative work to do. In 1965 they appointed me teacher of conducting and music literature in addition to my string-teaching responsibilities. McGill University ran extension branches in other cities across Canada, which allowed me to visit cities as far away as Banff and Victoria as violinist-teacher. Thus I was able to make my contribution through my students. By serving on juries for various competitions as well, I also found a happy way to be involved with the new generation of emerging violinists.

My Second Life – Violinists are Legion, Composers Rare

(1937–1980)

Ever since my schooldays I have always been attracted to composition. My brother Steve still reminds me how much I always enjoyed the creative outlet of interpretation in my violin playing. But composition allowed me another musical outlet with the extra benefit of seeing it preserved for all time. It could be interpreted by other artists and could enable me to see myself through their eyes.

My earliest efforts at composition were the short works I produced for my English teacher, setting the English Romantic poets to music. Later, I learned more about form and style and expanded my vocabulary with Douglas Clarke at McGill and then studied composition in New York. After receiving Clarke's inspirational letter at Juilliard, I made a vow to write at least one work every year.

Back home in Montreal in 1939, I received a Strathcona Scholarship at the Royal College of Music in London, England, to study with the great British composer Ralph Vaughan Williams. He had taught Douglas Clarke and I was dying to learn from him, but it proved impossible. To my everlasting regret, the war intervened and I was unable to accept the scholarship. I was not to reach London until after the war and then it was as a professional musician, no longer as a student. When I finally did get to meet Vaughan Williams and show him some of my compositions, his reaction was positive and encouraging.

At the outset of World War II, I wrote *Oracle*, a symphonic poem in which I tried to use realistic musical terms to express the feelings that prevailed at the time – the pessimism, doubt and restlessness, as well as the world-shaking quality of the conflict our country was entering. *Oracle* also asked where I, as an individual, was going in those worrying years. It is a work both personal and patriotic in its inspiration.

Oracle received the Elizabeth Sprague Coolidge Award for composition in 1939. *Two Symphonic Movements* had already won a year earlier when I was twenty-three years old. Certainly these awards encouraged me to write more music and to continue studying composition at Juilliard.

I don't think I ever wrote anything that I didn't perform or conduct at some point. It was a great advantage to write a piece and at the same time create the venue for performing it. Conducting your own music lets you bring the notes to life as you meant them to sound. I had the honour of conducting the premiere of *Two Symphonic Movements* in Montreal during the 1938-1939 season. Listening to a great conductor perform your music gives you a completely different insight. They often see and bring out things in those same notes which you never dared imagine. Sir Thomas Beecham gave tremendous support to my music. He had the capacity to breathe life into your notes, to make them sing and dance, so you would feel it was being created right there in front of you. He did this for *Oracle* when he conducted it with his Royal Philharmonic in London and on tour in Britain. He also presented its American premiere with the Seattle Symphony Orchestra in October of 1943. Most thrilling for me was his performance of it in Montreal in March of 1944, under the aegis of the Montreal Festivals, as it was the first performance of the piece in my home town. That a man of Beecham's reputation had chosen to conduct it gave it an imprimatur of international significance. When Sir Ernest MacMillan presented it with the Toronto Symphony Orchestra five years later, it was still a timely piece.

By the time *Oracle* was being performed I was already busy writing a more extensive orchestral piece, also on a war-related theme. Sir Thomas Beecham looked at the first part of *War and Peace* and urged me to complete it quickly. I later dedicated it to him.

Jean Beaudet conducted the premiere which was broadcast from the Plateau Hall over the CBC and NBC radio networks across North America as part of a program entitled *Canadian Music in Wartime*. That was an important program for Canadian music because Beaudet used it to introduce fifteen Canadian composers to his continent-wide radio audience. *War and Peace* was well received. Reviewer Thomas Archer, in particular, described the premiere as "an event of unquestioned importance in Canadian music." I'm embarrassed and secretly delighted to report that he went so far as to say that he felt certain passages were more direct and truly symbolical than some of Shostakovich's.

In undertaking the composition, I realized that my goal was ambitious. I had set out to suggest the transition from a state of war and destruction to a state of peace and construction. Perhaps my youthfulness emboldened me. After all, I was still under thirty when I began. I don't know if I would be so brave today but in retrospect I'm glad I was.

I was able to attend on the night that Sir Ernest MacMillan conducted the concert premiere of *War and Peace* with the Toronto Symphony Orchestra at Massey Hall on 20 March 1945. His sincerity overwhelmed me and I was extremely gratified by the several ovations from the audience. Désiré Defauw, principal conductor of our Montreal Symphony in 1945, chose to perform it in the orchestra's subscription concert series and again later that year with the Chicago Symphony Orchestra.

Another product of this period was *Ritual* written in 1942. It takes elements from the style of Ralph Vaughan Williams, and uses primarily the Dorian mode and superimposed fifths. The McGill Chamber Orchestra still performs *Ritual*, which I conducted with them most recently in May 2002.

Concordia is a major descriptive work written during this period and dedicated to Désiré Defauw. I took the title from the motto, *Concordia Salus*, on Montreal's coat of arms, so in a way it's a companion piece to *From Sea to Sea*. *Concordia* depicts the entente or concord between the various peoples of my city, in particular the founding French and English peoples. This is a recurring theme in my music.

From Sea to Sea is one of my most successful and well-regarded works. This suite is in five movements representing the Maritimes,

Quebec, Ontario, the Prairies, and British Columbia. I wrote it in 1947, a time when the main motivator of classical music in Canada was the newly-formed International Service of the CBC. One of its objectives was to mirror abroad our collective Canadian cultural and creative identity. It was Stuart Griffiths, assistant to the director, who suggested I write five movements under the title *From Sea to Sea*, evoking the nature and ethnic character of each province. He took the idea from the motto, *A mari usque ad mare*, on the Canadian coat of arms. Stuart was young and daring and I am grateful to him for his inspiration and encouragement. I have been told that mine was the first composition commissioned by the CBC International Service. The CBC not only ensured national and international exposure for many Canadian composers, but also provided them with recordings of their work to play for other conductors and performers to encourage additional performances. I was the beneficiary of many such commissions which stimulated me greatly as a composer.

To write *From Sea to Sea*, I consulted Canadian paintings, folklore materials and documentary films. Canadian ethnomusicologist Dr. Marius Barbeau of the National Museum of Civilization in Ottawa, who collected recordings of indigenous folk material from the farthest reaches of Canada, offered me valuable insights on the composition of melodies that reflected the nature of each locale and its inhabitants. Conductor Sir Ernest McMillan, who had accompanied Barbeau in one of his expeditions, added his perspective. I spent almost five months in its composition. Part of that time I hid away in a bucolic rented cottage at Fourteen Island Lake in the Laurentian Mountains – no running water, few interruptions, lots of inspiration. I united the work by composing an overarching noble theme which starts with a musical description of the small fishing villages of Newfoundland and builds to the final movement, British Columbia.

From Sea to Sea was broadcast over the radio networks in Canada, the United States and overseas. Eight hundred stations around the world tuned in for the premiere, which I had the good fortune to conduct. Sir Ernest MacMillan led his Toronto Symphony Orchestra to play it at Massey Hall on two November evenings in 1948. Later this work was also heard on radio in Europe thanks to the efforts of Mr. Pierre Dupuy, Canada's ambassador to Holland. It had been recorded by the CBC and distributed to Canadian embassies the world over, where it was often played during July 1 celebrations. RCA Victor re-released a Centennial recording of the work in 1967.

I have stopped entering composition competitions now but, over the years, a number of my works have been honoured. The Canadian Performing Rights Society worked to help Canadian composers achieve recognition with its own awards. I received several of those, including one for *War and Peace*. In 1946 *Concordia* was awarded a prize at the Prague Music Festival, where I was one of five Canadians entered in the competition. Jean Beaudet, who had earlier conducted my *War and Peace*, led *Concordia's* premiere in Prague with the Czech Philharmonic. When I returned to Prague with the McGill Chamber Orchestra some years later, the audience still remembered it fondly.

Few people realize that music was an Olympic event for many years. Composers competed in their own category as a cultural adjunct to the athletic matches, along with the contests of muscles of the body, went these competitions of the muscles of the brain, so to speak. This stemmed back to the days of ancient Greece when music was considered essential to a rounded education. Originally the works were featured in performance during the Olympics and those receiving the most votes won. I won Olympic music awards two successive times – in 1948 in London, for *War and Peace* (I thought it was a fitting composition to submit, given what England had recently lived through), and again in 1952 in Helsinki, Finland, for my *Violin Concerto*. To my regret I was unable to attend the medal ceremony, so I never got to see the athletic events. The cost of the trip was beyond my means as a working musician in those days. I didn't even travel to concerts where Sir Thomas Beecham played my works, although I know I should have.

My *Violin Concerto*, which was a commission from the Little Symphony of Montreal conducted by Bernard Naylor, is in a more neo-classical vein than some of my earlier works. As a violinist myself, I wrote it to stretch the boundaries of the violinist's role.

When *Violin Concerto* was conducted by Leopold Stokowski at Carnegie Hall in 1953, reviewer Olin Downes recognized this in his review in the *New York Times*, calling it, "Original, brilliant, technically resourceful, more than adroit and individual in the way that the form is handled...something really new under the sun in a composer's approach to the concerto form." This work too, has been recorded by the CBC.

In 1953 the CBC commissioned me to write something for the coronation of Queen Elizabeth II. I considered this a great honour and devoted myself to it. In the resultant composition, *Royal Tribute*, I tried to portray the circumstances of the coronation, the richness of the British heritage, and the new Queen's personal charm, as well as the turbulence of the times.

I premiered *Royal Tribute*, conducting the CBC Orchestra in Toronto during Coronation Year. Later Sir Malcolm Sargent of the BBC conducted the work at the London Promenade concerts at Royal Albert Hall in London, England. I was invited to attend. Backstage, I chatted with the great pianist, Dame Myra Hess and Sir Malcolm, who made me feel at home. Of course all this excited me greatly. The quality and size of the orchestra and the hall, their brilliance taken for granted, elevated my spirit.

Later, Otto Klemperer conducted the Montreal Symphony Orchestra in another performance of *Royal Tribute*. I conducted the same piece in one of the Prom Concerts – the Promenade Symphony Concerts in the Varsity Arena in Toronto. It was broadcast on radio via the CBC Trans-Canada network, and televised by CBLT in September 1954, the early days of televised concerts. Zvi Zeitlin, my old friend from Juilliard, played the violin on that program. I conducted the piece several more times, too, including once as part of a free outdoor concert at McGill. On that occasion we tried something really different – seating the orchestra on the terrace of the Redpath Library, and the audience on the lawn. I chose *Royal Tribute* for that concert since it was organized specially for the congress of the Association of Universities of the British Commonwealth.

Royal Tribute expresses the link I feel for the Royal family ever since Princess Margaret visited here in the 1950s, and was the guest of honour at the all-Bach concert we gave for the Montreal Festivals. When I met the Princess at the reception afterwards, she was very pretty and charming – the real vision of a royal princess. Princess Margaret died in 2002. So I sent a letter of sympathy to the Queen. As a show of respect, and since it was the fiftieth anniversary of Queen Elizabeth's accession to the throne, Boris performed *Royal Tribute* with his National Academy Orchestra in July 2002.

The 1950s saw many events that inspired composition. Space exploration opened up exciting possibilities and new musical techniques were coming into vogue. *Spheres in Orbit*, a commission of the Montreal Symphony Orchestra and dedicated to them, combined the two. It is one of the few works I have written using the twelve-tone technique. That seemed the most appropriate method to treat such a technological subject – the Russian satellite, Sputnik III. I had seen this wonderful scientific creation in1958, while sky-watching with my neighbours at our cottage on Lac des Chats in the Laurentians. I wanted to convey something about it in music, to express the feeling of weightlessness. On October 14th 1962 I took this composition to Russia and became the first Canadian to conduct my own work there, with the Moscow State Radio and Television Orchestra. They were wonderful to me – a standing ovation and eight curtain calls! It was especially meaningful since twelve-tone works were not well known in Russia at that time.

The Soviets organized a meeting between Aram Khachaturian, other members of their composers' union, and me. They were interested to hear about the twelve-tone system and why North American composers found it worthwhile as a musical language. My performance of *Spheres in Orbit* was recorded in Moscow and released by the Soviet *Melodya* label in Russia along with Respighi's *Pines of Rome* which I conducted on the same occasion. Later on the masters were purchased by Everest Records in Hollywood and released worldwide under their Contemporary Masterworks label.

I soon wrote *Three Astral Visions* on a commission from the Samuel Lapitsky Foundation. This was done using modified twelve-tone principles and dedicated to the heroes of our skies.

The McGill Chamber Orchestra premiered it in March 1959 and the CBC International Service recorded it. I later conducted *Three Astral Visions* as part of a program for the Stratford Festival. This was unusual. Although I often conducted works commissioned by the Lapitsky Foundation, they were usually by other composers, my colleagues, and, I guess, you could say my competition. It was a pleasure to conduct a work of my own, not just to feel the satisfaction of bringing my written notes to life, but to do it exactly as I had envisioned.

Although I wrote several pieces using the twelve-tone technique, I've never been particularly attracted by it. My early compositions were mainly Romantic and my other works were more along the Neoclassical line – some with a satirical bent, since I believe the greater truth can be told through jest. I did however, have some exposure to modernist composers. I once spent an entire day with Paul Hindemith in Montreal when he came to lecture to the Composers' League. He was wonderful with the students because he pared down everything they wrote. The moment they came to him they had to go right back to two-part writing. It was oversimplification for a good reason – he wanted to make sure their craft was such that they knew what they were doing. I admired Hindemith for his practicality as well as the individualism of his style. Hindemith has a compositional voice that makes his work immediately identifiable. He is one of the most original and forceful composers of the 20th century. A master of counterpoint, he combines modern devices such as atonality with polyphony that stems from Bach.

As a person I found him rather dry and unemotional. He was interested in the Canadian League of Composers. But like his music he seemed to be stimulated by fact rather than fancy. I was astonished that none of my colleagues seemed interested to meet him. I was particularly eager to talk with him about the number of major works he had written for chamber orchestra – the "Kammermusik" pieces, his *Four Temperaments* and the *Trauermusik*. We performed all of these with the McGill Chamber Orchestra.

When I had to give up playing the violin in 1960, I found one benefit of this disaster was that it gave me more time for composition. Commissions and requests came in steadily. Before the days of the Canada Council, composers looked to various foundations for sufficient funds to produce a new work. One such group was the Lapitsky Foundation, which paid the chosen composer a fee for the composition and the costs of copying the score and parts and guaranteed a first performance with the McGill Chamber Orchestra. Thanks to them I premiered many works by my colleagues, many of whom I counted as friends. When Lapitsky did commission a work from me, it had to go before the committee and compete just as all the other works did.

The Canada Council for the Arts played, and continues to play, a similarly vital role in encouraging composition and performance of Canadian music. They commissioned me to write several symphonic and chamber music works and, in collaboration with the federal government's Department of External Affairs, opened doors abroad.

The CBC was a major source of opportunity. Since the war, its news and public affairs programs attracted a large cross-section of listeners. The post-war years became the golden age of Canadian radio. They broadcast more opera, musicals, classical, chamber and choral music, plus many plays and documentaries, making it enormously popular in the intellectual and artistic communities across Canada. The CBC supported radio orchestras, in addition to the existing orchestras in our major cities, and gave our musicians and singers an audience both nationally and abroad.

The dramas and documentaries required musical background, so they frequently commissioned works from me. I composed the music for a series of radio shows called Playhouse Theatre, produced by Rupert Caplan. He would hand me the script two or three weeks before the rehearsals were due to begin. I would study it, then write around thirty minutes of suitable music. So for about eighteen months I wrote a score every week. In 1951, I even got to write the incidental music for three plays written by my brother, who had a regular program with CBC for several years. My mother insisted on keeping all the manuscripts. Thanks to her I still have them.

The advent of television increased the audience for and, therefore, expanded the development of theatre, ballet, drama and concerts. CBC music directors like John Peter Roberts did much to give creative incentive to worthwhile projects. I welcomed televised concerts since symphonies are written not only to be heard, but to be seen too. Just listening to a recording doesn't engage the eye. The visual enhances the experience. To see the movement, the pattern of it all, the strength of a performance by say, the tympanic section, creates an excitement. Those golden years of the CBC were a very stimulating period.

Today the CBC has fallen on hard times. At one time I and many other Canadian artists would receive a third of our annual income from the CBC. It is truly sad to see what has become of this vital engine of Canadian creativity.

Those were heady days. In 1954 the British Broadcasting Corporation in London, England added my name to their list of composers and conductors. In 1961 I was honoured with the title, "Composer of the Commonwealth" and received the Sir Arnold Bax Gold Medal. Again, I could not attend the ceremony. The wife of George Drew, the Canadian High Commissioner, accepted the medal on my behalf and the Drews sent it on to me with a lovely letter.

Six years later Canada's Centennial Year was upon us. I really was fortunate to be living and working in Montreal at a time when the city was celebrating so many events one after the other – Canada's Centennial, Expo '67, and then the Olympics in 1976. Each event yielded commissions and opportunities for me to compose and often to conduct special programs.

The CBC commissioned my *Centennial Colloquy*, which I dedicated to Boris, who conducted its premiere with the CBC Wind Orchestra. Boris performed the work in Wales where he was Chief Conductor of the BBC National Orchestra of Wales. Lotte and I were proud to attend the performance which was also broadcast throughout Britain on Radio 3. In fact Boris has conducted most of my orchestral compositions with the various orchestras with which he has been associated, often inviting me to conduct them myself. It is gratifying to have a son who believes in my works and continues my legacy.

Centennial Year was a rich source of inspiration and opportunities. I wrote several works which were played at Expo's Canadian Pavilion. *Les Grands Ballets Canadiens* asked me to compose the music for a ballet on the legend of La Corriveau. This work has been performed in Canada, America and Europe.

In a lighter vein, I dedicated what I hoped was a witty endeavour, *Centennial Cerebration*, to Mrs. Barbara Davis, then president of the McGill Chamber Orchestra. The piece, commissioned by the Centennial Commission, calls for a choir and employs a stylized version of *O Canada* as thematic material. I penned myself the lyrics. The premiere took place in the ballroom of the Sheraton Mount Royal Hotel, on April 17, 1967, with the choir of *L'Ecole Normale de Musique* and Jean-Louis Roux as narrator. In the lyrics I posed a few questions about the future of our nation and, with tongue in cheek, inserted some less-than-obscure references to the linguistic situation in Quebec and the federal policies of bilingualism and biculturalism. Afterwards I nervously wondered if I had gone too far, but much to my relief, none of the many telegrams and comments I received indicated anyone had taken offence.

While Canada's history was much on our minds, my American musicologist friend, Professor Barry S. Brook, was investigating French musical history. In his quest to discover what sort of music was being composed in France before and after their 1789 Revolution, he came across the giddiest, most frivolous music you ever heard – music that was incongruously in vogue while heads were rolling in the streets. A good many of the French composers' names from that period such as Filippo Ruge, Simon Le Duc, and Jean-Baptiste Breval are barely known today. Professor Brook had had the best of their concerti assembled and published by *L'Institut de musicologie de l'Université de Paris* in 1962, in a volume he called *La Symphonie Française*. Now he asked me to edit, bow and nuance these concerti, which I happily did. We later performed them with Les Jeunes Virtuoses. Let us hope the chaos of our times does not bring about results similar to those in France!

Montreal experienced Beethoven-mania from the mid-1960s leading up to the bicentennial of his birth in 1970. A Montreal-centric aspect of this was the discovery of a little scrap of music manuscript in Beethoven's handwriting, dedicated to the Quebec music teacher Theodore Frederic Molt in December 1825. Montrealer Lawrence Lande brought it home from New York in 1966, to great fanfare. The manuscript was a brief musical canon called *Freu dich des Lebens.*

Lande asked if I'd like to compose a fuller treatment of the canon for the McGill Chamber Orchestra. Since Beethoven has always been a favourite of mine and like me, he has an affinity for the marriage of head and heart, I gladly agreed. Lande personally commissioned me to write the work I called *Paraphrase in Polyphony,* which is basically a series of variants on the theme of the little canon. To get into Beethoven's mind I researched and chose musical ideas we know he was working with at the time – intervals and thematic material that appear in his late quartets and elsewhere. We premiered the resulting *Paraphrase* in November 1967, and the Montreal Symphony performed it again the following January under Roberto Benzi. The recording, which I conducted and Edward Farrant produced, was done by the *Orchestre de Radio-Canada.*

The music community in Montreal held many commemorative events featuring Beethoven's music and since I had intimate knowledge of the great man's works through research in rare volumes, I wanted to contribute to the celebrations. The CBC offered me a commission to orchestrate a group of Beethoven's preludes and fugues. After going for a walk with Beethoven expert Paul Loyonnet, I settled on the title *The Young Prometheus,* in reference to Beethoven's stature as a true giant of music and, in particular, to his contrapuntal art.

The preludes and fugues themselves I drew from a rare volume of collected Beethoven compositions that I had, and still have, in my possession. I had become aware of it while on tour through Scandinavia when a radio director in Stockholm showed me a collection of unpublished contrapuntal compositions by the young Viennese master. Later the Montreal book collector Heinz Heinemann found the original volume for me. It was an amazing find, because it was published in a limited subscription edition in Vienna in 1832, just five years after the composer's death, by Beethoven's friend, Ignaz Ritter von Seyfried. The publisher Tobias Haslinger had entrusted him to find whatever was available in Beethoven's house after he died and compile it into this collection. It contains several works never printed elsewhere, as well as sketches from Beethoven's notebooks. This is music from Beethoven's youth from about age nineteen to twenty-five, roughly 1789-1795, before he wrote the great symphonies. Among the original subscribers to the limited edition were the Grimm brothers of fairy-tale fame, Johann Strauss senior, Carl Czerny and Frederick Chopin. I occasionally show this volume to guests in my home.

When Otto Klemperer, the famous German conductor was with the Montreal Symphony Orchestra, he often dined at our home with his wife and daughter, Lotte. When I showed him the Beethoven volume one evening, he became so absorbed that we couldn't get him to eat. Everything was cold by the time he finally came to the table. The book holds such a fascination for Beethoven lovers.

My friends at the CBC had become interested in these works of the youthful Beethoven too. After discussing the possibilities with John Roberts, the CBC Head of Music at the time and Helmut Kallmann, chief music librarian, who went on to establish the music division of the National Library of Canada and the *Encyclopedia of Music in Canada*, the CBC offered me a commission to score and arrange the authenticated Beethoven preludes and fugues, with an eye to performing and broadcasting them. The pieces were an interesting puzzle for me to work on, because nowhere did Beethoven specifically state which instrument played, nor was there a single dynamic marking. My task was to set the preludes and fugues for a symphony orchestra of Beethoven's proportions, using the instrumentation typical of his time, with the dynamics that I thought applied.

Thus in 1969 the CBC commissioned me to orchestrate twelve preludes and twelve fugues. I used the title I had discussed with Paul Loyonnet, *The Young Prometheus*. I conducted the CBC Symphony in Toronto in the recording which was released by Select Records and chosen as Record of the Month.

While poring over the preludes and fugues I came across another find – some incomplete, abbreviated minuets and canons, also from Beethoven's pen. Although I already had enough material to keep me busy, I couldn't resist orchestrating those too, using as a basis Beethoven's own designation of how they might be dealt with. Beethoven had not worked out the canons fully as some were only partial sketches, in others, pieces of the manuscript were simply missing. The McGill Chamber Orchestra committee, interested in performing the final result, offered me a commission. So I went about weighing the evidence available and based on careful research, made my own decisions as to how Beethoven would have completed them. It took me most of a summer of painstaking work to orchestrate these canons and minuets. I am quite proud of the resulting work.

For the Beethoven Bicentennial in 1970 I produced sets of orchestrations of *Seven Minuets and Six Canons for Chamber Orchestra*, and *Three Preludes and Fugues for Strings*. These were recorded by the CBC and broadcast nationally. For these I conducted the McGill Chamber Orchestra at Redpath Hall. Our producer was the very conscientious Kit Kinnaird who headed CBC's English Network Music Department in Montreal for many years.

I have also enjoyed researching the works of other composers, usually to orchestrate or nuance the scores, or sometimes out of sheer interest. I have an antiquarian's fascination with rare volumes, even if my pocketbook hasn't always matched my tastes. Whenever I saw anything collectible and of real value, especially in Europe, I would try to get it. I own a volume containing the complete texts of the nine oratorios of George Frederick Handel, published in 1799, given to me by the German consul's wife before they left Montreal. In appreciation of our performance at Notre Dame Cathedral in Montreal of *Christ On The Mount of Olives*, one of Beethoven's really great works, she gave me another treasure, the original publication of this quite involved and barely known oratorio. It was beautifully set out in 1699 and remains in immaculate condition.

Some things I own are priceless. I possess a fragile, original bound manuscript of a mass written by no less a personage than Pope Urbanus VIII, the last of the Urbans. They are written in neumes (a type of music notation used centuries ago), in the Pope's own handwriting. The first performance of this papal mass took place in 1643 on the hills of Quebec. The last three pages titled, *Festa St. Joseph*, are his tribute to the patron saint of Quebec. Pope Urban had authorized special indulgences for prayers to St. Joseph as the patron saint of Canada and St. Joseph was formally installed at a ceremony in Quebec City on 19 March 1637, his feast day. This publication came out just a few years later in 1643.

Although historical events have interested me as subjects for compositions, I have been moved to write works based on people I have known. I was delighted to meet and professionally associate with several of the European immigrants to Canada, particularly those who contributed their talents to the Canadian fabric. In this regard, I must first mention Helmut Blume, who, in the 1940s was in charge of the German Section of the CBC's newly formed International Service, and, much later, became Dean of the Faculty of Music at McGill and, therefore, my boss. My suite, *Five Characterizations of Pianists Who Taught at McGill*, mirrors Helmut Blume and John Newmark with one movement each. The other three movements were for Samuel Levitan, Rose Goldblatt, and Charles Reiner, a graduate of the Liszt Academy in Budapest, Hungary.

Critic's Corner is possibly the best-known of my works about real people, but no one except me will ever know who they are. It is my Enigma. I was always intrigued by the assailant authority with which music critics pen their comments. I'm quite sensitive to musical criticism – positive reviews make my spirit soar. Fortunately, my work generally has received good reviews. But sooner or later every musician meets a puffed-up critic who makes you want to deflate him. Taking my inspiration from Debussy's *Coin des Enfants*, I wrote a work for percussion and string quartet and called it *Critic's Corner*. It has five movements in variation form, each of which represents a different type of critic. The first movement expresses the flamboyant, yet basically shallow type. The second movement lampoons the critic primarily interested in juggling words at the expense of content. The third movement describes the self indulgent sentimentalist, the fourth movement, the sly rather precious perfectionist and the fifth movement, the erudite busily in search of significance between the lines. I consider it valid even today. The Andante movement ends with a cow bell softly ringing, a reference to a Montreal critic who asked, "*Est ce qu'il pense que nous sommes des vaches?*" ("Does he think we are cows?"), to which I reply with a quotation expanding George Bernard Shaw. "Those who can, do; those who can't, teach; those who can't teach, just criticize."

Following the premiere of *Critic's Corner*, a number of people phoned to tell me that they recognized whose personality I had portrayed. But when the critics themselves called me, I had a fleeting evil image of the Last Supper in my mind, with each critic asking, "Lord, is it I? Lord, is it I?" It just proves that for composers, the eighth note can be mightier than the pen. Pieces such as *Critic's Corner* proved to me that I could always say more by composing music, than with lengthy verbiage about what clothes someone wore or how they behaved. Music is my language, truly.

There is another adage, "Write what you know." Although it applies mostly to writers of prose, I have found it is also true for musical composition. Each of my compositions reflects some event in my life. They mirror me, my circumstances, my times. Even my major orchestral works contain personal and introspective elements. In many ways my music is the story of my life.

I dedicated several compositions to individuals who helped or inspired me. *Analogy in Anagram* was for Pierre Monteux who often guest-conducted the Montreal Symphony Orchestra. I had worked with him closely as concertmaster and, in 1959, he asked me to write something for him. I didn't often attempt abstract music, preferring to have some kind of program on which to base my writing. But I made an exception that time. The *Analogy* is in variation form, a technique I use often in my compositions. The title *Analogy in Anagram* refers to the theme being manipulated in inversion and retrograde. The MSO premiered it while I was its concertmaster. He asked me to conduct the *Analogy* as part of one of his programs.

My family, of course, was a wonderful source of inspiration.

After our first son was born in 1944, I composed a little lullaby called *Lullaby and Procession of the Toys*. It is a sort of *Nutcracker* piece, in which a child dreams of his toys coming to life. *Arabesque* was written for Lotte after her radical mastectomy in 1958 when she was thirty-four. She had been booked for a solo concert no more than six weeks later. Naturally after such an operation a patient can't move her arm or fingers easily. While Lotte was recuperating in hospital, I went to visit her and opened the door quietly. There she was painfully climbing her fingers up the wall in an exercise the doctor had told her would regain her strength. I wrote *Arabesque* largely to encourage her to get well. She used this scheduled performance as the impetus for her recovery and, amazingly to all concerned, performed it on the scheduled date.

My Mother, My Memorial, was written for the other important woman in my life, my mother. My mother Annie passed away in January of 1978 and left an enormous void in my home and my heart. I was guest-conducting at the Festival of Youth Orchestras in Banff when she contracted pneumonia and was hospitalized. When Lotte informed me of her death, I rushed home to Montreal. After she was laid to rest, knowing my mother would have insisted, I returned to finish my engagement at Banff with a heavy heart, vowing to write a work in her memory. She had been an integral part of my career and had provided unconditional love and support for Lotte, our sons and me.

Circle, Triangle, Four Squares was inspired by a happier occasion. At age nine, my son Denis came home from school with a drawing which I liked very much. I congratulated him, "Denis, this is very good! How did you do that?"

He explained, "The teacher drew circles and triangles on the board and asked the class to do something with them. So I did."

The drawing really appealed to me because the question of form in music has always been of great importance to me. So I promised Denis, "The basis of your drawing is form. I'm going to use it as the motif of a piece. I'll use exactly your shapes, a circle, triangle and four squares, but I'm going to do them in musical terminology." It struck me that Denis' drawing was the perfect opportunity for a composition using a neo-classical concept of basic structure. To create the composition, I used a sheet of graph paper, one square per note, and matched the notes to the different shapes in his drawing. Denis' picture still hangs on my dining room wall.

Circle, Triangle, Four Squares was premiered by the McGill Chamber Orchestra in 1963. Four years later I conducted the orchestra in a performance of the piece for a Radio Canada International recording for Centennial year. On the same recording is a piece by Jean Vallerand, *Cordes en Mouvement.* He had composed it as a commission from the Lapitsky Foundation and the orchestra had premiered it. Jean and I were both Montrealers, born in the same year, so it seemed natural that we should share space on this LP.

I've worked closely with many Canadian musicians. Several have specialized in performing the works of their countrymen, and, luckily, many of them chose my compositions. Maureen Forrester made an excellent recording of my *Songs of Contemplation* with the Orford Quartet, when my son Denis was its cellist. Rose Goldblatt, the Montreal pianist, played my music on more than one occasion. She took my *Suite for Piano* to New York and played it at their Town Hall, in her first recital in that city, in October 1942.

I was especially pleased when Ethel Stark, the conductor of the Montreal Women's Orchestra, commissioned me to compose a piece for the Song Festival in Israel. At the festival, she conducted it with an all-Canadian choir. This was in August 1952 and I had not been to Israel, yet.

Now that Canadian musicians and composers are frequently heard outside our country it's easy to forget that this was not always so. There was a time – not too many decades ago – when the title "Canadian composer" or "Canadian musician" was interpreted to mean second-best. We were viewed as the colonials. So back in the 1950s and 1960s, it was not easy to have one's compositions performed abroad. I was fortunate that some of my works were played overseas, even in places like Spain where Canadian music was virtually unknown. In late 1952, Dr. Heinz Unger conducted two of my works, *Fancy and Folly* and *From Sea to Sea* (the Quebec and British Columbia movements) with the Valencia Orchestra.

As far as I know, it was the first performance of Canadian music in Spain. The newspapers were interested in the musical nationalism expressed in *From Sea to Sea*, (which is also known as the *Canadian Suite*), perhaps because their own composers were exploring similar nationalistic approaches. Unger had become acquainted with my work while conducting a new CBC radio symphonic series earlier that September.

I was fortunate that some of the great conductors who emigrated to North America because of the war presented my works in the United States. Leopold Stokowski had conducted the Montreal Symphony Orchestra and consequently I knew him quite well. He had dined at our home and we had worked together on bowings for the concerts he conducted in Montreal. He was a very imposing man with that infamous leonine mane of white hair. He was the very image of "The Maestro". Perhaps because of his Irish roots (his mother was Irish and his father Polish), he had a bit of the blarney in him. For example, he appeared at the end of the first *Fantasia* film shaking hands on screen with an animated Mickey Mouse! He had obviously left his English organist roots – where he was known as Leonard Stokes – far behind him. "Stokey", as his friends called him, was a very generous man who had a special place in his heart for new music and young people. For example, he preceded Leonard Bernstein in the establishment of a series of Young People's Concerts with the Philadelphia Orchestra in 1933. He championed the work of Gustav Mahler presenting his 8th Symphony, the *Symphony of a Thousand*, in its American premiere in 1916 when I was but one year old! I was thrilled when he chose to give the US premiere of my *Violin Concerto* in October 1953 as part of an all-Canadian program at Carnegie Hall. Canadian violinist Noel Brunet was the soloist. For that occasion, Stokowski included works by Pierre Mercure, Colin McPhee, François Morel and Healey Willan. I remember this performance well because Stokowski had a very personal way of interpreting music. He marked his scores meticulously in various colours and sometimes indicated individual bowings for each player in the string section. We had not really discussed my intentions for the *Violin Concerto* in detail and I arrived only for the dress rehearsal. I was both shocked and amazed. It was a marvelous interpretation, yet completely different than I would ever have intended.

That was not the only time my work was played at Carnegie Hall. *Delightful Delusions*, the piece I wrote for Désiré Defauw was performed there in January 1954 and Denis (while still in his teens,) played a solo recital at Carnegie Hall in 1968. He played the *Arabesque* I had written several years earlier for Lotte. Boris conducted my *Songs of Contemplation* with the New York Oratorio Society Orchestra in 1990 and I conducted my *Violin Concerto* there with the American Symphony. I am especially proud that my gifted sons have performed my music in that famous hall.

The elegant and clever Vladimir Golschmann conducted the world premiere of *Fancy and Folly*, (a little piece he had commissioned me to write especially for him), with the Saint Louis Symphony Orchestra in January 1948. I was not able to be there, but he wrote to me afterward to assure me that everything went beautifully and the audience reception was excellent. One of the Missouri reviewers, according to Golschmann, described it as a "cleanly wrought, intricate composition."

It is Canadian themes and subjects, however, that have been of enduring interest to me. When Justin Trudeau was born, I was inspired by the thought that here was a true Canadian, with a French father of Irish and French descent and an English mother, in a country with Inuit and Indian surroundings. To honour the occasion, the Canada Council commissioned me to create something suitable, and I penned *Songs of the Central Eskimos* and *Indian Legends*, two short works based on the ancient themes of these peoples. The date was 1972.

Some years later Pierre Trudeau invited me to play these pieces for a visiting Belgian delegation at 24 Sussex Drive. He phoned me at my home in Montreal but I didn't recognize his voice. I said, "Who's speaking?"

"Pierre," was the brief reply.

"But Pierre who?" I continued to press the unknown caller.

"For God's sake, it's Pierre Trudeau!"

I adopted a different tone with him after that.

Pierre wanted us in Ottawa in just two days' time. Somehow

Lotte managed to assemble John Newmark, soprano Henrietta Plattford and her baritone husband Kenneth Asch, who had just returned from a tour of the far north where they performed the work. We all headed off to 24 Sussex Drive in Ottawa.

Trudeau became a very good friend. I was fond of him and of his family. He was a man of tremendous character and courage. He attended Lotte's investiture as a Member of the Order of Canada. He occasionally attended our McGill Chamber Orchestra concerts especially after he left office as Prime Minister. He attended many special family occasions, for example my 80th birthday celebrations at Place des Arts when Boris conducted, Yo Yo Ma was soloist and Denis (who had been a co-student of Ma's with Leonard Rose) played Handel's concerto for two cellos. Trudeau attended his last McGill Chamber Orchestra concert at Notre Dame Cathedral. Itzhak Perlman was soloist and Trudeau attended with his son Sasha. Our daughter-in-law Ardyth sat with the Trudeaus and was charmed by Pierre's running commentary on the music to his son.

Denis invited Trudeau to give an address on the Canadian Constitution to my granddaughter Talia's class at Lower Canada College. To our astonishment he came and made quite an impression on these young minds. Trudeau always impressed me as an extremely modest yet highly intelligent and well informed man. He made a huge impression. We were all terribly sad when he passed away. He made you feel proud to be a Canadian.

* * *

In the 1970s, commissions became scarce for all of us, in part because few orchestras or commissioning bodies wanted to risk paying good money for an atonal or experimental piece which audiences would not buy tickets to hear. Even those of us who are not experimental composers were affected by this mindset.

Although I wrote the bulk of my work before 1980, I still compose from time to time. I tried to write a piece for Lotte after she passed away on January 6, 1998, but I decided it did not do her justice. Perhaps one day I'll produce something worthy of her memory. Recently I was asked to compose a few works in honour of the millennium, and since I love writing for and about significant historical events, I was happy to comply. The result is *Millennium Overture* and three separate movements which I conducted with the McGill Chamber Orchestra in the 2000 season.

There are a few other works that have not made it onto paper – the ones that got away. One was a prospective collaboration with Pierre Trudeau, for an opera. In 1968 an adaptation of Aristophanes' *Lysistrata* by André Brassard and Michel Tremblay was published by Les Editions Lemeac. I wanted to use it as the basis of a libretto for a perspective comic opera. We discussed it at the coffee and brandy stage of a dinner at the home of the Montreal based Greek shipping magnate Frixos Papachristides. Pierre was at his brilliant best that evening. He knew the play well and we discussed the characters and my projected dispersal of the musical arias. We debated the theme of how the heroine, Lysistrate, proposed to eliminate all wars by withholding her feminine favours. Since we were enjoying our conversation so much and Pierre knew the work so well, I suggested we collaborate. He replied regretfully, "Alex, I wish I had thought of it first, but I'm still writing my memoirs." Although Trudeau couldn't join me in this work, I've always believed that a collaboration on the theme of such an independent woman would have suited him perfectly.

My Third Life – Conductor and Entrepreneur

(1940–2004)

Conducting is the supreme classical music challenge. A conductor tries to bring his idea of the composer's intentions to life in a concert hall. For this he has the entire panoply of sonorities that can be produced by an ensemble of many instruments and voices. It is different from the challenge of playing an instrument, in that he must be able to convince others to accept his interpretation and make it their own.

Having watched the baton of many a maestro since age eleven, I was always intrigued by what seemed to me to be the ultimate in musical interpretation. As soon as I returned to Montreal in 1939, I discovered that the conductor's podium was a place I felt very comfortable.

I had studied conducting formally at McGill and Juilliard, but my real education began when I served as concertmaster and then assistant conductor, with the first Montreal Orchestra. It was led by some of the best conductors in the world and I used to observe them carefully. I knew I had much to learn from these great men.

I concluded that the interaction of a great conductor with an orchestra is really a form of hypnosis, based on the conductor's absolute conviction that what he is doing gives the poetry and the stance of the musical phrase. The best conductors I had worked with had an identifiable personality on stage which they communicated without uttering a single word. A baton makes no sound at all. With Markevitch the playing was very pristine, clean and precise, but emotionally detached. Stokowski painted in sound, so natural he seemed unaware of it. Vladimir Golschmann offered little criticism except to repeat, "They must understand the music." Then there were the perfection-seekers like Toscanini. I think he must have thought, play as fast as you can, keep their minds busy, so their main object is the mechanics of the music. Those conductors were giants.

During Dean Clarke's tenure with the orchestra we often discussed the symphonies of composers such as Brahms, Sibelius, and Vaughan Williams as he molded their works into human experiences. The transformation process fascinated me and continues to challenge me to mount the podium even now.

I had conducted the orchestra in several CBC broadcasts, but my first opportunity to conduct a full symphony on my own came when I was twenty-five. Just before the dress rehearsal in the last subscription concert of the Montreal Orchestra's 1940-1941 season, Douglas Clarke fell ill suddenly and was taken to hospital. I felt honoured, though not a little apprehensive, when he called and asked me to take over for him. For me it was a baptism by fire. The program was challenging – Brahms' *Variations on a Theme by Haydn*, Beethoven's *Eighth Symphony*, and after the interval the renowned pianist Henrietta Schumann was to play the Montreal premiere of Rachmaninoff's *Third Piano Concerto*.

Much to my relief and maybe to Clarke's too, the concert, in His Majesty's Theatre, was successful. The reviews, though not raves, were encouraging and cited my preparedness. When the *Montreal Gazette* noted that I, "had the makings of a first class conductor," I was intoxicated with joy. My path was set – I was going to become a conductor.

Wilfrid Pelletier, well-known French-Canadian conductor at New York's Metropolitan Opera, gave me further conducting opportunities whenever he needed an English-speaking conductor for his Matinée Symphonique education concerts. All these activities helped me gain experience and confidence.

I began to notice that my approach to the orchestral repertoire differed from Pelletier's whose instrument was the piano and whose expertise was opera. I sought to develop a conducting style that was emotional, that interpreted the score more deeply. I used my experience as a string player to provide bowings which would highlight dynamic contrast and shadings. I wanted the music to move and inspire the audience. To do this I first had to find inspiration myself, which I did in the thrilling performances of the great international conductors who visited, thanks to MSO Managing Director Pierre Béique.

When Klemperer, Ormandy, Mûnch, Monteux, Goosens, Beecham and their peers had to escape Europe, Béique invited them to conduct the Montreal Symphony Orchestra before 57th Street in New York City (sometimes called the management capital of the world) could ensnare them. We must have appeared provincial to these world renowned conductors. Our regular concert hall, Le Plateau, was a high school gym seating a mere 900 people on hard wooden chairs. We were good players but those conductors transformed us in two or three rehearsals. I used to marvel that the whole sound had changed.

Leonard Bernstein guest-conducted the MSO soon after he was appointed to the New York Philharmonic. He was quite young, in his early twenties. He scheduled *Le Sacre du Printemps* by Stravinsky, which the orchestra had never played. It is complicated even for the best orchestras – the last section is alternating rhythms of four, seven, nine beats to the bar. Monteux held forty-five rehearsals for its first performance at the Théâtre du Châtelet in Paris. Bernstein tried it once with us, then at the interval told me, "We're not going to do it."

I protested, "Shouldn't you speak to the management about taking it off the program?"

He responded, "I'm *not* doing it. We'll give an exciting performance of Rimsky-Korsakoff's *Scheherezade* and the players will enjoy it instead of struggling with the Stravinsky."

So the next rehearsal we played *Scheherezade*. I marvelled at this youth – to have the conviction to change the program simply because he believed the result would be better. Bernstein knew intrinsically that a good conductor must be absolutely sure of what he is doing and authoritative enough to act on it.

The non-playing conductor has existed only for the past two centuries since large symphony orchestras were established and opera put its players in the pit. Prior to this, Baroque and early Classical orchestras were led by the concertmaster/first violinist while he played, or from the keyboard by the harpsichord player. These playing conductors led with the hand or the bow when not leading with their head to indicate entries, and assumed the responsibility for interpreting the music and coordinating rehearsals.

It worked well with a small group of players. When orchestras increased in size it became necessary to have someone responsible for deciding tempi, style and content who was not distracted by also playing. So the non-playing maestro was born.

Conductors began to use a baton to be more visible to the stage and the extremities of a large group of musicians, and to devise a soundless system of communication. Through the language of gesture they re-enact the musical content and remind the players of decisions taken during rehearsal. It is a study and discipline unto itself.

Many of us have polished our conducting technique in master classes given by Pierre Monteux and Igor Markevitch, whose courses I attended in the late 1950s. Coincidentally they were also Boris' first teachers.

Markevitch was the most analytical conductor I knew. He taught us basic conducting technique and perfected a language of the art of conducting gesture. He taught me that the double-reed instruments (oboe, English horn, and bassoon) require a small precise upbeat, while players of brass instruments, such as horns, trumpets, trombones and tubas, require a gesture commensurate with the size and proportion of their instruments. The very opposite conducting gesture is necessary for the light percussion and all smaller woodwind instruments. Dynamics are communicated by the size of the gesture and the distance of the conductor's hands from his or her body. He stressed the independence of each hand – the right hand took care of the beat while the main function of the left hand was to indicate phrasing. The Markevitch technique is precise and easily communicates your interpretation to the orchestra.

Igor Markevitch came to Montreal in 1957 as Principal Conductor of Les Concerts Sinfonique, the French successor to Douglas Clarke's Montreal Orchestra. Our current orchestra called Montreal Symphony Orchestra/*Orchestre Symphonique de Montréal* traces its roots back to 1935, when Wilfrid Pelletier formed an ensemble called Les Concerts Symphoniques because of disagreements over the choice of repertoire and guest conductors. French Canadian members of the board, in particular Mme Antonia David, whose husband Louis Athanase had great political influence with the Quebec government, wanted to hire French Canadian composers and conductors. Clarke would not allow interference in what he deemed his musical decisions – conductors were much more autocratic in those days. So certain board members defected from Clarke's orchestra and formed their own. For a time the two orchestras functioned simultaneously in Montreal with basically the same musicians. Clarke's illness was the decisive factor that ended his Montreal Orchestra in 1941.

It was for me a great sadness. Clarke had been my mentor since I was young. He had taught me at McGill, directed me from afar while I attended Juilliard, encouraged me to compose, brought me on staff at McGill University and the Montreal Symphony, advanced me to the position of concertmaster, and provided my first conducting opportunities. He had guided my transformation from a child of poor immigrants on Napoleon Street to a musician of status across the continent. I respected him as a musician and was deeply fond of him as a person. It was my first lesson in musical politics.

But as they say 'every cloud has a silver lining' and from the conducting point of view, that for me was Igor Markevitch. In 1957 he invited me to attend a six-week summer course for conductors from around the world, held at the beautiful Institute of Fine Arts in Mexico City.

Mexico overwhelmed and inspired me as a most exciting country. The relics of its history stood in evidence everywhere. Public art in building frescoes and statuary graced almost every street corner. Folk music emanated from every doorway and public square. Its art and music were characteristic of its strength and independence. I saw the nation as a sleeping giant – colossal in size and geography, ripe with talent ready to develop.

Markevitch encouraged me to enter the Pan-American Conductors' Competition held at the end of the course. I was thrilled to win first prize, which consisted of a gold medal, diploma and most important, an invitation by Mexico's National Orchestra to conduct a concert during the following season. That concert took place in the spring of 1958, and the program included the *Roman Carnival* overture by Berlioz and Shostakovitch's *5th Symphony*. At the end of the concert the musicians paid me the ultimate compliment by breaking into *The Bull-fighter's Song* without conductor.

The winning of the Pan American Prize was not just the result of Markevitch's influence. I had learned good basic conducting technique and gained experience at university, and when Désiré Defauw appointed me assistant conductor in 1947, a position I enjoyed concurrently with my work as the Les Concert Symphonique's concertmaster and first violin in the McGill String Quartet.

Defauw was music director of the symphony orchestra from 1940 to 1952. During those twelve years the Montreal Symphony blossomed under the world's most distinguished guest-conductors – Sir Thomas Beecham, Erich Leinsdorf, Fritz Busch, Georges Enesco, Leonard Bernstein, Pierre Monteux, Charles Mûnch, George Szell and Leopold Stokowski among them.

What better instruction could I possibly have had? I watched, listened and studied how these conductors transformed a symphony from notes on a dry soundless page into a memorable emotional and musical experience. Defauw also helped bring some of the greatest guest soloists to Montreal – violinists Jascha Heifetz, Jacques Thibaud and Mischa Elman, cellists Emanuel Feuermann and Gregor Piatigorsky.

But they were foreign-born musicians and immigrants. Except for Sir Ernest MacMillan and Douglas Clarke, there was no internationally recognized Canadian conductor to look up to in Canada during the 1930s and 1940s. Nowadays, I'm glad to say, we are more self-sufficient – or should be. We produce excellent musicians and conductors here in our own institutions, who are making careers outside Canada. There is no greater incentive for a new generation of Canadians than to see the success of their countrymen.

Being a permanent assistant, even to such a talented and

likeable man as Defauw did not satisfy my ambitions. I was still young – only thirty-two – with a young man's dreams. I regarded the appointment as only a first step towards a conducting career and continued to seek out more challenging conducting experience where I could make decisions rather than respond to the choices of others.

I admired Defauw and dedicated my orchestral work, *Delightful Delusions* (the title composed of his initials) to him. He generously invited me to conduct it and even took my poking musical fun at him in good spirit. It was Defauw's habit to stamp his feet like a petulant child whenever he was perturbed at rehearsal, so I reciprocated in *Delusions* by having the members of the orchestra stamp their feet musically at their maestro as the last chord of the piece. He took it like the good sport he was.

Pierre Béique, the symphony's executive director, was Defauw's partner in obtaining the great conductors. I had known Pierre since his days in the Montreal Festivals office when Madame Athanase David was in charge. I'm grateful to him because much of what I learned and experienced in Montreal happened while he managed the symphony. He provided me with many opportunities as a violinist, conductor and composer. Pierre's achievements should be lauded – I described him musically in a composition for brass quintet entitled *MSO – Mutual Salvation Orgy* – also the acronym of the Montreal Symphony Orchestra. It was a commission by Sam Steinberg, owner of the famous Steinberg chain of grocery stores, and was first performed in 1962 at the Montreal Museum of Fine Arts.

In 1949 the legendary Leopold Stokowski invited me to assist him in New York by taking the first rehearsals for a performance of Shostakovitch's fifth symphony. We worked on the score at his beautiful penthouse apartment overlooking Central Park, in a room surrounded by mirrors on all sides. He stood behind me as we rehearsed together. He was most particular. He would instruct me, "Take it again from there. Now, how would you give the impression that the sound is suddenly disappearing?" He suggested that my hand should rise slowly up to the point where there was absolutely nothing. He had studied gesture intelligently yet emotionally. I was most impressed by Stokowski – a real human being with heart and soul and the knowledge to convey his intentions in elegant gesture. My time with him convinced me that my dream to conduct was achievable.

Since I was concertmaster of the MSO and the Montreal Little Symphony under George Schick at the time, the Stokowski opportunity meant my missing a concert with the Little Symphony. When I asked Schick for permission to be absent, he refused, saying I had to choose to be concertmaster or conductor. It was a watershed decision. I left the Little Symphony. That forced me to limit my playing to the Montreal Symphony and to give up many of the freelance positions that earned money but did not further my conducting ambition. I looked for other opportunities, more challenges.

In the late 1940s I guest-conducted the Quebec Symphony and was frequently invited to Toronto to conduct the Promenade Symphony Concerts, simply called "the Prom concerts." They were held in the Varsity Arena over the summer and generally featured Canadian performers such as violinist and concertmaster of the Toronto Symphony, Hyman Goodman, trumpeter Ellis McLintock, and contralto Evaleen Dunlop, as well as choirs and dancers. The CBC broadcast these concerts on the Trans-Canada Network on radio, then in the 1950s on television, extending our audience beyond the arena.

Royal Tribute provided me with an important conducting opportunity in England where I shared the podium at the famed London Promenade Concerts in Royal Albert Hall with the popular Sir Malcolm Sargent. The concert on 12 September 1955 was with the BBC Symphony Orchestra and featured the well-known English pianist Myra Hess. Lotte and eleven-year-old Boris attended. It was a career highlight.

The CBC had a fine orchestra in Toronto which I conducted each season during the 1950s. I conducted that CBC Symphony Orchestra on twenty occasions in programs which consisted of standard but less often featured repertoire and at least one Canadian piece in each program. I recall a particular concert with the internationally celebrated violist William Primrose in which we did Berlioz' *Harold in Italy* and Mozart's *Sinfonia Concertante* with Primrose and the orchestra's concertmaster Albert Pratz. On another program I gave the Canadian premiere of Vaughan Williams' *Pastorale* Symphony and on another Ernst Bloch's *Schelomo* with Zara Nelsova as soloist. The orchestra was wonderful at sight reading new works and the best Canadian orchestra of that time. Igor Stravinsky and his assistant Robert Craft had an association with the CBC Toronto Orchestra and the Festival Singers and made several Columbia recordings with them.

In January of 1959 I guest-conducted the Edmonton Symphony Orchestra in a program that included their first performance of Beethoven's *Eroica*. It was a privilege to introduce this magnificent music to an orchestra and its community. The fact they had never played so important a work gives you an indication of the development of orchestras in Canada compared to Europe and the United States.

Canadian orchestras outside Montreal and Toronto tended to be part amateur and part professional. They performed with great energy and commitment and appreciated the advice I gave, particularly as a practising string player. Conducting a first rate professional ensemble requires a different technique than leading enthusiastic amateurs.

In that context, a conductor depends far more on the players' knowledge of their instruments. His function is to refine interpretation and bring the music to life. Conducting willing semi-professionals puts him in the role of teacher, suggesting fingerings, bowings, instrumental techniques. With sufficient rehearsal, performances may be more exhilarating than those with a top professional ensemble where results may be more perfect, but lack heart.

I believe positive reinforcement and psychology are crucial to draw the best from an orchestra. Many of the great maestros were not too concerned with the players' feelings. The music was their only concern and the end product often justified the means even if the methods were temper tantrums and terror. There were exceptions of course, such as Pierre Monteux and Sir Thomas Beecham.

Before the establishment of the Canada Council for the Arts

in 1957, communities relied primarily on private donors to support orchestras and the creation of compositions. Generally, if a composer wanted an orchestra to perform Canadian music, he himself had to pay for the scores and parts to be copied.

It is not exaggeration to say that the CBC was central to the development of Canadian music. Through the 1950s many Canadian homes began to have a television set and CBC television embraced musical performance. In Montreal, the CBC French Television Network offered a weekly one hour series, *L'heure du Concert*. Eight full length opera productions were produced annually in Montreal. The English Network, headquartered in Toronto, produced a parallel number of programs. I conducted often for the CBC in Montreal, Toronto and in CBC centres across Canada.

By the late 1950s I began searching for more conducting opportunities, in part because I was beginning to have difficulties playing the violin. I knew, full well, that I would soon need to resign from the Montreal Symphony.

In June 1962, I was invited to contribute to a special evening the Boston Pops held in honour of McGill University. Why would an American symphony hold a McGill night? Several members of the McGill Society of Boston, an offshoot of the McGill Graduates Society, organized it and a delegation of McGill associates, including university governors Howard Ross and Anson McKim, were to attend the concert. Arthur Fiedler, the Boston Pops' director, was to be presented with a plaque making him an honorary member of the society. I accepted Fiedler's invitation to share the program conducting my own *Martlet's Muse*, a work I based on five traditional McGill student songs among them a song called *James McGill* and another called *Come, Fill Your Glasses*. The title of the work referred to the martlet, a mythical bird depicted on the coat of arms of James McGill, founder of McGill University. Three of them are on the McGill crest. Robert Silverman was the piano soloist. Hence there were two McGill grads, Silverman and me, on stage at the Boston Symphony Hall that night. Fiedler was in high spirits and so was the audience. I had the impression that the McGill spirits flowed that night!

I have been asked what it was like to be guest-conductor on

Arthur Fiedler's stage, since he *never* shared the conductor's podium at "his" Pops with anyone. Actually, I thought I would die! Not because I was shy and not because I was intimidated by the orchestra. Fiedler didn't leave enough time for me to rehearse the Boston Symphony. He kept practising the other works on the program that he was responsible for. I kept looking at my watch as the time sped by and he kept rehearsing. He finally left me fifteen minutes to rehearse my composition. I had little choice but to tell the orchestra, "Ladies and gentlemen, as you can see, the work itself takes more than the remaining fifteen minutes to play, so what we will rehearse are the crucial spots." I knew I was dealing with a first-class orchestra who could handle the rest of the piece.

Following the performance, Fiedler complimented me, "You needn't have worried. You chose the smartest thing to do." After that we became good friends. Though he seemed an outgoing person, he was really quite shy and required the help of a glass of Jack Daniels to metamorphose into his publicly jovial personality. He came to Montreal several times to guest conduct when we established the Pops series in Montreal and he lent his name to the Kingston Pops.

I have always loved conducting my own compositions since they allow me to be on both sides of the two staged process of making music as creator and interpreter. It's a pleasure which I still enjoy with the McGill Chamber Orchestra and occasionally in the United States. *Sept for Seven*, (seven movements, seven players), which I wrote to celebrate the fiftieth anniversary of the McGill Conservatory in 1955, is a work I've conducted often. For this piece I borrowed texts from Canadian poets such as Earle Birney (*Canada, Case History*) and E.J. Pratt (*Erosion*), which Don McGill narrated. Fittingly, we played this concert in McGill's own Moyse Hall.

As challenging as the variety of guest-conducting around Canada and the United States was, my main conducting commitment was, and remains, to the McGill Chamber Orchestra. I have truly enjoyed our great guest artists such as soprano Pierrette Alarie, flautist Jean-Pierre Rampal, violinists Menuhin, Perlman, David Oistrach and Szigeti, and cellists Yo Yo Ma and Rostropovitch.

Lotte once told reporters, "Give good musicians to my husband and he will be happy as a king."

I took the responsibility toward my fellow Canadian composers seriously and commissioned them to write music for the orchestra whenever circumstances allowed, with the help of the Lapitsky Foundation and later the Canada Council. I also regularly programmed existing works by Canadians because getting a second performance of a new work can often be more difficult than a premiere. I featured Canadian composers when we performed overseas, including works by Jean Coulthard of British Columbia, Harry Freedman from Toronto, Clermont Pepin and Pierre Mercure from Montreal.

In retrospect, Lotte and I became a team of entrepreneurs because of my desire to conduct music of all kinds, from chamber orchestra through opera to pops. I felt I had a gift for musical communication. People seemed to agree and our concerts drew extremely well. As a team, we brought all the elements together, from musicians, soloists, to interesting programs, sponsorship, publicity and audience.

Conductors' careers in the twentieth century have become increasingly peripatetic, with shorter and shorter tenures. They stay in one community for five to ten years, then move on to the next. Lotte and I wanted to devote ourselves to one place – Montreal. I was happy at McGill. When I had to change my focus from violin to conducting, we sought local opportunities that had not yet been developed in order to add to what was already around us and not to compete with it.

In the 1960s and 1970s, Lotte and I organized many full orchestra concerts. We started a series on the Chalet atop Mount Royal called "Concerts under the Stars." Since 1938 The Montreal Symphony Orchestra's season had been augmented each summer by a short season of concerts presented at the Chalet on the large porch of a structure called the Belvedere. A shell was constructed on this porch big enough to accommodate an orchestra of seventy players. The Chalet was surrounded by a large open area capable of seating over 3000 people and enclosed by a balustrade. What a breathtaking, spectacular location. It overlooked a magnificent view of the city below, the St. Lawrence River, the south shore and Mont St. Bruno. On a clear day you could see Vermont in the distance. On a warm summer evening people flocked to hear great music played by a symphony orchestra under the stars, with the lights of the Montreal skyline flickering below them as a backdrop.

Lotte and I sought to expand the Symphony's short summer season with one of our own. Once she had convinced Texaco to sponsor us, we presented our first concert on 21 July 1960, featuring violinist Ida Haendel. The series continued annually until 1968, funded by Texaco and later Dominion Stores. During those eight years, we gave concerts of the greatest classical music with international soloists and always to capacity paying crowds. Thousands more brought blankets and lawn chairs and listened to the music from the surrounding forests for free. One of the charming aspects of the Chalet was that no automobiles were allowed anywhere nearby. The audience strolled the fifteen minutes to the Chalet or rode there in horse-drawn carriages. It was very romantic and very popular. It also augmented the musicians' income.

Outdoor musical activity at the Chalet ceased after the 1968 season when Mayor Drapeau, intoxicated by the success of Expo 67, sought to bring people downtown to the more Francophone east end of the city. The Chalet, owned and operated by the City of Montreal, suddenly became "unavailable." But we weren't daunted. We believed the old saying, "when a door closes a window opens." That window was the concept of Pops concerts.

Pops is a vague term musically, but in this case it means well-known singers in the popular and folk genres, performing very popular classical short works, opera arias and Broadway scores played by a symphony orchestra. Often these concerts feature cross-over music and jazz. The genre probably dates back to the concerts given by Sir Henry Wood at London England's cavernous Royal Albert Hall. Its American embodiment was and still is the Boston Pops Concerts synonymous with Arthur Fiedler.

We initiated the concept in Montreal at the famous Forum on St. Catherine Street in the west end of Montreal. It was in many ways the brainchild of Arthur Carter, vice-president of Sherwin Williams Paints and our neighbour at Lac Des Chats in St. Sauveur. He had heard us perform "en famille" at concerts we occasionally gave on the lawn of our cottage. He knew about the Boston Pops, of course, but wanted to create concerts for people of the most modest means. The Forum held 13,000 seats, with the stage at one end and one third covered in velvet to dampen the echo. We presented our first series there in May 1961 under the banner Montreal Pops Concerts/Les Concerts Populaire de Montréal. When I look now at the programs they seem like the regular symphonic fare orchestras present today rather than the Pops format I described earlier. We invited Walter Susskind, then music director of the Toronto Symphony, to open the series as guest conductor. The program featured Montreal's young inter-national pianist sensation Ronald Turini playing Rachmaninoff's *Variations on a Theme by Paganini* and included Canadian composer Harry Freedman's *Nocturne*, Berlioz' *Roman Carnival Overture* and Dvorak's *New World Symphony*. The expensive seats were reduced to $2.00 plus twenty-five cents tax, and regular seating cost $1.00 plus tax. Sponsored by Canada Packers, the series became an an-nual event, increasing each year until four were given in 1964.

Montreal was still a city somewhat divided along linguistic lines. The Forum was considered in English territory. Montreal's energetic and popular Mayor Jean Drapeau was conscious of this perception and had a vision for greater cultural awareness among French Canadians. In May 1964, he was guest of honour at a con-cert featuring Beethoven's *Ninth Symphony* that Lotte organized and I conducted. A man of vision and enterprise, Drapeau called us to his office the next day. Without wasting time he asked, "Will you start a series of orchestral concerts at the Maurice Richard Arena?"

We were delighted, but full of questions. "What about acous-tics? What about sponsors? What about ... ?"

He replied, "For me, there are no problems, only solutions," and offered us the assistance of his staff to achieve these solutions. As part of his vision for the Montreal Pops, Drapeau proposed, "Let's do what they do at Fiedler's Boston Pops and serve a light meal during the concert." Thus was born the Maurice Richard Arena Pops series. The arena is in the east end of the city, predominantly French, and eventually became the site of the Olympic Velodrome.

We worked closely with Jean Dupire, the officer in charge of receptions and cultural affairs for the Mayor's office and his staff. Mr. Dupire was a sympathetic ally who loved music.

Maurice Richard Arena was quite a departure from our usual surroundings and its round shape presented acoustic challenges. Luckily it proved to be an exciting departure, financially and artistically successful. Lotte convinced Kraft Food Products Ltd. and the Montreal Parks Department to sponsor the concerts. To our knowledge, ours was the only series of orchestral concerts in Canada that featured exclusively Canadian conductors and soloists. This made us very proud.

I directed the four concerts in the first season which took place on 8, 15, 22 and 29 July 1964. Lotte and the city of Montreal staff set up a cabaret-style atmosphere – café tables seating four and draped with cheery checkered tablecloths set the stage for the most sophisticated, culturally enjoyable evening people had ever spent in the arena. This was very different from the cold and noisy, rough-and-tumble hockey games for which the arena had been built. They even provided a special selection of wine with "Bottled Expressly for the Montreal Pops" labels, cheese and pastries and, the crowning touch, a fireworks sparkler for each guest. These were manufactured to order since Lotte's plan was to turn the lights off for the playing of the national anthem during which everyone would light their sparklers and she wanted to ensure that they burned just long enough. The audiences positively loved it. Again, the formula of pops music was less intimidating to audiences than some of the more musically demanding repertoire of the Montreal Symphony or the McGill Chamber Orchestra. Seating at the pops concerts became much in demand.

Mayor Drapeau continued to show his support by attending each of the four concerts in the Maurice Richard Arena series. At the last concert on July 29, he mounted the podium. We had no idea what he was going to say. He turned to the audience. "My friends, I have one question to ask you – would you like another four concerts?"

They applauded wildly and long. We gave annual series of concerts at the Arena until 1969. By 1965 the series had grown to sixteen concerts given from June 2 to September 16, thirteen of which were televised by the CBC. So successful was our format that the Maurice Richard Arena is still used this same way to this day.

The orchestra we used for these concerts was not the McGill Chamber Orchestra. During the summer many musicians, including Lotte and I, had a break from teaching responsibilities and regular concert series. But they welcomed the extra engagements. Many Montreal musicians benefited substantially from those concerts.

During Canada's Centennial and Expo '67, Montreal overflowed with concerts. The MSO extended its regular season by an unprecedented forty extra concerts. We filled Maurice Richard Arena, the Verdun Auditorium, Villeray Arena on St. Helen's Island, and the Chalet on Mount Royal. The City of Montreal, Kraft Foods and Dominion Grocery Stores supported us, thanks to Lotte's entrepreneurial talents.

Being an entrepreneur is risky, especially in the field of orchestral music which is a non-profit venture. Success means being able to pay your bills. Profit is impossible. Failure means you personally are responsible for the loss. It is always easier to be employed by an established orchestra as conductor and music director, but then your vision is hampered by the collective. Matters of program and format become group decisions that must encompass the interests and ambitions of all stakeholders. Those who taught me my craft considered the role of conductor as that of decision maker and I have difficulty seeing it any other way.

As it so often does, our success bred envy. During the Expo year of plenty, the Montreal Symphony extended itself so much, the result was severe financial problems. In order to solve its problems, it appealed to Mayor Drapeau to transfer the city's extensive support from our concerts to the MSO. The Mayor felt it his civic duty to do so.

Pierre Béique from the MSO, John Tobin and René Laporte representing the city, Lotte and I, and representatives from Kraft Foods (our major sponsor) all held a meeting at the offices of J. Walter Thompson. There Lotte and I agreed to turn over our format, administration and sponsorship to the MSO on condition that I retain the title of music director of the series and conduct the majority of concerts.

It seemed like a good solution. We collaborated amicably for the first season in the summer of 1968. In the interests of collegial benefit to both the MSO and my conducting colleagues, I agreed to reduce my conducting activity to only two programs, opening and closing the series of eight concerts with repeats. These colleagues included Boris, who by now had a flourishing career and had just won the prestigious Mitropolous International Conductors Competition in New York and was Leonard Bernstein's assistant with the New York Philharmonic. His concert featured the very popular Quebec pops singer Ginette Reno. For that final concert I was joined by my friend, pianist and composer Neil Chotem. After we finished Tchaikovsky's *Symphony No. 4,* which received thunderous applause from the capacity crowd of 3000, the Quebec chansonnier Gilles Vigneault sang and received several ovations. Unrelated styles of music to be sure, but Montrealers are sophisticated and appreciate the various cultures that make up our city. The concerts were performed twice and the following night's concert was sold out, too.

In 1969, Kraft Foods discontinued their sponsorship. We weren't happy about this loss. As Lotte knew so well, sponsorship relationships required constant contact, seeing to the sponsor's needs before they even realized them themselves, and being proactive. In a large organization like the MSO, there was, perhaps, not the time or personnel with the talent to continue that grooming of what was now only one benefactor among many. The MSO found a new sponsor, the French language newspaper *La Presse.*

During that fertile and lively period, the CBC televised a special Montreal Symphony Orchestra pops series on both the English and French networks, during July and August of 1969, from Salle Wilfrid Pelletier at Place des Arts. In addition, this

MSO series was presented at the new National Arts Centre in Ottawa.

In May 1969, Mayor Drapeau invited me to sign the city's Gold Book, celebrating our accomplishments in support of Montreal's cultural scene. The symbolism was not lost on us, for we were indeed coming to regard this as our golden period.

Alas, gold has a way of being spent. The second season saw our relationship with the MSO suddenly evaporate. In a letter dated 25 June 1968, Béique had promised me his commitment. "I have reviewed with Yvon Lussier and René Laporte the labeling of the Maurice Richard Arena concerts. Hereafter they will be known as the Popular Concerts with you as Music Director with the support of the City of Montreal and Kraft Foods and the participation of the Montreal Symphony Orchestra." But in 1970 they let me go as conductor. We felt betrayed and heartbroken. It seemed so horribly unfair! We had been willing to help the Montreal Symphony but the moment they were on their feet again, we were dismissed. Unless we were willing to take the matter to legal adjudication, a decade of our life's work seemed simply gone.

We are not litigious people. We did not have the stomach nor for that matter the money to finance a protracted legal battle. So we wished the MSO good luck and redoubled our efforts in our own enterprises with the McGill Chamber Orchestra and the Kingston Symphony.

During the golden period of the 1960s, I also conducted more than one choir. One of these was the female choir of L'École Normale of the Congregation Notre Dame. I taught there for fifteen years and found the experience pleasurable and edifying. The girls were full of fun and the choir was fresh and flexible, so I could encourage them in an interesting repertoire. The person in charge was Soeur Marcelle Corneille, one of the most charming people I have ever met, who could discipline with a wilting smile. Before every concert I sent each young lady a corsage of roses or carnations because I referred to them as "mes petite fleurs." I wrote my *Centennial Cerebration* expressly with them in mind and dedicated it to Sister Marcelle. Sometimes now at a reception or concert, a middle-aged woman will approach me and remind me she was one of the members of that choir.

In the 1970s and 1980s I led a Jewish amateur choir of over forty mixed voices, called Ron-Am, Hebrew for "happiness of the people". It consisted of school teachers and synagogue congregation members. Together we performed a lot of interesting Hebraic music. Besides the music of Bloch, Achron and Bernstein, our programs included works by Srul Irving Glick, John Weinzweig, Harry Freedman, Oskar Morawetz, Marvin Duchow and compositions I wrote for them. I led the Ron-Am choir in Haydn's *Ten Commandments* and Mendelssohn's ecclesiastical works. We performed in public and synagogue and over radio stations CKAC and CFCF. I enjoyed my relationship with the choirs and the expanded repertoire I learned as a result of leading them.

I have also derived great pleasure conducting several large choral works with local and visiting choirs. These were highlights not only in my career, but in Montreal's musical calendar as well. To my astonishment, people still remember them such as, Mozart's *Requiem* in Notre Dame Cathedral, filled to capacity; Verdi's *Requiem*, on 27 May 1965 with the legendary Beverly Sills singing solo soprano, and Beethoven's *Ninth Symphony*, both at Place des Arts; the oratorio *Christ on the Mount of Olives;* and the Canadian premiere of Mennotti's *The Bishop of Brindisi*, sung by a choir of 350 schoolchildren directed by Gifford Mitchell, to celebrate the 100th Annual Convention of the Association of Protestant Teachers of Quebec, held on 8 October 1964.

In 1965, I was presented with the possibility of becoming music director for the Kingston Symphony Orchestra. I still had the odd, free weekend left and I decided to take it on, too.

Before the 1960s ended, I encountered a challenge of another type. I began to notice an inability to distinguish voices at faculty meetings at McGill. Of course, this alarmed me. I knew the history of composers like Beethoven who suffered so greatly from hearing loss and Georg Frideric Handel, who was both blind and deaf at the end of his years. In the 1960s, physical problems were still seen as disabilities instead of challenges, as they are today. I remembered Viennese-born Toronto conductor Heinz Unger. When he experienced hearing difficulties, he had to weather both them and the prejudices heaped upon him by colleagues. This can be a cruel profession!

I worried that if people became aware of my hearing difficulties, I'd receive the same prejudice. But I also realized that tremendous advances were being made in hearing aids that could allow me to function fully without discomfort. So I obtained a hearing aid and grew my hair longer to cover it. My new hairstyle fit right in with the sixties hippy fashions, as did my love of semi-precious stones and outlandish adornments, especially necklaces. My students nicknamed me, "the old hippy." Secretly, I was flattered.

If only Beethoven were alive today, he could have lived a more fulfilled life. He would have heard his beloved *Ninth Symphony* and, perhaps, written a tenth. One has only to read his *Heiligenstadt Testament* to recognize the depths of his despair. It is true that a composer afflicted by gradual hearing loss as an adult doesn't need to listen to his music played by instruments to know what he is writing. He or she also "hears" the tone colour of each instrument and various instrumental combinations he sets down. Part of the skill of composition is the ability to hear music in your head much like a reader can hear the words as he or she reads this text. Even if one cannot really listen to the music as it is played, one can enjoy the whole composition and orchestration in his head.

For a conductor, the ability to hear others playing is more essential. I am certainly not so deaf that I can't hear at all, but for social and professional reasons I gave myself the tools to hear as nature intended. It's much the same as wearing glasses to see properly. I continue to upgrade my hearing devices as improvements become available.

Despite this potential setback, we finished the 1960s successfully. The following decade was equally fruitful for Lotte and me, even when Montrealers had their minds on gold of a special kind, Olympic gold. As it turned out, Montreal's Summer Olympics in 1976 did not produce a gold medal for Canada, but they contained golden moments for both me and Montreal's orchestral musicians.

The organizers of the Summer Olympics were pulling out all the stops for a global success and we decided to do the same musically. I was asked to conduct an orchestral concert for the event and what better way to do it than with Olympic music? Having won two Olympic medals myself (1948 in London and 1952 in Hilsinki, Finland), I was aware that the Olympics had once included competitions for performing artists as well as athletes. But I knew few works written expressly for sports occasions. So in 1973, we got to work preparing Olympic repertoire for concerts to be presented at the same time as the Montreal Olympics in 1976.

After extensive research Dr. Walter Kunstler, a surgeon and member of the McGill Chamber Orchestra program committee, came up with an astounding list of musical works written on Olympic themes. He uncovered works by famous and lesser-known composers, including Pergolesi, Beethoven and even Vivaldi, who many people wrongly assume lived too early to be writing Olympic music. I selected the compositions most suitable for our concerts, added my own Olympic offerings, and re-scored many of them for symphony orchestra and its modern instruments. This included orchestrating the *Hymn to Apollo*, which Gabriel Fauré had set to music for the first modern Olympics three-quarters of a century earlier, as well as the overture and three acts of Antonio Sacchini's opera *The Olympiad*.

This lengthy exercise culminated in three concerts of Olympic music which we performed in July 1976 at Place des Arts. The first one was a sort of dress rehearsal for the main event, which was the concert of July 18, attended by Her Majesty Queen Elizabeth II, the Shah of Iran, Queen Juliana of Holland, and Prince Rainier of Monaco. We wanted everything to be perfect. Premier Bourassa and his wife sponsored the concert, the Greek ambassador to Canada recited Homer, and Jon Vickers and Clarice Carson, among others, sang solos in the choral movement of Beethoven's *Ninth Symphony*.

The following week we gave what I believe was the concert premiere of the mid-18th century opera *The Olympiad*. Our research revealed that this work was based on a text by the seventeenth century opera librettist Metastasio and was, thus, historically significant. We were proud that the relatively unknown works of former composers were enjoying a certain revival at our hands. I planned those evenings carefully, taking care to include well-known composers like Vivaldi, as well as less familiar names, like

Leonardo Leo. All in all, the musical aspects of the 1976 Montreal Summer Olympics were a Herculean effort, but among the most artistically gratifying of my career. I have retained my interest in music on Olympic themes and still have my own small Olympic music library in my home.

There remained one further notable event in 1976. I received the Canadian Music Council medal. This is an annual award initiated in 1971 to honour musicians for outstanding service to Canadian musical life, so, of course, it was a tremendous honour. The banquet and presentation were held in Guelph, Ontario that May. Nicholas Goldschmidt, John Cozens and I all received the awards from Lieutenant-Governor Pauline McGibbon, a gracious and elegant lady.

In the 1980s I concentrated mainly on conducting the McGill Chamber Orchestra. We were busy planning and rehearsing our regular concert series in Montreal, as well as planning the extensive travel for the large ensemble. The McGill Chamber Orchestra and I have visited almost every far corner of our country, or, for that matter, the globe. During our tenure with the orchestra Lotte and I toured 17 countries on six continents and in Canada, from the Yukon to Newfoundland.

Canada's capital city hosted us on several occasions, performing in salons and concert halls for the highest-ranking dignitaries, and at outdoor festivals in the mosquito-infested woods, playing for ordinary concert-goers. One of the many prestigious opportunities the McGill Chamber Orchestra and I were offered was to perform at the investiture of the new Governor General in 1984. Jeanne Sauvé's ceremony took place at historic Rideau Hall, a grand old mansion by the Ottawa River on picturesque Sussex Drive. Her Excellency was a highly cultured woman and had requested music that reflected the English, French and immigrant elements of Canada. With that in mind, Lotte and I included original compositions by one composer from Ontario and one from Quebec. We engaged Sara Kang, a young violinist, to play featured works by Mozart, Vivaldi and Handel. The whole orchestra was invited to dinner at Rideau Hall afterwards. As Madame Sauvé and I chatted at the reception, she wondered aloud, "How is it possible for such a young girl to play as she does?" A question, of course, to which there is no answer.

The orchestra was presented with new and interesting challenges for the outdoor concerts at Camp Fortune, a ski hill in West Quebec, very close to the nation's capital. It had a natural amphitheatre that doubled as a location for summer concert series. Audiences and performers quickly learned to come prepared for both the elements and the hungry insects. Along with the sounds of Corelli, Haydn and Bartok, the musicians and I were preoccupied by the quite audible wind, which sometimes blew the music right off the stands. Despite it being July, it was numbingly cold and, at least one member of the orchestra wore an overcoat. Denis played the Haydn cello *Concerto in D* that night, without overcoat, and carried it off exceedingly well. Most of us would have preferred an indoor concert.

Leading a professional chamber orchestra exacts a lot from the conductor, but it also has its humorous side. You deal with many different people under various circumstances in a business where everyone seems to know one another. One "don't-I-know-you-from-somewhere," incident stands out in my memory. The McGill Chamber Orchestra had given a performance in St. John's, Newfoundland, featuring the violinist Angèle Dubeau, playing on a Strad violin. The next day I was amused to read a review entitled, "Maybe I should have paid more attention," in which the critic, Berni Yablon, made some laudatory personal reference to me and explained that he was a former student of mine from McGill days. I didn't know quite how to take it when he described me as an "autocratic taskmaster" of a professor and added he was grateful some things never change. Maybe I too should have paid more attention, to Mr. Yablon, back then.

I'm pleased that Boris has followed in my footsteps as a professional conductor. His active global career takes him to the four corners of the world and I'm proud of his accomplishments. We have worked together many times and he often asks me to conduct his orchestras. When he was conductor of the Northern Sinfonia in Britain in the late 1960s, he invited me to conduct his orchestra on tour with the noted bassist Gary Karr as soloist, featuring my concerto. We travelled by bus throughout the beautiful north of England, stopping for fish and chips wrapped in a London newspaper handed up to us through the bus windows. It was fun.

I conducted the Lakehead Symphony while Boris was developing it in Thunder Bay. In fact, for one concert in October of 1968, the whole family participated. Lotte and Denis performed as cello soloists in an adaptation of a Handel concerto for two cellos with me conducting. Boris conducted my *Cradle Song* which had been written for his birth; Denis conducted Boris playing Mozart's *Third Horn Concerto;* and Boris conducted for Denis who played Tchaikovsky's *Rococo Variations.* We didn't often perform as a family so this concert meant a lot to us.

During Boris' twenty-three year tenure with the Hamilton Philharmonic I guest conducted several times. We also exchanged concerts, with the MCO playing in Hamilton and the HPO playing on our series in Montreal. I was guest conductor for Symphony Nova Scotia in Halifax just after Boris founded it in 1983. It has been a pleasure to share my conducting career with my eldest son, to offer him opportunities at the start of his career. We don't agree on all aspects of interpretation by any means and have lively discussions on musical and administrative subjects. After I handed the reins of the McGill Chamber Orchestra over to Boris as music director, he still asks me to rehearse and conduct one work in each concert. This ensures a solid connection with the orchestra's traditions and keeps my hand in what I love to do.

The training of young orchestral musicians has long concerned me. I know the agonies young graduates can go through trying to find a post in which they can prove themselves. I've seen generations of students come out of McGill not knowing whether they'll be able to find work. Lotte and I discussed how we might be able to help some of them out. Finally we received some assistance.

Late in the summer of 1986, we invited the Honourable Flora MacDonald, our friend and MP for Kingston and the Islands, to our Kingston home. Over a luxurious lunch of B.C. salmon prepared by Lotte, Flora said, "You know so many people and so many people know you. I think you could be helpful to me and to my constituents."

Lotte and I always took care to be politically non-partisan, so I answered, "What can *we* do?"

"I want to do something constructive for this riding. Do you two have any ideas?"

So within a few weeks I prepared a report for her proposing an educational project to build fine young people into fine young musicians. Flora was absolutely wonderful. By December we received a letter promising an allocation of $150,000!

With this generous government grant we created our training orchestra for string players and called it Les Jeunes Virtuoses, The Young Virtuosos. This orchestra, which I directed until recently, is open to all Canadian musicians and provides intensive training for twenty weeks at professional union rates. We have had sessions each year for seventeen years, during which we've prepared many talented musicians for professional life. There is hardly a professional orchestra in Canada that doesn't count a graduate of Les Jeunes Virtuoses among its members. Though I remain president of this orchestra, in 1999 I passed the baton to Denis, who for several years continued the tradition we started and incorporated performances into his very successful *Festival de Musique de Chambre de Montreal*.

Over my long conducting career I've seen the orchestral scene, in Canada and elsewhere, evolve in many ways. Orchestras used to be all-male bastions, where a rare female soloist was occasionally engaged. Gradually, orchestra leaders came to their senses and began to hire women instrumentalists. The McGill Chamber Orchestra was quite progressive, at least since the war, because we had opened up positions for Mildred Goodman and Lotte from the days of the McGill String Quartet. I have observed that the presence of women in the present-day orchestra has changed the entire pattern of behaviour, both of the other players, as well as the conductor, usually for the better. Certainly it is impossible to imagine any successful orchestra now without its female musicians.

Part 2

On Tour

(1948–1988)

Europe 1948, 1949

When Lotte and I began our European tours in the summer of 1948, we were excited by the ground-breaking nature of our mission. The musicians and cultural officials we met also felt the novelty of our visit. They enjoyed hearing about Canada's music as much as we wanted to learn about their contemporary music.

The idea was pioneered by Jean-Marie Beaudet, music director of CBC, who performed a concert at The Prague Festival with the Prague Philharmonic. Then, Stuart Griffiths of the CBC offered me the CBC International Service's very first commission to compose the orchestral suite *From Sea to Sea*. The suite was broadcast over eight hundred stations in Canada and the United States and was chosen for performance in America and Britain by Sir Thomas Beecham. Shortly afterward I received an invitation to conduct it for European radio broadcast.

We felt like musical missionaries. At that time, neither the Canada Council nor provincial arts councils existed and Canada's foreign relations and cultural exchange programs were in their infancy. Lotte and I undertook these trips entirely on our own initiative and at our expense. We carried ten scores of Canadian works with us to Europe – my own compositions, as well as works by Claude Champagne, Jean Vallerand, Sir Ernest MacMillan, Oscar Morawetz and John Weinzweig. These composers were in vogue then, but none of their compositions had ever been presented in so many European venues. The timing was right. It was a creative period for Canadian orchestras and Canadian broadcasting and short-wave radio was thriving.

Performing Canadian music overseas generated so much publicity it gave currency to our own composers in our own land, which encouraged our orchestras to program more Canadian works. When I was interviewed by Canadian reporters before I left, I told them the media's job was to recognize artists before they leave the country and that Canadian musicians are not appreciated enough at home. Regrettably, this is still the case today. "Europeans are less self-conscious about new music," I told them. "Canadians are inclined to undervalue the work of their composers . . . We're too self-conscious about our own work. We need a more positive and active policy on the part of Canadians to present their own musical product." These were bold statements, but I knew this was my chance to promote our work not only outside our borders but in Canada, too.

Boris was only four years old and, although we hated to leave him behind, we felt we had to grab the opportunity – "Carpe diem." Our two and a half months away taught us what my mother had meant when she said, "You will be alone, but together with us." We were incredibly lucky to have the support of my mother, my step-father Abe and brother Steve, who took good care of Boris and held the homefront together for us. In her spare time, Talosa Timmins, secretary to the President of the Royal Bank, managed our correspondence and affairs so we could go to Europe relatively worry free.

Our ship, the *New Amsterdam*, landed in Southampton on a Saturday in June and we immediately took a train to the capital. Lotte and I arrived in London, laden with my violin, music scores and recordings. We found a fantastic mix of everything in London, all the music and all the arts. Then we realized we had forgotten to book accommodations. Luckily the Cumberland Hotel took pity on such obviously inexperienced travelers and gave us rooms, even though they were booked for the entire summer. We found Londoners were eager to help us and give all kinds of advice on what we should hear and see.

A representative of the world renowned music publishers Boosey and Hawkes extended an invitation to us. "Please come as my guest to a luncheon in the Queen's Hall in London. All of Britain's major musicians and music executives will be there." We were introduced to influential composers like Arthur Benjamin and Benjamin Britten, Sir Shouldam Redfern of the British Arts Council and BBC's Head of Music, Stuart Wilson and we encountered many artists whom we later invited to perform with the McGill Chamber Orchestra, among them Peter Pears and the oboist Eugene Goosens. I recognized Vaughan Williams at the head table. I eventually performed his Third Symphony, the *Pastorale*, in its Canadian premiere in 1953. Among my treasured possessions is a letter from him congratulating me on that performance.

My publisher introduced me around as the composer of *From Sea to Sea*, although I had to bite my tongue when he described me as belonging to, "One of our more intelligent dominions." I turned down his offer to publish *From Sea to Sea* providing I re-scored it for a smaller and less expensive orchestra. I was young, idealistic and unwilling to consider the compromises one must sometimes make to get ahead. At times I have regretted that decision as it would have made these works more playable by more orchestras and introduced them to an international audience. It was better when Lotte handled the promotion of my work herself. It is always more professional when someone else acts as your advocate. And she loved telling me what to do and when to do it.

From that luncheon, we proceeded to the offices of the BBC to play my recordings to several officials and music critics. I was thrilled when they engaged me to conduct their orchestras in Manchester and London. Through my CBC and BBC contacts I was introduced to many influential people in Britain. Grateful though I am to all those who helped, my true musical mentor in England was Sir Thomas Beecham.

The highlight of our stay was our visit to Sir Thomas Beecham's elegant home in St. John's Wood. Our new contacts were instantly impressed by the mere mention of this invitation. One telephone call from him would open almost any musical door in Britain. Our full agenda also included meetings with such luminaries as Sir Adrian Boult and Sir Malcolm Sargent.

We soon had to descend from the rarefied atmosphere of Britain's classical music scene and see first-hand how much London had suffered during the war and was still suffering. Good food in England was scarce, no meat, no eggs, no fats. Even at the finest restaurants we had to choose between soup or a piece of bread, dessert or a lump of sugar in your coffee, never both, because there was strict rationing. You would never have guessed this from the way they set their tables with the best silver flatware and linen tablecloths.

Rationing even extended into Sir Thomas Beecham's home. At the end of his lovely garden stood several crates of live chickens whose eggs Sir Thomas used to supplement his household rations. To see this great man keeping chickens in his yard was sad. Not that he was living in poverty – far from it. He was simply too honourable to do any black-marketing to obtain the foods we, in Canada, took for granted. I immediately wrote to my mother asking her to make up an air-mail parcel of a smoked ham, sugar, condensed milk, anchovies and other small tinned items. For anyone else I would have hesitated to offer such a gift, but I knew Sir Thomas well enough!

He invited me into his handsome, very masculine, very English drawing room resplendent with heavy leather furnishings. In greeting, he pointed to one particular armchair and said, "Last Saturday, old (Richard) Strauss sat there when he came to collect his British royalties. Now you sit in it!" He explained that it was the first time since the war began that the German composer had been permitted to come. I hoped that chair, still warm from the great Strauss's visit, would transfer the muse to my work.

I attended a concert where Sir Thomas conducted the music of his great friends Gustav Holst and Edward Elgar. Shortly before the concert, he called me to his dressing room. As I entered the maestro's inner sanctum, I wondered why he had summoned me. Did he want to acquaint me with some detail of interpretation or share some insight on the music he was to perform? No. He asked in an exasperated tone, "Help me with this bloody necktie, will you? I can't put it on!"

I laughed. "Sir Thomas, I can't tie those things for myself, so I can't do it for anybody else!"

He snatched up the receiver and called his wife. "Will you send somebody along to help? Brott here can't do it up either!"

This was characteristic of the warm relationship we shared. I consider him one of the conducting giants of all time. But more, I valued his friendship tremendously and admired his wit and wisdom and his British accent. I was flattered by the genuine concern he showed for Lotte and me. Such friendships are rare!

Lotte and I spent a wonderful week-end at the splendid estate of Lord and Lady Christie in Glyndebourne, Sussex. During the war years, the beautiful soprano Audrey Mildmay had been one of a number of foreign musicians seeking refuge in Canada. After hearing her sing Mozart in Montreal, I had engaged her at once for a concert. We became slightly more than good friends. (This was before I married Lotte.) Later her millionaire husband, John Christie, founded the Glyndbourne Festival Opera. So when we were planning our tour, I wrote to Audrey who invited me to attend their Mozart festival at Glyndebourne.

A chauffeur met us at the train and drove us to the castle which had been in their family since the twelfth century. The grounds were heavenly acres of terraced gardens and swans graced the ponds. As the finishing touch, Christie had built an opera-house in one of the barns a decade earlier. The acoustics, stage, seating, artists' quarters and equipment were all worked out to the last perfect detail.

When we arrived I introduced Lotte to Audrey, who didn't know we had married. Immediately she asked, "When did that happen?"

I replied, "Only after you left."

Lotte was not yet accustomed to my sense of humour and Audrey didn't appreciate it either. Once we got over my *faux pas*, Audrey was most charming and full of good suggestions, as was her husband. They were also friends of Sir Thomas Beecham, who was directing the Mozart Festival with the Royal Philharmonic Orchestra in these wonderful facilities. Lotte and I felt privileged to be the guests of honour seated next to the aristocrats. We were also ecstatic with the performance, the location and their luxurious estate.

That evening, as the reception went on and on, I realized that our train time was approaching. Our hostess, a glass-half-full type of person, offered to take us to the station. Just as we arrived the train left. "Don't worry. I'll get you to the next stop," she said and sped like mad only to discover she couldn't make it. "Never mind," she said, "I'll get you there in the morning."

When we returned to the mansion, Sir John was in his slippers and pyjamas, which reminded me that I had no night attire. Lotte could be more easily accommodated, but for me Audrey suggested, "I'll put you both in Sir Thomas's room. You'll find his pajamas there." Well, after several efforts to put on the pajamas – Sir Thomas was not quite as svelte as I was in those days – I abandoned the project and slept *au naturel*. Before we knew it, the blinds were drawn and the bright sun shone in. There stood the energetic Audrey with two servings of sumptuous strawberries and farmer's double cream. I kept the covers discreetly around me until she left the room.

On our way back to London later that morning, we shared a train compartment with the great Belgian violinist Arthur Grumiaux, who invited us to dine with him the following day at a Greek restaurant in Soho.

The adventures that the CBC had helped launch continued. I directed the BBC Northern Symphony Orchestra at a special July 1st Dominion Day program from Manchester, which the BBC broadcast on short-wave radio. Sir Thomas had already planned to take *From Sea to Sea* on tour that October, to Belfast, Dublin and Liverpool and he would direct my symphonic poem *Concordia* in London with the Royal Philharmonic Orchestra. I didn't know how fortunate I was.

Although new and exciting things were happening quickly for us, Lotte and I missed Boris. We had never been away from him for so long. We each wrote to him, addressing him by pet nick-names and exhorted him to drink lots of milk (we had been alarmed to see many undernourished British children) and to play his violin.

The International Service of the CBC had created an enlightened audience for Canadian works to radio listeners overseas. The CBC recordings of my works as conductor and as a solo violinist introduced my work to many European countries and *From Sea to Sea*, being a musical travelogue across Canada, sent a thematic portrait of our vast and multi-cultured landscape. The next stop on our overseas musical adventure was Scandinavia where I was to guest-conduct their national and principal radio orchestras and play some engagements as a violinist.

Lotte had been born in Germany, but this was my first visit to the continent and I was excited by the delights of Sweden, Norway and Denmark. The people seemed friendly, down to earth and very welcoming. But I had one big problem. Since the musical scores and the parts for the orchestra were not available in Europe, I had to pay to transport them myself and I had to lug those bulky papers plus the conductor's scores from one country to the next. In addition, we carried many heavy and fragile 78-rpm recordings. Being a Canadian cultural ambassador required physical stamina. But it was worth the effort for it put Canadian music in Europe. I only regretted that the printing costs in those pre-copier days made it impossible to leave scores with any of the orchestras for further study or performances.

My engagements as a solo violinist on the Continent were arranged by the British Arts Council, who were quick to step into Europe after the war to re-establish and even increase the flow of cultural activities. They arranged for the pianist, Jon Oien to perform with me, they set up press coverage and receptions to meet local musical notables and handled the myriad details that such a tour requires. In Stockholm 28 July to 2 August 1948, I gave concerts as a violinist and guest-conducted radio broadcasts, as well. I was delighted to be the first Canadian musician to conduct the Stockholm Orchestra, which gave an enthusiastic, brilliant performance of *From Sea to Sea*.

Travel was broadening my mind. In Stockholm, Lotte's close friend from her Neuchatel days, Günile Florman, met us in a Cadillac convertible. Such cars being a weakness of mine, I was impressed by the vehicle, as well as the young lady. She invited us to Skansen, near Stockholm, to go swimming the next day. I hadn't expected this so I had no swim trunks. We went to several men's clothing shops, only to find that Swedish men didn't wear such apparel. Perhaps my two *au naturel* experiences inspired me later to write *The Emperor's New Clothes*.

Our concert at Skansen had an interesting feature. During the intermission, they held a musical contest. The regular conductor performed short snippets of contemporary music and a panel of five men and five women from the audience were asked to name the composer or the work. The prize was dinner at a Skansen restaurant. I found this a palatable way to teach an audience and decided to try it at home, though I wondered how much our audiences knew about Canadian composition.

For our last evening in Skansen, Dr. Lindfors invited some distinguished personalities to dine with us. Lotte thoroughly enjoyed the festivities and would not stop *skolling* (toasting) with aquavit, the notoriously powerful Scandinavian liqueur with everyone who could join her. When we left we had to physically lift her off the chair while she giggled helplessly. The next morning she didn't feel quite that cheery. She never did it again.

Stockholm's Grand Hotel was truly grand and included its own dock. Our boat sailed directly from the hotel out to the Baltic Sea on a beautiful starry night. We looked back to see "Neptune" beckoning us to return.

Scandinavian audiences were receptive to Canadian compositions and applauded enthusiastically. In Denmark I conducted John Weinzweig's *Interlude in an Artist's Life*. The Canadian Embassy in Copenhagen arranged to have a recording of it played on Danish radio, which catapulted Weinzweig's work to immediate popularity. Successes of that kind made the trip worthwhile.

We took every opportunity to be tourists. Travelling on tour gives you an advantage over the normal tourist in that you are immediately immersed in the culture of that country and you work alongside its citizens. Lotte and I were curious to visit the popular attractions. Often we found ourselves introducing those attractions to our musician hosts, since locals rarely go to their own tourist sites. The first thing I did in Norway was to visit Edvard Grieg's house, a small simple wooden structure. I wondered how he could have conceived the assertive opening solo of his *Piano Concerto in A Minor* in such humble surroundings. With that pilgrimage out of my system, I joined Jon Oien for some violin and piano sonatas for Oslo Radio. Oien lived in Oslo and he, his wife, and mother-in-law went to a lot of trouble to make our stay pleasant.

Our trip to that northern city was absolutely fascinating. We took the train to Oslo, climbing high up the mountain and arriving at twilight. Norway is a spectacular land with vivid natural beauty. Despite the mountains, one never seems to get away from the bounty of the sea. Once we saw the ocean shimmering with thousands of silvery sardines. Lotte dived in for an impromptu swim, jumping out quickly when a boat unexpectedly came around the bend and honked its horn. Perhaps it was a fishing boat. Certainly every dinner we ate in Norway featured huge plates of raw and cooked fish of all types. Norway remained a cherished memory for Lotte and me and I looked forward to returning the following year.

In addition to the Scandinavian countries, my 1948 and 1949 summer tours included France, Holland, Luxembourg, Belgium and Italy. We quickly formed positive impressions of the people around us, finding a fascinating array of cultures – a mix we were reminded of when we visited the USSR fifteen years later. In Western Europe we also found wonderful liqueurs, superb chocolates, fourteenth and fifteenth century churches *sans pareil* and impressive heavy horses hauling tons of coal. All round us we saw reminders of the past, such as Luxembourg Broadcast House, which was surrounded by a moat with a drawbridge to exclude undesirables.

There, as in Scandinavia, we had arranged to showcase the compositions of Canadians. Henri Pensis, music director of Radio-Luxembourg, featured *From Sea to Sea* over their network as a Dominion Day tribute to Canada. In Holland I guest-conducted the Radio Philharmonic Orchestra in two more performances of *From Sea to Sea*. Hilversum Radio featured a program of Canadian music. The typical program I presented in these radio broadcasts was forty-five minutes long, featuring Canadian works for string chamber orchestra, including Claude Champagne's *Danse Villageoise*, my *Songs of Contemplation*, Jean Coulthard's *Music on a Quiet Song*, John Weinzweig's *Interlude in an Artist's Life* and

Ernest MacMillan's *Two Sketches*. If the station could afford a larger orchestra, I chose a symphonic program with an hour of works including Oscar Morawetz' *Carnival,* Claude Champagne's *Symphonie Gaspésienne,* Douglas Clarke's *Piece for Orchestra* and my own *Concordia.*

Holland gave us many musical and magical experiences. I performed the three Brahms sonatas for violin and piano with Oien again. The Canadian ambassador, Pierre Dupuy, had a palatial residence on extensive grounds with beautiful old trees where he occasionally presented Mendelssohn's *Midsummer Night's Dream.* Apparently it was the very place for which Mendelssohn had written it.

Next we travelled to Italy where Canadian ambassador Jean Desy had invited me to Rome to conduct Canadian music. Their radio network RAI played the recordings I had sent them, including *Ritual.**

Bolstered with promises of return engagements, our ears ringing with the strains of our Canadian musical premieres on European airwaves, Lotte and I boarded the ship to return home. We already knew there would be a return trip to Europe. Stuart Griffiths of the CBC had suggested we write to the director of Danish Radio in Copenhagen to arrange a performance in 1949 and I had an engagement to guest-conduct the Oslo radio orchestra that June. I planned to present more symphonic music by our principal Canadian composers Jean Coulthard and Oscar Morawetz.

So the next year, I again carted my musical bag of tricks and luggage to Europe. I took the works of nine outstanding Canadian composers and conducted programs built around their works and *From Sea to Sea.* Before leaving home I had also obtained and studied the scores of Scandinavian composers. In addition to a radio broadcast from Sweden, I was to conduct an all-Canadian

---

* Interestingly, soon after I wrote this paragraph in 2003, *Ritual* was performed again in Rome, under the direction of Maestro Vincenzo Mariozzi, principal clarinet of the Santa Cecilia Orchestra.

Denis Brott and family

Boris Brott and family

Alexander and Lotte with Yehudi Menuhin, 1989

. to R) Mayor Drapeau, Alexander Brott, Helmut Blume, Lotte Brott, and Barbara Davis

oto courtesy of Schiret Photo Studio

McGill Chamber Orchestra with Mstislav Rostropovich at Place des Arts, 1985
photo courtesy Basil Zarov

(L to R) Alexander Brott, Major Sarto Fournier, Princess Margaret, 1959
photo courtesy Canada Wide Photo

(L to R) Alexander Brott, Prime Minister Pierre Trudeau and sons
photo courtesy Jack Markow

(L to R) Denis, Lotte, Alexander, Boris Brott and Yitzchak Perlman
at Notre Dame Cathedral, 1999

Anne Fixman–Brott
with Steve and Alex,
1922

on the steps of Juilliard
Alexander Brott, Sascha
Jacobsen abd Madame
Faneroff, 1936

the first McGill String Quartet Barn, Lac Manitou, 1939

Concertmaster Alexander Brott, CBC Radio Orchestra, 1936
photo courtesy Editorial Associates

*(L to R) Wilfred Pelletier, 5-year-old Boris and Alexander Brott
with the Montreal Symphony Orchestra, 1948*

Otto Klemperer and Alexander Brott, 1954
Courtesty Studio Jac-Guy

Lord and Lady Christie,
Lotte and Alexander Brott,
Glyndebourne, 1948

(L to R) Lotte Brott, David Oistrakh, Yaela Hertz, Alexander Brott, 1960

(L to R) Rostropovich, Lotte and Alexander Brott, Galina Vishnevskaya and Tania Plaw, 1988

McGill Chamber Orchestra in rehersal with Yehudi Menhuin

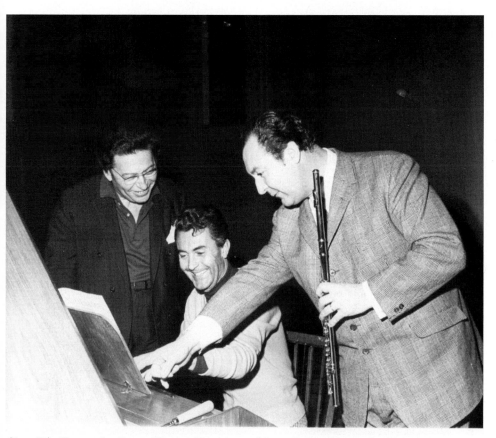

(L to R) ALexander Brott, Vernon Lacroix and Jean–Peirre Rampal, 1960

Dr. Alexander Brott

program with the BBC Scottish Symphony Orchestra and to perform a violin recital at the Glyndebourne Festival.

Pierre Monteux was in Amsterdam at the same time and asked me to escort his wife to his performance of Maurice Ravel's opera, *L'Heure Espagnole*. We attended together with Ineke Cronheim of the British Arts Council's Amsterdam office. Some time into the performance we were astonished to see Maestro Monteux lean toward the music-stand, turn off the conductor's light, walk out between the players and disappear backstage. The performance halted. *L'Heure Espagnol* is a one-act opera without intermission, so the audience whispered among themselves at this strange premature ending. Madame Monteux was worried. She urged Ineke to go backstage and find out what happened. Ineke was gone nearly fifteen minutes while we waited anxiously and the audience grew restless. She returned smiling. "He's fine," she reported. "He wants me to tell you that at his age, when you have to go...you really have to go!"

Monteux returned to the podium smiling with satisfaction and finished conducting the opera without further interruption. The performance was crystal clear and seemed to fit both the text and theatricals. No explanation was ever given to the audience. We went backstage and congratulated the maestro on his success.

I repeated my musical tours of Europe each summer for a few years, until the birth of our second child and the beginning of the pops concerts kept us home.

Israel 1959

My mother and her half-sister were the first of my family to arrive in Canada as teenagers and, when they saw there were no Indians rampant, they solicited the help of various societies to bring their parents to Montreal. My maternal grandfather was a religious man who believed that his real homeland was Jerusalem – this was before the establishment of the state of Israel. For thousands of years Jews throughout the Diaspora have prayed for a return to

Yerushalayim shell sachav — Jerusalem of gold. I remember my grandfather repeating the traditional phrase from the Torah after each
prayer, *L'shona ab'a b'rusholaem,* next year in Jerusalem.

Imagine how thrilled I felt to be invited to conduct a con-
cert in 1959 celebrating the tenth anniversary of the state of Israel.
Allan Bronfman sponsored the trip and was in attendance. It was
quite an event as it celebrated the inauguration of the Hebrew
University's law faculty building constructed with the assistance
of Canadian funds. For the occasion, Canada contributed the
Sir John A. Macdonald Chair to the law faculty of the Hebrew
University. March 30th was declared Canada Day in Jerusalem.

Even though Israel was ten years old, the military presence
was everywhere. We were transported to the library in an army
jeep with helmeted soldiers, which took some getting used to.

On that first trip I spent three days in the desert with a group
of professors and musicians. We navigated across the sand wearing a strange sort of slipper with four inch soles. We carried our
own water and food, including figs and dates. As we travelled on,
members of this distinguished group began to act more and more
giddy. We didn't know why until we realized the power of fruits
that had fermented in the heat.

I was astonished at the variety of Jews – blond Jews from
Scandinavia and Poland, black Jews from Ethiopia, Sabras, Jews
born within Palestine or Israel's border who looked down upon
the Jews from the European Diaspora, orthodox Jews and secular
Jews.

Despite the unfamiliar middle-eastern environment, I felt
very much at home in Israel. In Canada or anywhere else in the
world, I will always be a minority. All of a sudden I was in a society
where I belonged to the majority, which affected me deeply on an
emotional plane. I guess I was brought up with a deferential attitude to the people in the majority. In Israel I felt free from these
restraints. I could be entirely myself.

I also felt at home with the Kol Israel Orchestra where I met
a number of outstanding musicians. I especially remember Joseph
Tal, one of their most creative composers. Again I included compositions by my Canadian colleagues – Murray Adaskin's *Serenade*

Concertante, Claude Champagne's *Danse Villageoise* and my own *Critic's Corner*.

I gave a lecture on Canadian music at the Ruben Academy, recorded some of our music with the Kol Israel Orchestra and helped Ambassador Margaret Maegher present several scores of the Lapitsky Foundation's commissioned compositions to the Kol Israel library. It embarrassed me when the old rabbis would neither shake her hand, nor look at her as she passed, because she was a woman.

I returned to Israel several more times to guest-conduct the Kol Israel. I eagerly anticipated each trip for different reasons. On the second one, I brought Lotte and Denis. Boris was invited to conduct there in 1985 and now returns annually to lead the Israel Chamber Orchestra, the Jerusalem Symphony and the Haifa Orchestras.

I had other reasons to look forward to my Israel trips. I wanted to visit King Solomon's mines, Beersheba and the many biblical historic locations, which couldn't all be managed in one trip. And I wanted to thank personally the percussion player who presented me with a pair of ancient finger cymbals he used in our performance of my *Critic's Corner*.

USSR 1962, 1966, 1972

I had seen my religious homeland and was eager to visit the birthplace of my parents. My mother emigrated from Russia, bordering the Ukraine and my father from Riga in Latvia. They had told me many stories about both places, but sadly, never taught me to speak, write or read Russian. My parents felt it was a language best forgotten so they could quickly assimilate and become Canadian.

In 1962, I was delighted when the Soviet Embassy in Ottawa invited me to bring Canadian music to Russia, an immense land with multitudes of peoples of many origins. It is one thing to read about a country and quite another to experience it. As the guest of the Soviet government, I conducted the Moscow Radio Orchestra and other Soviet orchestras in three of their capitals – Moscow, Tiflis in the province of Georgia, Yerivan, in Armenia and also in Leningrad.

I had the honour of being the first Canadian composer to conduct his own work in the USSR. Lotte and I were conscious of our responsibility as Canadian cultural ambassadors, hoping to connect through the universal language of music and perhaps paving the way for political dialogue. With the Canadian Department of External Affairs and Soviet Ministry of Culture I carefully selected the program featuring my most recent composition, a twelve-tone work which I called *Spheres in Orbit*. The piece conveys the seeming weightlessness of the Sputnik satellite, which we had seen in the sky over our cottage in 1958. My first taste of what I thought was Soviet censorship came when I noticed that the posters changed my title to *Sputnik na Orbite*. Then I learned that the Russian word for sphere was – you guessed it – Sputnik.

Our premieres of Canadian works in Moscow were grand successes. The Soviet audience in Moscow's Hall of Columns received my *Spheres/Sputniks in Orbit* with unbridled enthusiasm. For a people who on the outside appear to be dour, the Soviets are wonderfully demonstrative, much more so than North Americans. They love their classical music as well as vodka. They clapped in rhythm, stood for up to twelve curtain calls and came to the foot of the stage to throw flowers.

I received a further education in the differences between Western and Soviet musical life when I was invited to a meeting of the Soviet composers' union, with Aram Khachaturian. I had assumed we might compare training methods and concert opportunities but it was not conventional music-writing that interested the Soviet composers. They wanted to discuss the electronic and twelve-tone music with which Western composers were experimenting.

At one point they took me into two adjoining chambers where I was amazed to see a copy of every new work that had been played anywhere outside their borders. They didn't officially recommend these pieces for performance, but they collected this music to keep in touch. Even in music, the Soviet system was very thorough at information gathering. They also asked me to send them scores of some Canadian works which I happily did. Despite the politics that emphasized Soviet creation, the musicians and music directors were anxious to learn new Western music.

I found their procedures for encouraging new compositions equally enlightened. They explained to me how their officials would select promising composers whose submissions they liked, liberate them from normal duties and send them to a country *dacha* for up to four months, all expenses paid, to devote themselves to composition. When the work was completed, if the committee approved it, they would distribute the score and a set of orchestra parts to every major orchestra in the country. I tried to imagine myself as one of the chosen, enjoying life in a comfortable cottage, with staff to serve me, a peaceful lake inspiring me to compose my next concerto and no worries about where my next cheque was coming from!

The *dacha* idea certainly appealed to me, but I'm wary of committee approvals of artistic work. A few years later, our own Canada Council adopted a peer review committee approval system for commissions. Since I don't believe any composer should be constrained by a government official's notion of acceptability or worse still a government official hiding behind a committee of 'peers' because it is after all they who choose the peers and can control the decisions in that way, I thereafter commissioned new works only through non-governmental routes such as the Lapitsky Foundation.

The variety in the USSR astonished Lotte and me. Tiflis, (or Tbilisi), was beautiful, with flowers, fragrances, fruits and endless variety. Yerevan, our stop in Armenia, was the only city where I saw a twenty-foot statue of Stalin. The others in other Soviet republics had been torn down by then. Armenia was very poor, but in puzzling contrast, the Tiflis orchestra was huge (like the statue) and their concert hall fully equipped for television and recording. Their regular conductor had graduated from the *Paris Conservatoire*. The Soviets held classical music and composers in very high social and financial esteem and children were exposed to it from their earliest school years.

In Yerevan, the Orthodox priest, called "Katolikos", memorably attired in a stove-pipe hat and black cape, invited us to visit the seminary. The next day he sent an official Mercedes-Benz to call for us. We drove regally into the church square where we saw peasants in straw shoes leading birds and beasts to be blessed on a ten-foot stone table. The Katolikos later told us that this church dated from the third century and was the first church to practice Christianity outside the Holy Land. Inside, the church displayed the most impressive array of garments, white ermine and jewellery, all gifts from the nobility. Later, the Katolikos attended our concert in the company of other priests.

My visit to the USSR clarified for me the nature of their music. I came to appreciate that Russia's warm, emotional music reflects the temperament of the people themselves. I also understood, for the first time, that the USSR was not just Russia, one nation. From the Nordic peoples of Latvia to the Orientals of the southern regions, they made me acutely aware that people may belong to one political state yet have different cultures and that a government does not necessarily reflect the character of all of its peoples. In our inaugural cultural exchanges, my modest goal had been to learn about the Soviet music system. The real lesson I learned was that the common element of music had the power to overcome our political and cultural differences.

In all our travels and dealings with our Russian hosts I focused on the music and avoided politics. I must have earned their trust, for upon my return to Canada the Soviet Ministry of Culture invited me to come back and bring my entire chamber orchestra with me. Thus in 1966 and again in 1972, I returned to the Soviet Union as the conductor of the first Canadian chamber orchestra to visit the USSR, and only the third foreign chamber orchestra in the world to do so.

It still took three years of negotiations and grants from the federal, Quebec and Montreal governments, before my wife, this time with her cello, the fourteen other members of the McGill Chamber Orchestra and I could set off. The only non-musician to accompany us was our resident Russian-speaker, Mrs. Tania Plaw, then on the Board of the orchestra and soon to become our most important president. Tania was an organizing force who, together with Lotte, expanded the musical horizons of the MCO on a truly worldwide basis. Boris, as music director of the Northern Sinfonia, had just conducted a joint concert with Rudolf Barshai's Moscow Chamber Orchestra and arranged to join us at the last minute.

Upon our arrival in Moscow in April 1966, we were received like royalty, with flowers, gifts and chauffeur-driven vehicles. We performed for a packed audience of over 1,000 in the Moscow Conservatory and the Soviet news agency, *Tass*, praised the orchestra's beautiful tone. The Canadian ambassador, Mr. Robert Ford, a highly cultured and well read individual with a keen appreciation of the arts, hosted a dinner for us. Ford was a gifted poet, author and linguist as well as a consummate diplomat. Lotte and I felt proud that Canada had so distinguished a representative in the Soviet Union.

We went on to perform in Riga, Latvia and Tallinn, Estonia and, then in May, in Leningrad, followed by a television broadcast from Petrozavodsk, the capital city of Karelia. No foreign group had given such a telecast from that location before. In all, we had nine performances. Our tour repertoire included Mozart, Handel, Vivaldi and Corelli, as well as compositions by Eastern European composers Bartok, Dvorak and Schoenberg. We gave the Moscow premiere of Canadian Pierre Mercure's *Divertimento* and of my own *Circle, Triangle, Four Squares*. Someone suggested that the Schoenberg *Transfigured Night* (*Verklaerte Nacht*) had never been played in the USSR but we could not confirm it. Either way, it was received as if it were the premiere. The Soviets were just as enthusiastic about the Canadian music. In each city I was requested to leave extra orchestral scores for them to study. It seemed obvious that Soviet audiences were thirsting for new musical stimuli probably more than our audiences at home. Classical music was encouraged – American popular music was forbidden.

The celebrated violinist David Oistrakh and composer Aram Khatchaturian, whom I had met on my earlier trip, both attended our concerts and warmed us with their enthusiasm. The concert halls were full and compliments were showered on us. The orchestra distinguished itself and more than earned their praise. "Each musician is a fine artist in his own right," and "Among the best ensembles in our time," wrote the Soviet newspaper *Pravda*.

We had great fun together as tourists. There is no better team building exercise for an orchestra than a tour. We took group photos in front of Glinka's statue, which stood right around the corner from Tchaikovsky's house. It was exciting to see the historic home of our role model.

In Tallinn we performed in open-air facilities on a stage unbelievably large for the size of audience one could expect for a "Les Canadiens" evening. I compared it to the opera house in Riga. My father used to tell me about the magnificent doors of that opera house. The morning after we arrived there, I got out of bed, pulled aside the heavy drapes of our hotel room window and there they were. Delighted at my good fortune I shouted, "Lotte, I know those doors!" Later we were surprised to hear band musicians playing vintage American jazz in the hotel lobby, even though such influences were frowned upon.

From Riga, we traveled all night by train to reach historic Leningrad. Each car was equipped with a coal fired Russian samovar to keep us supplied with freshly brewed tea. On arrival at around 8:00 a.m., we were met by the mayor and various city officials, each carrying a cellophane package of flowers. Lotte and I were ushered into the back seat of the mayor's car while he sat up front with the driver. The mayor was heavy-set and looked to me like a real Russian *muzhic* (peasant). He kept glancing back at me. Finally just before we reached our destination, he asked me, *A yiddish vort ret hir?* (Do you speak Yiddish?) I was amazed but later learned that his family had lived there for generations and somehow had escaped the pogroms and gulag. It was a nice welcome to Leningrad and totally unexpected.

After our Leningrad performances we made our way to Petrozavodsk for our broadcast. We broadcast and recorded a number of programs, each containing at least one Canadian composition, works by Roger Matton, Pierre Mercure and Harry Freedman, as well as some of my own such as *Songs of Contemplation*. The Canadian soprano Gaelyne Gabora, who toured with us, sang this piece to perfection. I still possess a copy of the recording.

Then it was back to Moscow for our voyage home. Despite the demands of the great distances we covered, we had had wonderful times, very warm and enthusiastic audiences and the intense satisfaction of showcasing Canadian music in new areas. The McGill Chamber Orchestra's second trip to the USSR in 1972 was equally memorable and successful.

France and Switzerland 1971

Since we were from French-speaking Quebec, it was natural for the Canadian Cultural Branch of the Canadian Department of External Affairs to send us to perform in France. It should surprise no one that Lotte made sure that Switzerland was included in this tour. It was the first cultural exchange between our two countries.

Through the Swiss Consul General we arranged to give concerts in Zollinberg, Zurich and Berne and we squeezed in a radio broadcast from Lugano. We performed at the Interlaken Music Festival and stopped at the Canadian Embassy in Berne. We also arranged for the Vivaldi Players of Zurich to come to Montreal the following April.

On 28 May we arrived in Paris. The orchestra played Corelli, Mozart and Bartok, as well as *Circle, Triangle, Four Squares* at the Canadian Cultural Centre in front of many distinguished guests. The renowned musicologist, Marc Pincherle called us, "a group of virtuosi led by a virtuoso conductor."

Not only did we revisit the French and Swiss locales of my solo tours, but we encountered what seemed like divine approval of our orchestra's trip. On an afternoon break in Strasbourg, Lotte and Yaëla dropped in to the famous Strasbourg Cathedral. As they stood in front of a pillar of an angel, Lotte was annoyed that one had to pay to have it illuminated in order to see the art clearly. "Ah, commercialism has penetrated even the thick walls of this holy place of worship!" she said.

Just then someone paid to have it lit. At once they recognized the angel. It was the same angel the McGill Chamber Orchestra had used as its symbol since the early 1950s.

North American Travels

The McGill Chamber Orchestra often gave "run-out" concerts during the summer at various colleges and festivals in New York, Maine, Vermont and bordering states. Hydro-Quebec sponsored the McGill Chamber Orchestra's tours of upstate New York and Vermont, an easy and pleasant trip. We put on all-Mozart concerts at a summer festival, which included a stop at the popular and gracious Trapp Family Lodge nestled in the mountains of Stowe. We repeated these programs in the Canadian Maritime provinces and the Eastern Townships of Quebec, often playing at festivals in Saint Sauveur in the beautiful Laurentians. One year we made a tour – a short one because it's a small island – of the Ile d'Orléans in Quebec, playing in seven churches across the island.

Over the years, I have guest-conducted in New York, Boston, Phoenix and other major American centres. In 1960 I exchanged podiums with director Francois D'Albert of the Chicago Conservatory College – presenting Canadian music to Chicago, while he conducted the McGill Chamber Orchestra I was deeply honoured when Dr. D'Albert proposed me for an honorary Doctor of Music degree from the Chicago Conservatory College.

In the early days McGill University's music department conducted examinations in 57 branches throughout Canada. Hence I often travelled from east to west to adjudicate violin examinations and competitions after the end of term in late April and early May. On these trips I discovered where the talent was. I was impressed by the quality of the excellent teachers, many of whom had arrived in Canada from overseas, or in the case of western Canada, most had arrived from eastern Canada.

The McGill Chamber Orchestra has toured the Maritime provinces more than once, including an appearance at the inauguration of the Charlottetown Festival in Prince Edward Island and opening a major concert venue there in the mid-1960s. The whole orchestra flew from Halifax to each of the other cities in the region. Like Moscow, Halifax was the hub for air travel in the Maritimes, so we got to know it well.

Seagram's sponsored that tour, but when Centennial year rolled around, purse-strings loosened around the country as agencies of-fered arts groups funds to celebrate. The Centennial Commission gave us a grant to tour Quebec, Newfoundland and Prince Edward Island, so we made a short Centennial tour in September of 1967 to Jonquiére, Quebec City, St. John's, and Charlottetown, where we played at Confederation Centre, site of the historic signing that began it all.

Twenty-five years later, in 1992, the MCO's trip to the Yukon and Northwest Territories also took us to places where classical music performed by Canadians was rather foreign. We inaugu-rated the Yukon Cultural Arts Center at Whitehorse and gave additional concerts in Dawson City and Klondike City. Boris and I shared conducting duties. It was a tremendous experience to re-trace the steps of the miners in the very halls where they ogled the original can-can dancers. One of the antique honky-tonk pianos was still functioning. Some of the places were still decorated *à la* Goldrush.

On that trip, the entire Brott clan participated. Boris and I conducted, Denis was principal cellist and Lotte played beside him. Sopranist Gaelyne Gabora sang my *Songs of Contemplation*. Boris led a family concert. (He has become well known for these very innovative concerts. He has the Bernstein knack of communicat-ing successfully with young people.) We played André Gagnon's *Petit Concerto* with a local red-headed girl, aptly named Rusty May, as violin soloist. So successful was this work that we repeated it as an encore at all the concerts. Our performance was broadcast over the CBC.

Mexico. 1957, 1974

My first trip to Mexico was for the Pan-American Conductors Competition put on by Igor Markevitch in 1957. Since I won it, my second visit, in July 1958, was to direct some concerts of the Mexican National Symphony Orchestra in their Palacio de Bellas Artes.

Fifteen years later, Lotte and I used our contacts in Mexico to arrange an official invitation from the Instituto Nacional de Bellas Artes y Literatura de Mexico. It was to be the first time a Canadian chamber orchestra would perform in that country.

In 1974, the McGill Chamber Orchestra embarked on its first Latin American tour to Mexico to preach the gospel of Canadian music and performers. We received help from the National Institute of Fine Arts of Mexico as well as from the Quebec and Canadian governments. And we added one more Brott to our ensemble – Denis played the principal cello next to Lotte.

We went again to Mexico in 1975. We played in Cuernavaca on 26 October, two days later to San Luis Potosi and we finished the month in San Miguel Allende. By 1 November we were in Guanajuato, then on to Toluca – five towns in some beautiful and ornate halls. At our inaugural concert at the Palace of Fine Arts in Mexico City, we played Pierre Mercure's *Divertimento* and a Mozart *Divertimento* (K 136) for contrast.

Eastern Europe 1977

Flush with our Mexican success, Lotte and I decided to tour even further. After two trips to the Soviet Union, Eastern Europe seemed to be the next logical destination. As soon as we returned from Mexico late in 1976, we began to plan the orchestra's trip to Czechoslovakia, Hungary and Poland. Tania Plaw did much of the necessary legwork again and we received support from the Department of External Affairs in Ottawa.

Our orchestra made history in Poland and Hungary. It was the first time a Canadian ensemble had performed in these countries. From 11 to 22 December 1977, we did five concerts – in Warsaw's National Philharmonic Hall, in Wroclaw, Ostrava, Nagykanizsa and Budapest and then home.

We performed Dvorak and Bartok, of course and, for Canadian content, I included my own *Circle, Triangle, Four Squares*, as well as *Three Astral Visions* and *Divertissement,* a work we had commissioned from Pierre Mercure. One of the European reviewers commented on my "very interesting habit," of asking a Canadian composer to write something for us every year.

As we had discovered in the Soviet Union the previous decade, European audiences were most receptive, giving us standing ovations from sold-out halls and calling us back for several encores. "Their playing is disciplined, their sound is clear and their performance has high emotional warmth," said a reviewer.

Our Polish musical colleagues and hosts were warm and welcoming, but I felt uneasy in this Soviet police state. I sensed an anti-Semitic sentiment and could not escape my knowledge of their history. I was haunted by my Polish step-father's stories and I was tormented by the cries of the oppressed in the ghetto and the screams of the victims in the death camps. Some of our musicians wanted to visit Dachau. We chartered a bus, but my wife, who had lost her grandparents there, wisely refused to leave the bus. I went into the museum to see for myself. It was truly frightening to witness man's inhumanity to man. Stacks of eyeglasses and other personal effects of the victims were piled high, telling their cruel stories without words. The musicians were all relieved to get back to their instruments.

In contrast to the horrors of the camps, central Europe was full of natural beauty. Poland had its treasure in the form of the amber mine and I went in search of amber with insects captured within. From the point of view of my rock-polishing hobby, it was the best amber in the world. It's a pity that despite these natural riches, Poland was so poverty-stricken, as was the city of Prague, despite its happier intellectual reputation.

In Budapest we performed in a concert hall with first-rate acoustics. The hall stands out in my mind for its beauty, with its interior décor, all red plush with gold trimming. And most beautiful for an orchestra – it was fully attended.

South America 1981

In 1981, the McGill Chamber Orchestra tackled a tour of South America, with performances in Santiago, Chile; Bogota, Columbia;

Buenos Aires, Argentina; Brazil; Venezuela; and Peru. I'm not sure whether this was the first time any Canadian orchestra had travelled there, but we thought it was. We were part of a series which included *I Musici* (the *real* one from Italy), the *Beaux-Arts Trio*, Rampal and Starker.

We performed a Canadian work at each one of our South American concerts. I also carefully selected Shostakovich's *Chamber Symphony*, an arrangement by Rudolf Barshai of his *String Quartet No. 8*, now known as *Op. 110A* for string orchestra, which is dedicated to those who fell in the fight against Naziism. I felt that South America was a suitable location for this piece.

The South American countries are rich in minerals and precious stones but masses of its people live in grinding poverty. The geography and landscape are breathtaking. A lapidary like me could easily go mad with the superabundance of gem mines, emerald, lapis lazuli, rhodochrosita, rhodonite, as well as gold, silver, nickel and above all the salt mines. I see rocks, their colours and patterns, the same way as I see music. Elements of form and feeling are involved in both – actually, in everything we do. And we loved their magnificent tangos, a national treasure of another kind.

We were treated superbly, but we did get the impression they thought we were an oddity because we were Canadians proficient at classical music. There we met many Germans and other Europeans and we were invited to ambassadors' homes for private concerts. Our sponsors were interested in the arts, knew a great deal about music and spoke several languages. The Brazilians even presented me with a medal from their *Academia Brasiliera de Ciencias*.

The orchestra performed four concerts in Buenos Aires. As always, the orchestra members displayed a wonderful camaraderie on tour. During a dress rehearsal, first violinist Martin Foster, now concertmaster of the MCO, announced that a severe toothache might prevent him from playing the concert. His friend and fellow violinist, Latin American Adolfo Bornstein, who was a recent arrival to Montreal, offered to take Martin to a dentist he knew, so that the offending molar might be extracted. With two violinists bowing out I stopped the rehearsal and said, "We'll all play better when we feel better." Later at the performance the orchestra surpassed its usual excellence, Martin with a swollen jaw and Adolfo proud of his service to his friend.

On our departure the Argentineans presented me with a bronze plaque of appreciation. Press reviews were very positive. "Perfection of execution maintaining a technical mastery with great detail to dynamic and expressive inflections. The quality of the strings was noble and majestic"; and "A precise chamber music style rising above all technical difficulties, individual virtuosity of all members, noble expression, fine attention to detail"; and "Great praise belongs, first of all, to the conductor, Alexander Brott, who was able to evoke masterful interpretations from his ensemble."

The Orient 1987

In 1987, we undertook an ambitious three-week tour of the Orient, with stops in Japan, Hong Kong, South Korea and Taiwan. I believe it was the first time a Canadian chamber orchestra had been to China and Taiwan. The violinist Angèle Dubeau accompanied us as our headliner soloist.

Like many North Americans visiting Japan for the first time, I experienced a degree of culture shock. To me there is no country more distinctive than Japan and its archipelago. No country is as disciplined as Japan; few are as organized. And there are fewer countries where I *cannot* make myself understood, except through music. People every foot, umbrellas every six inches. The citizens seemed to be engaged in silent conversation. The Japanese are a keenly introspective people to whom extroversion is a capital sin, but their seeming detachment is misleading. They replace emotional displays with a preference for finesse and perfection of form. Their attention to beauty, colours and detail reflects their acceptance and performance of music.

Our orchestra found Japanese audiences most receptive and quietly respectful, quite unlike the boisterous Soviets. In Japan we gave concerts in Tokyo, Nagoya, Iwanuma and Sandai, followed by Seoul in South Korea, Taipei and Taichung in Taiwan and finally Hong Kong.

In Asia, as in the USSR, I discovered how different cultural values can be, including those toward classical music. The music created in the Orient tends to rely on beautiful, sparse melodies, rather than on rich European harmonies. It is less emotional or personal than Russian music but precise, clean and delicate, re-flecting the characteristics their culture values. In our performanc-es, we naturally chose European selections we felt the audiences would know and understand, Corelli and Handel, Shostakovitch's *Chamber Symphony*, two Bach concerti and Vivaldi's *Four Seasons*, in both of which Angèle Dubeau was featured. In Nagoya, the reviewer termed our performance of Mozart's *Divertimento*, "plain and sober." Perhaps something was lost in the translation. He did seem to like *Ritual*, calling it, "spiritual music based on deep philosophical thought." The reviewer visited us backstage after the concert and congratulated me, "Your half-century [the orchestra's anniversary] comes brilliantly alive."

In Taiwan, we were assigned to play in a colossal hall. Normally our orchestra plays in chamber-sized rooms that do not exceed 1,200 seats, so we were surprised to discover this one held around 3,000. Concerned about the acoustics and the reach of our delicate stringed instruments, I quickly requested microphones and ampli-fication.

The McGill Alumni Association was particularly active in Hong Kong and they entertained us royally. They presented us with a large photograph of the ensemble, which still hangs on my wall at home. As always, Canadian embassy officials outdid them-selves on behalf of the orchestra.

We returned to Canada after three weeks laden with not just tourist acquisitions but also with examples of contemporary Japanese and Korean music to study. Later at home, I programmed the work *Elegy for Strings* by Korea's Hai Jung Yoon, president of their Contemporary Music Society in Seoul. It is a softly undulat-ing piece, which will forever remind me of their beautiful land.

Bermuda 1988

In 1988 Yehudi Menuhin invited the McGill Chamber Orchestra to give some concerts as part of the prestigious Bermuda Festival. Menuhin also ran a violin school there and he asked me to lecture to the students. The French-Canadian violinist Angèle Dubeau came with us again for Vivaldi's *Four Seasons* and Bach's Violin Concerti.

I've known and admired Menuhin since his youth which, of course, was my youth as well. He was phenomenal in so many ways. We took every opportunity to engage him and he performed with the McGill Chamber Orchestra at annual gala concerts at Notre Dame Church. Once, following his appearance as soloist with the Montreal Symphony (when I was still associated with that orchestra), we all attended a reception at the Ritz Carlton Hotel. As Lotte and I shook Yehudi's hand in the receiving line, he murmured, "I'll meet you in the restaurant in twenty minutes." True to the clock, we met him there away from the crowd and he ordered a massive meal. I sensed that he was reflective and asked why. He replied with the usual soloist's complaint, "It's so demanding."

I was taken aback, because he didn't appear pressured. I coaxed him, "Yehudi, you're so successful, you speak several languages, you're admired internationally. Why should you be unhappy?" He thought for a moment, then replied enigmatically, "But Alec, what do I know about higher mathematics?"

Of course. How could I have forgotten that!

Part of the adventure of all these travels for me, was that I was living a dream (not to mention my mother's dream) in achieving so many musical firsts. Sometimes I find it hard to believe that Lotte and I did so much in a lifetime, but we did it by working constantly and sacrificing recreation, rest and precious family time. We wore "career blinders" . Work was our primary concern and everything we did got folded in with our work. And Lotte's organizational abilities were incredible – if she wanted a particular engagement, she would move mountains. Our tours over several continents and five decades stand as tributes not only to the talent and professionalism of the orchestra, its committee and its volunteers, but also to Lotte herself.

As I recount all these travels I reflect that in spite of many short trips within Canada and the United States, we never made a formal North American tour. There were just too many regular concerts and numerous commissions to compose.

Distinguished Artists

Throughout my career I've been privileged to make music with distinguished musicians. They taught me many things about conducting and playing, but also about leadership and living to the fullest. These giants fuelled my dreams. Many had survived hard times and worse in Europe. I understood their motivations because Lotte and I had also experienced hardship. But we all shared the love of music.

All of them had totally different personalities but they all shared making music come to life. That's really what it's all about. We in the orchestra soaked up their talent, professionalism, and inspirational qualities. We were always in awe – they were people and musicians like us, yet not quite like us at all. We knew we were in the company of the best and that brought out the best in us.

In the 1940s I worked with a fine French Canadian conductor, Wilfrid Pelletier, another success story from Montreal's east end. This handsome portly man, with a kindly face, liked to wear a vest and watch set over his stomach. He always made you feel he was interested in you. He, along with Pierre Béique, made an essential contribution to music in Quebec by bringing international artists, conductors and teachers here, transforming the Montreal music scene from musical backwater to sought-after venue.

Pelletier was named director of the *Conservatoire de Musique et de L'Art Dramatique de la Province de Québec,* an all-scholarship school with satellite campuses in Hull, Sherbrooke, Trois Rivieres, Chicoutimi, and Quebec City as well as Montreal. The *Conservatoire* created a huge talent pool of singers, instrumental performers, composers and conductors – to the point of almost oversupply today! It enabled young Quebecois, from the furthest reaches of the province, to have their talent identified and nurtured without cost to them. Even instruments were supplied free. Pelletier brought the school to international status by importing members of the New York Metropolitan Opera and the New York Philharmonic as instructors. When he was criticized for not hiring local people, he replied that eventually those teachers would be replaced by the graduates of our Quebec conservatories.

In the early years, many of the students were singers. Pelletier was head of French repertoire for the Metropolitan Opera and, thus, had an immediate entrée for these Quebec talents onto the international stage.

Although Pelletier recognized the English element of the province too, he seemed to favour French-Canadians in an early kind of affirmative action. Some people thought that policy may have caused other difficulties, but no one could fault him for doing his best to ensure that French-Canadians were not overlooked. He had an excellent ability to communicate with young people and he helped develop both talent and audiences with his Matinées Sinfoniques in Montreal and Sherbrooke. Since he was not as comfortable in English and considered the English audience equally important, he often invited me to conduct the English matinées.

"Uncle Pelly" seemed happiest in the company of young people and the performance of a promising young musician could move him to tears. Both of our sons attended and benefited from his *Conservatoire*. He took a personal interest in the development of their talent and featured them in his Matinées Sinfoniques. When Boris was five, I wrote an orchestral piece for him to play at one of the matinées. When Denis was studying with Walter Joachim, an excellent pedagogue as well as performer who created an internationally acclaimed cello program at the *Conservatoire* in Montreal, Pelletier invited him, too.

"The grand man of music in Quebec," had a consummate knowledge of opera, particularly the French repertoire. He was an excellent coach, precise and exacting. I also benefited from his wisdom. One incident stands out. It's common that young people starting their careers like to assert themselves. I was no exception. During my early days as concertmaster of the Montreal

Orchestra, the players were petitioning management for improved conditions. I spoke out in their favour and against management. One day, Pelletier took me aside and said, "Do not close the door behind you!" I took his advice to heart and have passed it on to other young concertmasters. He was right! A leader must keep the channels of communication open. Another example of Pelletier's wisdom is that whenever Pelletier's parents attended his Youth Concerts, he always introduced them to his young audience. I so admired this touching gesture of respect and appreciation that I, too, had my mother and stepfather attend as many of my concerts as they could.

The famous Russian-French conductor Igor Markevitch influenced my technique of conducting gesture. A short thin man, with a pinched face and beaked nose, his personality made him seem taller. Part madman, part genius, Markevitch was also a master of intrigue. He liked to play people off one against the other and to keep you unsure of your relationship with him. He was a respected devotee of "Les Six," the group of early twentieth-century French composers which included Darius Milhaud.

As a conductor he was highly organized. Each gesture and note of every Markevitch performance was superbly planned. His trademark was exemplary clarity in performance, detached from any intervening emotion. He used to brag to us, *Ça ne me touche pas. Vous voyez, je ne transpire pas.* ("It doesn't touch me. See, I'm not perspiring.")

He gave excellent performances, crystal clear. But they always left me wondering – is this the climax? Why doesn't he express it? Why won't he take a little more time? I always felt Markevitch's performances required an ounce or two more. Though I never fully agreed with his approach, I considered his baton technique exemplary and his way of teaching it superb. I later used his method to improve my own teaching of the art of conducting.

Markevitch was a great influence on Boris. In his early teens, Boris was losing interest in music, so Markevitch introduced the idea of a conducting career to him. He invited my son to study with him in Mexico and even to continue his studies in Paris, where he could live with Markevitch's mother.

Leopold Stokowski was totally different. He was passionate. He breathed music. It wasn't just a question of being precise. He convinced you emotionally – playing for him meant something. Like him, I believe that music directs me in a certain way and I search for the message.

Stokowski conducted the MSO many memorable times. Once we performed in Quebec City and our venue was a cold reverberating hockey arena. That didn't daunt our elegant conductor at all. He inspired us to transcend the limitations of the location to play as if we were in the great concert halls of Europe. We finished such a great and moving performance of Tchaikovsky's *Pathetique Symphony* that our first violist, Lucien Robert, couldn't keep from weeping. We were all wrung out, but we were exuberant in our exhaustion!

Stokowski was an escapist, trying to get away from his background as Les Stokes of Manchester, making himself five years younger and adopting a strange East European/English accent. He was famous for many things including composing the music for Walt Disney's *Fantasia*, for his several wives including Gloria Vanderbilt, and for a public affair with Greta Garbo.

Many musical colleagues mocked him and accused him of being a libertine, "over the top". But I loved it. He dared to do the unusual, even if he was criticized. Where the music called for imitative echoes, he placed the players distantly off the stage, and got the real thing. One had to admire his courage. You could always tell a Stokowski performance because of the deliberately wrong things he did. Often in music it is not what you do right that counts, it is what you do judiciously wrong that is distinctive. His were beautiful, though I have to say they were personal choices. His critics were scandalized that he had no qualms about making changes to the scores of the great masters such as Beethoven or Bach, if it suited his interpretation

I had a remarkable opportunity to witness this from the standpoint of the composer. Stokowski selected my first violin concerto to perform in Carnegie Hall. I appeared partway through the dress rehearsal and was shocked that I could barely recognize my own music. He had changed so many things, all the dynamics, phrasing, and emphasis. He completely changed the colour of the work. When I received the orchestral parts back from him, I found that he had written all over them using a system whereby the violins and string parts were all marked up in blue ink, the brass part in red, and so on. I still have it, but I can never use it. It's personal only to Stokowski.

Afterwards I felt lucky that I hadn't come in time for the entire rehearsal. As the composer, I would probably have insisted or tried to insist he make no changes and we would have missed the once-in-a-lifetime chance of hearing it *à la Stoky*.

I have some wonderful photographs of Lotte and Stokowski when we were doing Wagner with him. Lotte knew the German operas very well. During one rehearsal, there came a turn of page, but since Lotte knew by heart what was to follow, nobody came in except her. "Bravo, Madame!" Stokowski exclaimed. Later he gave her a beautiful autographed photo on which he had written out a musical staff with the excerpt she had played.

Great conductors communicate from the podium. Their presence and gestures change how the musicians perform. Their personalities and intellect bring life to the composers' notes. It is impossible to write these things down, which is why music is a two-stage creative process, with the notes coming alive only when they are played.

Vladimir Golschmann conducted with extraordinary style. He was an elegant and refreshing musician. Because of a leg injury, he limped onto the stage, his clothes beautifully cut and his shoes made specially for him. Gatsby-like, precious, he wore glorious rings with heavenly stones. It was he who sparked my love of flashy rings.

He postured like an ink drawing by Picasso. "I don't know vot, but I vant somesing," he would vaguely instruct the orchestra. I remember him as a charming man who depended on the men and women "wishing" to play well. Sometimes they did, and sometimes they didn't, but it never seemed to bother him, because he was doing his part and was thoroughly immersed in it. What he heard in his head was all that seemed to matter to him. I'm not sure he even listened to the orchestra.

Golschmann gave my composing career an early boost. In January 1948 he conducted my *Fancy and Folly* with the Saint Louis Symphony Orchestra, where he was principal conductor. On the occasion of its US premiere, he wrote me:

> Cher ami – You would have enjoyed it because everything went beautifully. The reception of the public was very good, particularly Saturday night, the audience being much more "modern music conscious" than the Friday afternoon one which is somewhat conservative! The *Star-Times* speaks of a cleanly wrought, intricate composition.

Some of our illustrious guest conductors had lengthy sojourns in Montreal but some left more quickly. Bruno Walter conducted the Montreal Symphony only once. As the high priest of Mozart and Mahler, he devoted himself to both these composers with meaningful authenticity. My former teacher Eugene Schneider, who was playing first viola in the Montreal Symphony Orchestra, was intensely looking forward to Walter's appearance. That evening, having achieved his goal of playing with Walter, in full view of the orchestra and of the audience, Schneider quietly put down his instrument and keeled over in the grips of a heart attack. Sadly, but perhaps fittingly, he died during that concert. Walter never returned to Montreal.

Pierre Monteux was a moderator of the best order. Quiet in demeanor, he threw no tantrums as other conductors will do. He made no special personal requests. He did everything with a smile. He had a wonderful ear for pitch and an excellent sense of musical balance. His mastery of French music was exceptional. After all, he remembered Debussy and he knew Ravel. He became an entrusted grand-papa of that movement. When Toscanini was hired to form the NBC Orchestra, he asked Pierre and Artur Rodzinski to prepare the orchestra for him. They chose personnel who were outstanding, with Mischa Mischakoff as concertmaster, Leonard Rose as principal cellist, and William Primrose, violist, among the strings.

Monteux always called me Sasha, the diminutive of Alexander.

He taught Boris at his conducting academy in Maine, and gave him his first job as his assistant with the London Symphony and on his tours in Europe. Monteux and his wife Doris took Boris to museums, art galleries, the theatre and acted as real mentors to him. Unlike some of the more egotistical conductors, Monteux was, above all, human. He knew his job well, but didn't seek the limelight. Once when he was asked to address the orchestra's subscribers, he was most reluctant. Instead he said to the audience, "For so many years, I have turned ze back on you, I haven't ze courage to face you. I give you my wife."

Madame Monteux spoke for the next forty-five minutes.

Monteux never raised his voice or lost his temper. Boris tells of an incident on a car trip between Quebec City and Montreal. Doris could be demanding and talked incessantly in a nasal Maine twang. She was in the midst of haranguing Maitre about something he had done or neglected to do, when he calmly picked up their miniature French poodle Fifi. Ceremoniously he handed the dog to her saying, "Darling, here's your daughter."

Lotte and I went to see Monteux at his home in Maine a few years before he passed away in 1964 and walked with him in the flower garden he was proud of. We thanked him again for his kindness to Boris. Despite advancing frailty, this remarkable man conducted the London Symphony Orchestra on the fiftieth anniversary of Stravinsky's *Le Sacre du Printemps* at the age of 87 – from memory!

Sir Thomas Beecham guest-conducted the MSO several times and took us to a higher pinnacle of music-making. What a delightful person he was. I can't imagine playing anything with Beecham without thoroughly enjoying it musically and on a personal level. He could change the shape of music, giving it a human quality, charm, vitality. Pierre Monteux called him, "Le Grand Baton."

Sir Thomas not only influenced my life as a composer but as a concertmaster, too. He led the Montreal Symphony in several programs, providing memorable experiences of his wit as well as his musical mastery. During a performance of Berlioz' *Symphonie Fantastique* in the Eglise Saint Laurent, the orchestra and audience could clearly hear a train rushing by. The sound came so close and so loud that it seemed the locomotive would pass right through the church. Beecham stopped the performance. "I would hate to think that this was a critic," he told the audience. His choice of words was always unique. He was a wonderful gentleman of the old world, with all the old-world courtesies.

And he could be hilarious. The British public loved him for the stories of his wit, such as his opinion, "Brass bands are all very well in their place – outdoors and several miles away." I watched him conduct Richard Strauss's *Til Eulenspiegel* and imitate every one of the characters and situations. He was having fun, bringing the comical elements of this score to life, in sharp contrast to Strauss himself who would perform the same piece with a dour poker face. His love of music was infectious. His Rossini was so joyful and effervescent it made us giggle. Yet he had a romantic side. His Mozart was magical, his Schubert was infused with indulgent romanticism.

He was an example of a generation of British intellectuals, who like George Bernard Shaw, could find the perfect word for any occasion. He was the one conductor who could elegantly criticize your playing and make you laugh with him. However, he could make sharp and hurtful remarks that stung the recipient perhaps more than he intended. One had to get used to the Beecham humour and not everyone could.

He was not rude and often took pains to conceal his reactions. On one occasion, he brought with him Betty Humby, the British pianist of some reputation. I believe they were married at the time. Humby played the Grieg *Piano Concerto* for a concert held at the Forum, home of the Montreal Canadiens in their glory days. We had rehearsed together in the morning and she played beautifully. But at the evening concert she didn't do as well. The Grieg was played, as is customary, just before the intermission. When Sir Thomas and I went backstage to our dressing room, he shared his displeasure about her performance with me. The stage manager asked Sir Thomas whether he should remove the grand piano from the stage.

Beecham answered, "Let it be, it will slink off all by itself." It was potentially embarrassing, because a moment later Betty came in, but Sir Thomas was gracious to her. He had let off steam and didn't need to make things worse.

Beecham's personal relationships caused a problem. Each time he came here he was accompanied by a different woman. This upset Montreal's society matrons who didn't know where to seat the women at dinner parties, so they usually ended up sitting somewhere at the end of the table, while Sir Thomas occupied the place of honour next to the hostess. On one occasion, Madame Athanase David was the hostess. Having sat through several of these dinners each with a different Sir Thomas companion, she asked him in a loud stage whisper, "Sir Thomas, tell me are you *really* married?"

He replied sarcastically, "Not seriously, you know."

I wonder what he would have answered in our modern time of political correctness.

Beecham wasn't the only conductor to let his musicians know when he was unhappy with them. A public outburst by Victor Di Sabata, who was in Montreal to guest-conduct the MSO, remains burned into my memory. Di Sabata opened the concert with the Verdi overture of *La Forza del Destino*. This overture calls for three chords fortissimo and one full measure of silence, which is repeated, then it recurs at the very end for a nicely rounded structure. The utmost precision is required to play it absolutely together. We practised it often and thought we had it just right. But at the concert, Maestro Di Sabata was not satisfied and at the measure of rest, he muttered, "Stupido!" for all to hear. The orchestra was shocked, but I was hopeful that the uninitiated in the audience would think the impromptu vocals were part of the score.

Dealing with the fractured English of our maestros could be a challenge. Many humorous misinterpretations could result. Guest-conductor, Josef Krips, once said to our first horn player, Joseph Masella, "Cho, komm, I brink you an omelette!"

Wondering why the maestro had singled him out for an egg dinner, Masella went forward.

Krips reached into the breast pocket of his full-dress suit and handed Masella an amulet to wear, "For the high Richard Strauss horn parts."

Did the good luck omelette help Masella? Maybe, maybe not,

but it did serve as the beginning of a hobby for me which has become somewhat of an obsession – the collecting, polishing and setting of precious and semi-precious stones. Like most men, I dislike the restrictive nature of neckties, yet in my profession one has to wear a tie of some kind. My polished-stone pendants are a tie substitute and allow me a little individuality, as well as an opportunity to show off my lapidary labours.

Many of the lighter moments in an orchestra's life happen during the rehearsals and often the international blend of people and languages comes into play. One of the great German conductors to appear with the Montreal Symphony Orchestra was Dr. Fritz Stiedry, who at one time conducted the Wagner *Ring Cycle* at the Metropolitan Opera in New York. At our first rehearsal, the cleaning staff was noisily working on the second balcony, which bothered the maestro no end. In desperation he turned to the cleaning ladies and shouted, *Vimmen, vimmen, don't kair* ('Kair' in German means to sweep) and turned back to the orchestra.

The resident wise guy, cellist Jack Cantor, punned, "Maestro, they don't care!"

After exchanges of English, German and French, someone in the wind section shouted to the cleaners, *Arrêtez donc*.

After two minutes of silence, the cleaners left.

Otto Klemperer was a giant of another order. He was not pre-occupied with the finesses of gesture with which other conductors, especially Markevitch, were concerned. His approach was power, drama and intent – strength of gesture in the execution of form. His Beethoven was towering. His slow movements were profound indulgence. His scherzos were not fleeting moments amongst the clouds, but heroes at play.

In 1951, while disembarking an aircraft in Montreal, Klemperer fell and broke his hip. After surgery, he was kept in hospital to recuperate for about six months. Finally he was released and able to plan his return to the podium. He called me to his hotel to go through the concert program with him. The work in question was Beethoven's *Fifth Symphony*, which Klemperer had performed more frequently than any other conductor in the world. But his long illness and recuperation seemed to have taken some of his confidence. After we had inspected every bowing, nuance and relative dynamic, he timidly posed an unexpected question. "Do you think I'll be able to do it?"

I assured him that if he, the great Otto Klemperer, couldn't do it, then no one else on earth could.

In the end, his performance was powerful and moving. He brought the house down. The giant was back.

A giant-to-be, Leonard Bernstein came to Montreal as an extraordinarily gifted young man. I remember attending one of his famed Young People's Concerts in New York. Until that time, the New York Philharmonic had trouble during the educational concerts, because the kids would fold the programs into paper airplanes and create all kinds of havoc. But Bernstein knew how to reach them without speaking down to them. This made me realize the value of the child psychology courses they made us take at Juilliard. Bernstein really applied that psychology. He explained a musical canon to the children this way.

He asked the audience, "How many of you have been to a fair or the circus?" It was probably the first time anyone had asked a Carnegie Hall audience such a question.

Of course, all the kids shouted, "Yay!"

"Okay," said Bernstein. "How many have taken a ride on the ferris wheel there and know what it feels like?"

Most of the children responded.

So he explained, "Every time you hit the top of our musical 'ferris wheel,' you will hear the same tune come back. Tell me when you hear it." Then he played the canon until the second entry of the same line appeared again. He looked at the audience.

Of course, they all yelled again. He had made a connection with them and they loved it.

Bernstein had a wisdom beyond his years and his extraordinary talent brought him success at an early age. He was so lucky that everything he touched seemed to turn to gold. I often think it was too bad he wasted his talents on Broadway instead of devoting himself to serious music. On the other hand the popular success of his music created a curiosity among young people to attend his concerts.

As first prize winner of the Mitropolous International Conducting Competition in 1968, Boris served as Bernstein's assistant with the New York Philharmonic. He shares his natural talent for exposing young people to music and learned a great deal more from him. In June of 2000, Boris realized his mentor's dream by conducting the Vatican premiere of Bernstein's controversial *Mass*. I attended and was deeply moved.

Lotte and I liked to invite our guest conductors home for dinner, which provided many unique memories. Many of the great names sat at our table. Otto Klemperer brought his wife and daughter Lotte. Most came alone. Gregor Piatigorsky arrived from the hotel and complained, "Vot a life I ave – I'm alvays alone. I even 'ave to zo my own botenz!"

Enesco arrived carrying a hand-powered flashlight to light his way up the stairs. Charles Münch used to plead with the orchestra, *"Mes enfants, con amore, espressivo, plus tendre, tout a fait à la point."* (My children, play it with love, expressively, tenderly.) As a gentle hint for us to play better in performance than we had in rehearsal, he ended one rehearsal exhorting, *"Alors, au revoir, mais pour ce soir, apportez vos meilleurs instruments."* (See you this evening, but bring your best instruments.) After one of these sessions, he came to a wonderful dinner prepared by Lotte, whom he loved, and declared, *"Mais Alec, vous êtes donc un homme heureux."* (Alec, you're such a lucky man.)

"C'est vrai!" (True!) I returned the compliment. After all, he had enjoyed my wife's dinner too.

At one of the most memorable meals we hosted, Leopold Stokowski was our guest. Who would have thought that this theatrical maestro was really a family man at heart? We discovered this secret when in the entr'acte of the morning rehearsal, Stokowski came off the stage and asked me, "What is a really fine place to eat here?"

I started naming some restaurants when Lotte walked towards the podium and said, "I know a good place."

"And where would that be, Madame?" inquired the maestro. He didn't know we were married, so he was surprised when she laughed, "At our house!"

"What sort of cuisine?"

"Swiss," Lotte said with assurance.

"With real Neuchatel wine?"

Lotte didn't realize that real Neuchatel wine may be easy to get in Switzerland but, in those days, it was not so simple in Montreal. I spent the rest of the afternoon going from one liquor shop to another, until I finally found three bottles.

When I got home, Lotte had a lady there to help her with dinner and I went into the front room to play with Denis, who was about eight months old. Stokowski was to arrive at seven, but the doorbell rang a full hour early. He explained, "I know I'm early, but I want to feel at home."

You have to know what he looked like – over six feet tall, with a wonderful leonine mane of white hair. His fine herring-bone coat and white silk scarf made an elegant impression, but that didn't stop him from dropping to the floor to play with Denis.

At this incongruent picture I exclaimed, "That's a far cry from Capri," referring to his well-publicized escapade with Greta Garbo.

He looked up wistfully and remarked, "Ah yes, those were the days of all rehearsals and no concerts."

Over the sixty-odd years since I founded the McGill Chamber Orchestra, many guest artists have graced our stage from Canadian pops pianist André Gagnon, to flautist Jean-Pierre Rampal, to violinist David Oistrakh. A prime example of the star-studded line up the McGill Chamber Orchestra offered our audiences is our 1973-74 season, in which the above three virtuosi appeared along with the baritone Donald Bell, harmonica player Larry Adler, and guitarist Alexandre Lagoya.

Internationally known Canadian artists including Pierrette Alarie, Leopold Simoneau, Maureen Forrester, Lois Marshall, Glenn Gould, Marc Andrée Hamelin, Neil Chotem, Karen Kain, The Canadian Brass, Rosabelle and Kelsey Jones, Walter Joachim, and Jacques Lecompte appeared with us too. There was never a shortage of talent at home.

Another good season was the McGill Chamber Orchestra's 1956-57 series, in Redpath Hall at McGill University. We were able to offer violinists Hyman Bress and Mildred Goodman, harpsichordist Kelsey Jones, internationally known Canadian flautist Mario Duschenes, Geoffrey Waddington guest-conducting *Music for Mourning* on the death of King George VI, pianists Rose Goldblatt and Neil Chotem, soprano Patricia Neway, and Jean-Pierre Rampal in a return engagement by popular request. English oboist Leon Goossens and French cellist Maurice Gendron rounded out the season.

We found Jean-Pierre Rampal by a lucky accident. As Lotte and I took a walk around the Opéra House one sunny afternoon in Paris on one of our European tours, we met Vladimir Golschmann. During the conversation he said, "Leesten, eef you want to hear great flute playing, go to the Opera."

We did as he advised, heard a young man playing absolute magic, and hurried back-stage to offer him an engagement in Montreal. At first he demurred, "Oh, dis-donc, I don't know, I am so busy," but finally he agreed. That is how Jean-Pierre Rampal got his first of many, many notable engagements in Montreal. Headliners like Rampal have been what distinguished our orchestra from other ensembles.

Over the years, Maureen Forrester often appeared as soloist with the MCO. She was one of my favourite Canadian guest soloists and, of course, she was highly popular with the audiences and orchestra. Another native of Montreal, raised in the east end, she too began humbly. She sang with her mother in the CBC radio choir where I was playing in the orchestra. They looked alike – big-boned, tall and attractive. Her husband, violinist Eugene Kash, and I were both struggling "fiddlers" together in our youth.

Maureen achieved fame during the tremendous influx of immigrants like her coaches Bernard Diamant and John Newmark. Her type of voice, Germanic alto, was well suited to the German repertoire, which she came to specialize in, and her performances of Mahler were exemplary. When she sang the Mahler *Kindertotenlieder* (on the death of a child), she touched everyone. She was a very natural talent, with an excellent memory and the power to project her voice, and she loved to mingle with a crowd. The last project I did with Maureen was a recording of my *Songs of Contemplation*.

146

The newly arrived Joachim brothers, Walter and Otto, were welcome assets to music in Montreal. Walter became principal cellist in the MSO as well as the MCO, for many years. He was wonderful as leader and as a teacher at the *Conservatoire du Québec*. Walter's brother Otto is a fine violist but his forte is contemporary composition – laconic, electronic, with fascinating devices.

Maestro Luciano and Madame Edith Della Pergola were a great motivating couple in the McGill faculty. They emigrated from Italy, land of opera, and contributed greatly to the growth of the Opera Department at McGill. The Della Pergolas asked me to conduct the McGill student body in the chamber opera *The Apothecary* by Haydn. Our royal standard french poodle, Alphonse, had a walk on role in it, but luckily he was not required to sing.

Mario Duschenes, flautist, conductor, expert narrator and recorder player, was another talented McGill colleague. He narrated our premiere performance of Stravinsky's *L'Histoire du Soldat* on the McGill University grounds and made us all feel as if we were in a Swiss village. He was part of a trio consisting of himself on flute, Melvin Berman on oboe, and Kelsey Jones as harpsichordist. Duschenes once asked me to compose something for him using his entire family of recorders. I wrote a piece in which each movement used another recorder. I'm rather proud of my title, *Three on a Spree (Twixt Thee and Me)*.

Tenor Peter Pears, whom I had met in 1948 at the Queen's Hall luncheon in London, was one of the many British musicians we engaged. He came to sing Benjamin Britten's *St. Nicholas Cantata* with us in 1976. Pears was a refined artist and his communication with the audience was transcendental.

On the day of the concert, we had just about finished the last rehearsal when Pears received an urgent call. His partner, Benjamin Britten was dying. He wanted to get back to England immediately and I was frantic because there was no time to prepare a substitute for the program. But Lotte, cool as ever, confidently said, "You go ahead and finish the rehearsal. I'll be on the phone for about twenty minutes. Don't worry about anything." She telephoned the airline, got the president, explained the urgency of the situation, and convinced him of the magnitude of the service he would be performing if only he could delay Pears's flight. Then she invited him to attend the concert he was facilitating. Pears's flight to England was postponed and he was able to perform at the concert. We quickly switched the visiting Ottawa choir's place in the program to facilitate his new schedule.

To complicate matters, it was the night of the Quebec provincial election in which the Parti Québecois came to power and emotions were running high. Noisy crowds, traffic jams and jubilation echoed in the streets, but tears flowed backstage in the concert hall. Most of us had great lumps in our throats, so upset were we about Britten's illness.

We heard later that Pears made it home just in time. I wrote to him afterwards –

In the light of circumstances I hesitated writing you before to thank you for your memorable performance of the *St. Nicholas Cantata*. For all those present at Notre Dame Church, it will remain a treasured moment in time. Benjamin Britten has left us, but his music has not …. Your presentation of his music reaches the very core of this expression and we are grateful to have shared in this experience.

I meant every word.

McGill also enjoyed visits from many distinguished musicians, among them Paul Hindemith, the renowned German composer. He came as a guest of the Composers' League and I was asked to entertain him. I thought it would be an opportune moment for me to bring along one of my scores to the old Queen's Hotel at the bottom of Peel Street where he was staying. During our conversation, Hindemith made a remark criticizing the extroversion in the music of Richard Strauss and Shostakovitch.

It gave me the feeling that my music which had similarities particularly to Shostakovitch would probably not be to his taste. I tried to hide my score behind my chair, but he saw my gesture and insisted on having a peek. His comments were illuminating. He told me that he found my music too outwardly bombastic, likening it to that of Richard Strauss. This helped me understand his approach to creativity in the intellectual sense. I performed several of his compositions… but not too often. They're too arid for me. He himself called it, *gebrauchtsmusik* (music for the occasion.) His approach to inspiration was also revealing. He said "I wake up every morning, have my coffee and sit at my desk at 9:00 promptly. The muse has learned to be on time."

I have especially enjoyed performing British music, perhaps because of my relationship with Douglas Clarke and my early visits to England. In my lectures on English music at McGill, I taught that it was mainly two people who brought English music back to its roots which were with the sixteenth century composers Christopher Tye, John Taverner and Thomas Tallis, and away from the clutches of Handel, Haydn and Mendelssohn. Those two were Gustav Holst and Ralph Vaughan Williams.

Douglas Clarke had studied with Gustav Holst in England and, to pay tribute to his teacher, had invited him to conduct a concert with the Montreal Symphony Orchestra. We musicians knew of Holst and his music through his recording of the great suite *The Planets*, which was on the program that night. When Clarke presented Holst to the orchestra rehearsing in the Mount Royal Hotel ballroom, the entire orchestra stood up and applauded him for the next ten minutes. In a soft, almost humble voice, Holst protested, "Thank you, please don't. I'm only a trombone player." It was an altogether moving experience.

Some of the musicians we entertained had chosen a different path. Many years ago, I conducted for the pianist-comedian Victor Borge with the Montreal Symphony at the St. Denis Theatre. Mayor Jean Drapeau asked me to bring Borge to City Hall the next morning to sign the Golden Book. I picked him up in my flamboyant white convertible Buick and had the funniest drive downtown in my life. Borge's comments about what we saw as we drove through the streets were priceless.

At City Hall the press had been coached to take photos just as Borge was to sign the book, but he kept talking about his ViBo Farms and the fact that he raised 4,000 Cornish hens every month.

Finally, Mayor Drapeau asked, "How is all this possible, that you travel so much, you practise the piano, you write your own humour, and yet you raise so many hens?"

"Ah," said Borge, "it's not really a problem – they do it all by themselves!" With this example of the Borge humour, the press cameras flashed.

I'm convinced that the success of our orchestras has been largely due to the high-caliber artists and conductors who performed with us. The best and brightest graced Montreal's stages and inspired us to reach ever-greater heights in performance and communication. We truly experienced Robert Browning's meaning when he said, "A man's reach should exceed his grasp, or what's a heaven for?" As an orchestra, as musicians, as individuals, under the guidance of motivating guest-conductors and alongside virtuoso soloists, we rose to their challenge, and set the bar ever higher.

The Kingston Adventure

By the 1960s, the struggles of the Depression and the war years were well behind us and we felt economically and professionally secure. Now opportunities in business and the arts were opening up. Lotte and I were busy. The Montreal Symphony Orchestra concerts at the Chalet atop Mount Royal were repeated at other locations, concerts like those at the Maurice Richard Arena also took place at three other venues surrounding Montreal and our McGill Chamber Orchestra concerts continued. We performed in church concerts and educational concerts, we taught and lectured, sometimes I even took a few moments to study my scores. Many evenings I think Lotte and I embraced each other out of sheer fatigue. But we could not have been happier.

In 1965, Queen's University English Professor George Whalley and Michael Davies, publisher of the *Kingston Whig Standard*, invited me to assess the Kingston Symphony Orchestra. I was to take a rehearsal one Sunday afternoon and report my findings. The invitation from this historic Ontario city, the home of Sir John A. Macdonald, intrigued me. I assumed I would study the orchestra briefly, suggest additional players and maybe recommend a McGill student to take over as conductor.

I fully intended not to get too involved. But the entire situation was just too tempting. Having the full responsibility to select personnel and artists and to plan repertoire was a dream challenge. I found a way to fit the role of conductor of the Kingston Symphony Orchestra into my schedule. The larger orchestra also meant I could program full symphonies, concerti and other works for which my smaller McGill Chamber Orchestra did not have the people.

Besides, I never could turn down an invitation to stretch myself musically. It's always interesting to build anew. Boris, too, has thoroughly enjoyed being responsible for creating and improving seven symphony orchestras – two in the United Kingdom, five in Canada and he is now working on an eighth in Los Angeles, California.

As it turned out, my affiliation with Kingston was substantial, spanning from 1965 to 1980 with the Kingston Symphony Orchestra and extending beyond that with the Kingston Pops concerts series. Of course, I didn't give up my chamber orchestra and I retained my teaching position at McGill University. Lotte continued her work with the Montreal Symphony Orchestra, too. We became inter-city commuters, rearranging our affairs to keep weekends free for rehearsals with the Kingston Symphony. We spent four days of the week in Montreal, took the train to Kingston on Thursday nights and then headed home to Montreal on Sundays.

My first advice for Whalley was to engage a young professional string quartet-in-residence in Kingston. I was sure a resident quartet would go a long way toward establishing uniform bowings and phrasing in the symphony and act as standard bearer, setting goals to which the predominantly amateur and student musicians in the Kingston Symphony could aspire. I had found this practice of resident ensembles successful in Montreal and at Juilliard. It was the first of many ideas I imported to Kingston from Montreal and New York.

For recommendations for the string quartet members, I consulted a friend from my Juilliard days, who was, by then, a renowned pedagogue and music coach. I knew I could trust Professor Dorothy de Lay. George Whalley went to New York to meet and hear the quartet that de Lay recommended and he was as impressed, as we thought he would be.

The Vághy Quartet consisted of Dezsö Vághy, first violin and his brother Tibor, violist and two other members who changed over the years. The Vághys had fled Hungary in 1956 and then studied at Juilliard. They first played in Canada at Expo '67, where I heard them. When Whalley and I asked them to become section leaders of the Kingston Symphony, they accepted the posts on condition that all four members of the quartet become teachers on the Queen's University music faculty. So they were invited to become Queen's quartet-in-residence and, in the fall of 1968, they moved to Kingston with their families. A resident professional woodwind quartet was later created from the excellent supply of young Canadian wind players, which provided the orchestra with principal players of professional quality in all sections.

We insisted on regular rehearsals and full attendance for the full orchestra, as well as sectional rehearsals when needed. These common-sense changes raised the standard of the Kingston Symphony so we were ready to invite soloists of distinction.

As their sound and confidence grew, we made our programs a little more challenging each year. At the same time we included pieces representative of every musical period from Baroque to Impressionist to contemporary. With this new professional approach they improved radically within a few years.

The basic orchestra consisted of fifty-five members, but for larger works we imported additional players from Montreal or Toronto. By 1971 the symphony's extremely modest budget of $20,000 had more than tripled to $67,500. Fund-raising activities, government grants, business sponsorships and a donation from the City of Kingston made up a significant portion of this annual budget, over and above ticket revenues.

A symphony is a strange animal whose appetite is never satiated. It continually needs funds to guarantee creative activity and steady artistic development. It's a constant struggle and, as I alerted everyone, it would be no different for the Kingston Symphony than for any other orchestra. As I well knew, the financial demands of maintaining and developing an orchestra are every bit as daunting as its musical challenges.

Knowing Lotte's consummate ability as a manager, I asked her to take a sabbatical from the Montreal Symphony and come live in Kingston to help me out. We determined to repeat our earlier successes by applying the lessons we had learned managing the McGill Chamber Orchestra. If our techniques worked on the intellectual and artistic citizens of Montreal, the sophisticated university town of Kingston would surely appreciate our musical wares too.

This was just after the Montreal Symphony broke my contract as musical director of the MSO Pops Series. There's no doubt that our distress over that had a lot to do with our accepting the Kingston challenge.

In Kingston, our strategy included imaginative concert programs of works by a single composer, such as all-Bach concerts, programs focussed on a specific musical period such as the Baroque or Romantic era and the engagement of top-flight internationally renowned soloists. We copied our Maurice Richard Arena concerts at Kingston's Memorial Centre Arena, complete with wine and cheese, of course. As we had on Montreal's Mount Royal, we staged outdoor concerts at Kingston's Fort Henry. Again, we attended to every detail and innovation, such as making the last number a waltz, to which the audience would dance.

All this meant I had to find a residence in Kingston. By this time, Boris was music director of the Hamilton Philharmonic Orchestra and living with his family in Hamilton and Denis was in California, studying under famed cellist Gregor Piatigorsky. Since the Thousand Islands fascinated me, I contacted a real estate agent who offered a gem of a location on one of the numerous picturesque islands in the St. Lawrence River. Clutching glossy photographs of the proposed property, I gleefully brought them to Montreal to show Lotte.

She looked for a brief moment, then pointed out, "It's beautiful. But where will I find a doctor or drugstore?" By that time, she could no longer hide the encroachment of her multiple sclerosis and her healthcare was an important consideration.

Well, I felt quite stupid and was heartily sorry for having failed to consider her needs. I never mentioned those islands again. Instead, I searched for a home bordering Lake Ontario and found a gorgeous house at 86 Lakeshore Drive. I first saw it in winter, from the lake where the agent and I walked across the ice and admired that the back of the house was all windows with a magnificent view of the lake. Lotte loved it, too, so we purchased it. That home gave us much pleasure during our years in Kingston.

This made us a two-home family, since we continued to maintain our Montreal address, where I lived during the week. Boris found a 1968 white Rolls Royce for me, which I drove with pride and pleasure. (I confess to a weakness for interesting British automobiles.) We kept our own 21 foot pontoon boat, a happy orange colour with a fringed canopy. It was beautifully outfitted with a centre helm and upholstered seating, perfect for Denis, Boris, their young families (we now had several grandchildren) and us. We spent many happy times on it, often packing lunches and sailing out around the islands for the day. We counted ourselves very fortunate.

Now that Lotte was beside me in Kingston to keep things operating smoothly, we could aim even higher. Keeping that "hungry animal" image constantly in mind, we knew the Kingston Symphony Orchestra had to attract between 2,200 to 2,500 subscribers in order to remain financially viable. Luckily, this did happen because as a small and vibrant university community, Kingston considered having a fine orchestra a civic asset and people supported its development by their attendance and fund-raising efforts. In Kingston there was also less competition for the entertainment and cultural dollar than in Montreal or Toronto.

By 1973, we had long-range plans to become a regional orchestra, often giving repeat performances of Kingston concerts in nearby towns such as Brockville and Belleville. We hoped eventually to establish a regular touring schedule to centres all over Eastern Ontario. Members of the orchestra were encouraged to form unconducted chamber ensembles to perform educational concerts and play in various outlying locations, as audience development measures. We began to present special education concerts for the schools, for which the children were bussed to the Grand Theatre. The Vághy String Quartet and the St. Lawrence Wind Quintet were often booked for school ensemble concerts. I planned to hire more resident professional musicians and to create a more narrowly focussed chamber orchestra. Lotte and I thought we could build something that would last. We weren't afraid to dream big.

Through our international connections we brought some of the world's greatest artists to Kingston – pan flautist George Zamfir, André Gagnon, Jean-Pierre Rampal, Janos Starker, Leonard Rose,

Gary Karr, David Oistrakh, Ravi Shankar, Ida Haendel, Henryk Szeryng and Lili Kraus, to name a few. We could attract such luminaries to Kingston by close-booking them near their Montreal dates with the McGill Chamber Orchestra.

Yet, I don't think the Kingston Symphony Board fully appreciated our achievements. They appeared to take our success for granted. The Board members were all very nice people individually, but they didn't know the field like Lotte and I did. In my more frustrated moments, I used to think, uncharitably, I admit, that some of them would not have been able to spell these artists' names, let alone know how to engage them.

Our symphony animal with its voracious appetite led us to seek corporate support. Thanks to Lotte, a wide selection of corporations such as Royal Trust, Bright's and Andrès Wines, Imperial Tobacco, Imperial Oil, du Maurier and others sponsored our Kingston concerts. She was one of the first concert promoters in Canada to successfully obtain corporate sponsorship for classical symphony concerts and Kingston musicians and audiences benefited from her energy and expertise.

During this period I continued to compose. I wrote music to Andersen's fairy tale *The Emperor's New Clothes*, with the text edited by George Whalley, who was a skilled poet. We performed this new work together at one of the Kingston Symphony concerts. I enjoyed working with the charming tale about a powerful poseur who fools everyone until a child exposes him and brings them all to their senses.

The work employs a violin cadenza to represent the part where the Emperor parades naked through town. Later, a critic suggested I should have extended the cadenza to give the audience time to absorb the situation, so I rewrote that section. Sometimes a critic does hit the nail on the head!

In June 1973, my efforts with the Kingston Symphony Orchestra were rewarded at the Queen's University convocation where I was granted an honorary Doctor of Laws degree. It was one of my proudest moments. As the citation was read out, I mentally relived my last eight years of Kingston activities –

Alexander Brott, composer, conductor, violinist, teacher of music at a sister university; musician extraordinaire; whose music-making activities have been familiar to enthusiastic audiences on both sides of the Atlantic for a quarter century and more; whose appointment as conductor of the Kingston Symphony eight years ago presented a stimulating challenge to Kingston instrumentalists and audiences alike; and whose charming cajolery and subtle pedagogy have lifted the capacities and ambitions of both to heights they hardly suspected possible, thus earning for Kingston a proud and permanent place in the annals of orchestral development in Ontario; an impresario, as well as conductor, who has brought to us as soloists some of the great musicians of our time; a versatile virtuoso who imparts style and grace to all he does and who can reveal through musical imagination the fun and fancy to be discovered in a circle, a triangle and four squares, or in *The Emperor's New Clothes*.

This was a very happy time. We had overcome difficult obstacles and achieved many successes together, Lotte, I and the Kingston Symphony Orchestra and my future seemed to include both the Kingston and McGill orchestras. We loved our lakeside home in Kingston, the only truly gracious residence Lotte and I had ever owned. There I kept my Rolls Royce, my boat and my hopes of eventual retirement. At 58 years of age, I occasionally thought of retirement in the distant future. But, as these things have a way of doing, the future arranged itself sooner than I was ready for.

My mother passed away in January, 1978. She had been an important beacon in my life and left a hole in my heart from which I still cannot quite recover. Her devotion to me, to my training as a musician and to my family, was selfless and constant. Despite her limited education and income, she had raised Steve and me almost single-handedly and given us a strong foundation in music. She had encouraged us when I married Lotte and her support had allowed Lotte and I to fully practice our profession, secure in the knowledge that Denis and Boris were loved and looked after when we were away. It was hard to accept she would no longer be in our lives. In appreciation and commemoration of her life, I wrote *My Mother, My Memorial* and gave its premiere with the Kingston Symphony.

In addition to that loss came my break with the Kingston Symphony. That story is still an emotional one and not easy to write about. I now understand the most important lesson of that experience is that there's a destiny to all things, which is sometimes impossible to change. In hindsight, I realize that Kingston, wonderful town that it is, was never meant to be a cultural capital. There are parochial aspects of the city – they called our plans "too rich for our blood" – that Lotte and I were simply unable to overcome. Ultimately a community orchestra is the creature of that community and without far-sighted leadership, financial support and a willingness to reach for a shared global vision, it will not grow.

In retrospect and with hindsight I can see that my departure was caused by a collection of events, each trivial on its own, but taken together, they were an erosion of my musical authority. For instance, the Queen's University staff often invited me to listen to their music graduates' final examinations, with a view to hiring them for the Kingston Symphony. These invitations caused problems. During the examinations, the principal teachers always wanted to know immediately whether I would accept their students into the orchestra. But I had to consider not only the young musicians' ability to deliver musically, but whether their personalities would mesh with the rest of the players, the needs of the orchestra and our budget. I just couldn't hire everyone as there weren't enough positions or money. No matter how much they pressured me, I had to answer, "Let me think about it. It's not just up to me." This noncommittal reply did not make me a friend of those professors.

And, indeed, they wouldn't leave it up to me. Certain members of the orchestra's board persuaded other members to admit students from the community into the orchestra. I suspected they may have promised positions that were not theirs to give. I considered it really small-town stuff. A conductor is invested with the artistic and financial responsibility for the entire orchestra. He cannot allow special whims and favours for a few.

I wonder if familiarity undid us, too. When I was commuting from Montreal, I had the benefit of distance and distance lends mystery, awe and authority. Once we were both in residence and even though we spent at least half of each week in Montreal, people resorted to the small town mindset, "If he's here living among us, he can't be that great." They began to take us for granted and tried to tell us what to do and how.

As problems cropped up more and more frequently, I grew uncomfortable. It became clear to me that the lobbying and pressures jeopardized the quality I sought in the orchestra.

Then a prominent and influential member of the symphony board tried to get the Canada Council to support a residency of the McGill Chamber Orchestra in Kingston. It looked to me like an attempted takeover of my McGill Chamber Orchestra and its support base, by the less established, less prestigious Kingston Symphony.

A meeting was called in Ottawa which was attended by Canada Council officials, Michael Davies for the Kingston Symphony, Tania Plaw in her capacity as president of our board of directors of the McGill Chamber Orchestra and me. Michael Davies brought forth a proposal for the Kingston Symphony to take over the McGill Chamber Orchestra and a study to show how the merger should be accomplished. This was an unexpected blow! I had not approved or even known about it. Thus ambushed, I could not examine the ideas presented or dispute them. Tania Plaw was just as shocked at this apparently hostile takeover. She categorically refused to consider it. The Canada Council representative called the plan clearly unfeasible, as it had not been thought through carefully enough. It turned out the takeover would be impossible, since in those days the McGill Chamber Orchestra was made up principally of the leading players in the Montreal Symphony. Michael and I had to drive back to Kingston together. It was a long, chilly and silent trip. We were never really friends again.

Despite these behind-the-scenes tensions and internal politics, the Kingston Symphony continued to present incredible concerts. Lotte and I still engaged world-renowned soloists. We had a tremendous following, which was most gratifying. But the board claimed we had gotten them involved in bigger projects and larger expenditures than they wanted to risk. On this point we were at odds. Lotte and I firmly believed that any concert you give must be of the best quality. The board didn't realize that an orchestra cannot go back. The public expects the quality it has become accustomed to. When that is lowered, people know instinctively that there's been a step backwards and they are not keen to return.

Most of the board members didn't understand our careful, expert planning and scheduling. For example, by repeating concerts in two or even three towns, we saved money because one set of rehearsals would suffice for all concerts. The only person who understood that what we were doing was great business for the city and who spoke up for us, was the mayor, Ken Keyes. I began to feel that unless I could govern the orchestra at least musically, if not financially, it was not worth retaining my position.

In the end, the Kingston Symphony made up our minds for us by not renewing our contracts. Lotte and I were deeply hurt, given our years of toil and effort. In retrospect though, we were there for fifteen years and it was long enough.

We made a clean break with the Kingston Symphony in 1980 and everyone in our family was in solid agreement. Although the orchestra wanted me to come back as a guest conductor, I thought it best not to accept the invitation. They invited Boris to guest conduct for them but he declined also.

Because we had been so serious about putting Kingston on the world's musical map it was painful to go, especially since some of our dreams for the Symphony remained unfulfilled. As soon as we left, most of the projects we had launched collapsed or were abandoned. It was distressing to watch the Kingston Symphony return to being the parochial orchestra I had encountered on my first visit.

We can look back on fifteen great years of outstanding concert successes. We made some wonderful friends in Kingston including the Honourable Flora MacDonald, George Whalley, Dr. and Mrs. Westenberg, Dr. John and Mrs. Loretta Fay, Dr. and Mrs. S.R. Beharriell, Allen Brooks, Gordon Eligh and Dr. Ronald Watts. I'm very grateful to Queen's University for the honorary Doctorate of Laws. When I left the Kingston Symphony Orchestra to return to Montreal, they kindly presented me with a specially bound set of volumes of several years of our concert programs. It's a wonderful and treasured keepsake.

We still loved our beautiful Kingston home. All our collections of souvenirs, antiquities and precious manuscripts were there and we were so near to nature, right in the pathway of the Canada geese. We maintained it as a pied-à-terre, a place to visit, with and without our family.

Lotte and I found it impossible to live in a place where we were not musically active. Since the symphony claimed not to have enough funds to undertake my projects, we decided to give our own concerts that would bring in enough money. We organized a new board and established the Kingston Pops Concerts, presenting performances in the summer when the Symphony was normally dormant. This benefited them too, as it provided additional income to their professional string quartet, woodwind quartet and the core of their resident musicians. In fact, the Kingston Pops concerts series orchestra consisted of leading Kingston Symphony members, with Deszö Vághy as concertmaster as well as musicians from Montreal and Toronto.

The Pops concept in Kingston wasn't entirely new. We had already initiated it during the winter season with the Kingston Symphony some years earlier, with concerts by pianist André Gagnon in 1972. We secured many popular headliners to appear with the Kingston Pops in the early 1980s, Canadian stars such as jazz pianist Oscar Peterson, the *a capella* pop group The Nylons, Liona Boyd and Boris' friends the Canadian Brass. They were lovely affairs, held at Kingston's Memorial Centre, complete with candle-lit café tables, wine and cheese.

Our devoted volunteer committee, without whom the Kingston Pops concerts would not have been possible, worked tirelessly. Lotte and I became manager and conductor respectively. The summer concerts were supported by the City of Kingston, the Ontario Ministry of Citizenship and Culture and the corporate sponsors Lotte attracted.

For several years, we did Pops concerts tributes to my friend Arthur Fiedler, since he had offered his assistance with a festival I was planning at Fort Henry in 1979. For one such concert, Gheorghe Zamfir, the internationally known Rumanian specialist on the pan flute, was soloist at Old Fort Henry. Zamfir lived in Hudson, Quebec, not far from Montreal, so he was part of our musical community there. The stone walls of the fort and its buildings provided interesting acoustic challenges so we held one rehearsal right on location to test the acoustics. The sound bounced off the stone and created a wonderful experience.

Our Kingston Pops performed so often outdoors at Fort Henry that Kingstonians counted on including our music-and-fireworks event in their annual summer activities. We played at a fundraising concert for St. Mary's Cathedral restoration project, for which I brought my Young Virtuosi with Angèle Dubeau.

Astronaut Marc Garneau helped us present one especially interesting concert. I had met him on an earlier occasion where I had been surprised and delighted to discover that Garneau loved chamber music so much, he had taken tapes of The McGill Chamber Orchestra with him to listen to up in space. I invited him to appear as guest soloist with us in Montreal and then repeat the performance in Kingston. While we projected a film of the space shuttle behind him, Garneau stood onstage and narrated his experiences and reactions in space. During that concert, our symphony played live the same music Garneau had listened to on his amazing voyage.

I conducted the Kingston Pops Orchestra at Fort Frederick, the home of the Royal Military College, in a natural amphitheatre on the waterfront. People picnicked on the lawns as they listened to the music. Unfortunately we had uninvited competition at that event because the wind wafted in rock music from the nearby bars in the entertainment district. For our finale, we exploded fireworks over the water to Borodin's *Polovetsian Dances* from the opera, *Prince Igor*.

Now with a little less upheaval and a bit more time to spare, we devoted ourselves to the McGill Chamber Orchestra in the winter months and to the Kingston Pops in the summer. We continued to build on our successful ventures in Montreal, borrowing many ideas from our experiences with the Maurice Richard Arena Concerts Populaire de Montreal. One such borrowed idea was presenting evenings dedicated to the music of one particular nation. So the Kingston Pops presented a *Viva Italia* evening and one called, *Ole Espagna*, for which the door prize was two return air tickets to Spain on Iberia Airlines. The public was eager for more themed evenings and given my love of ballet, it seemed natural to combine the two. In 1981 The Kingston Pops paid tribute to ballet with Karen Kain and Frank Augustine dancing to selections from *Sleeping Beauty, Swan Lake* and the *Nutcracker Suite*.

For the opening concert of the Kingston Pops 1982 series at Old Fort Henry, I naturally selected programs to suit the military setting. We hosted the Fort Henry Guard and *La Compagnie Franche de la Marine* of Montreal to stage a mock battle between English and French forces on the parade square, choreographed to Beethoven's *Wellington's Victory*. The music, the mock battle in historically accurate blue and red uniforms, wigs, tri-corner hats and sword salutes, all set in the historic old fort, stirred everyone emotionally and gave us a sense of witnessing history. What a unique and memorable concert!

As professional musicians, Lotte and I liked to stretch ourselves and attempt new experiences, rather than safely plod the same old routes. We were also mindful of our artistic responsibilities and the financial appetite of the Kingston Pops, so in the later years of our Pops concerts we decided to reach farther than the classical audience. The first half of these programs was classical and the second half was popular. That served another purpose. We saved half the cost of rehearsal for the players, so the orchestra could make ends meet without a government grant. This strategy succeeded until we secured a Wintario grant in 1983.

Thus, with our finances in place, our Old Fort Henry series continued with a special tribute concert to Arthur Fiedler, featuring his favourite works such as Tchaikovsky's *1812 Overture*. Cannon fire is required in that symphony and the Fort Henry Guard were pleased to oblige with the real thing. The guardsmen and their costumed ladies also danced the *Blue Danube* waltz and then the audience joined them on the square.

The same year, we held an imaginatively themed series of three Kingston Pops concerts. For the Birds and Beasts program we played Saint Saëns' *Carnival of the Animals*, Vivaldi's *The Bullfinch* and Rimsky-Korsakoff's *Flight of the Bumblebee*. My friend Flora MacDonald narrated Prokofiev's *Peter and the Wolf*. The second concert, on the theme of Nature, included Handel's *Water Music*, Smetana's tone poem on the Moldau River and the popular theme from *Star Wars*. Music and Love, the final concert in the series, featured several great love themes such as Glinka's *Rusland and Ludmila*, Tchaikowsky's *Romeo and Juliet* and Mendelssohn's *Wedding March*. The entire series was sponsored by Andrès Wines, a natural choice given the café ambience.

As the Kingston Pops summer series thrived through the early 1980s under the Brott family management, we continued to reach out to the community. One such event was the Kingston Pops Tall Ships Festival concert in 1984. The harbour provided an absolutely majestic setting. Tourists and festival-goers crowded into Confederation Park, spilling out onto the docks and nearby boats. People stood as far as the eye could see. Despite some problems with the amplification, which didn't quite project the sound enough to the park area, the concert was received enthusiastically.

Their appreciation helped compensate us for the challenges we encountered performing aboard the tall ship, the *Western Union*. This impressive vessel was a two-masted gaff schooner, 130 feet long. Built in 1939, she serviced the Western Union Telegraph Company's cables for years. I've been a week-end sailor who found pleasure owning a boat, but as a conductor I encountered difficulties one would never find on a stationary stage on land. First, it was a challenge just to climb up on the decks of the ship. I almost fell into the drink. Even though the ship was tied up and docked, it still rocked in the water, making it difficult to balance and perform. Eventually, with the proper placement of stands and music and longer pins to hold the music down against the wind, we managed to give the concert. Afterward, we were presented with beautiful souvenir flags. The whole experience made me marvel at the ability of long-ago sailors to negotiate huge ocean waves.

All of these memorable experiences and successes kept us happily involved with the Kingston Pops concerts for several years, but gradually, Lotte and I felt the lure of partial retirement beckoning. We began to wind down our Kingston commitment.

Brian Jackson took over as director of the symphony and I was pleased to continue to be associated with them in a friendly way. With fond memories of our time in Kingston and gratitude that our Pops enterprise would not be allowed to collapse, we closed our Kingston chapter and returned our full attention to our affairs in Montreal, in particular to the McGill Chamber Orchestra.

A Personal Note

During my life music and the violin have absorbed most of my time and thoughts, but several other interests also intrigued me. At public school we received a well-rounded classical education with an emphasis on literature. The teachers read poetry aloud and taught us about form, cadence and rhythm. I know this benefited me musically, and it left me with a lifelong appreciation of poetry and art, which I have enjoyed dabbling at. Around twelve, both animals and Spanish galleons fascinated me, so I drew them in pencilled detail for hours. My sons still keep some of those pictures displayed in their homes. Behind me on the wall as I write, hangs my watercolour of two affectionate robins, that I'm still fond of.

While I was at Juilliard, where the ballroom dancing classes were a lot of fun and a good way to mix with young ladies, I smoked a pipe (an excellent one, ornately carved of Oriental wood) and fancied myself as Beau Brummel, a romantic character in French literature. In my room on Claremont Avenue I kept some aquatic and reptilian life – tropical fish, turtles and a baby crocodile. I fed my crocodile a quarter pound of meat a week, and walked him along Riverside Drive with a miniature leash and collar every morning. His stay with me ended abruptly when he surprised the cleaning lady as she dusted under my bed one day. The health department took him away.

Tropical fish have always fascinated me. I raised them as a boy in Montreal, as a student in New York and after I married. To the growing curiosity of my young sons, I cross-mated our guppies, curious to see what colours and patterns would emerge. Their shapes, colours and designs are always intriguing.

Once I could afford it, my next obsession was old scores of

Gregorian vintage, Baroque music, and early classical music. At Patelson's Music, behind Carnegie Hall, I found some real treasures, and my later travels provided more. I have derived great pleasure collecting first-edition books, (one of which set me off on my Beethoven adventure in 1970), music manuscripts, and precious volumes such as a rare early bound copy of oratorios, including Handel's *Messiah*. The combination of music, history, literature and rich leather bindings is intoxicating.

I was bitten by the collecting bug early on, and later my offspring sent me on the trail of diverse items, as families are wont to do. When I left for one of my conducting trips to England, Boris asked me to bring him an English bobby's (police officer's) tall black hat. An English barrister helped me get the bobby's hat, and from then on I collected hats from every country I visited. In Switzerland I discovered that each Swiss canton has its own distinctive hat insigne badge, so of course I had to obtain those.

With the next tour, I gathered walking sticks from every country that would sell them. I brought home a Moor sword stick with pewter handle from England, a delicate baton from France, a peasant stick from Pietrozavodsk, Russia, and a marriage stick with snake and neck rings from Africa. When my grandson David found out the chamber orchestra was going to Japan, he begged me to bring him a Japanese sword and kimono, since he was studying karate. I located a sword but it became a major problem, since I had to register it as a weapon and leave it with the police, at a fee, in every city I travelled through!

Since my fifties, rocks have been my passion. I have developed quite a collection of semi-precious stones and fossils. Working with stones relaxes me completely. Conducting a concert requires a substantial amount of concentration and adrenaline, making it hard to unwind after the show. So in Montreal and in Kingston, I developed the habit of retiring downstairs to my basement workshop after a performance. There I focused on the intricate tasks of cutting, polishing, and setting stones until I felt calm enough to sleep. My workshops were outfitted with the best equipment, including a diamond-tip saw to cut minerals. Fossils a million or more years old are very humbling. They will outlive us mortals many times over, and put our vanities and our worries into perspective. At least one other composer shares this hobby. Apparently Ernest Bloch used to polish agates in his garage while Zara Nelsova practised her cello upstairs in the guest apartment.

Everywhere I travelled, I was always on the lookout for interesting-looking minerals. Some were for sale; usually I just had to search for naturally-occurring samples. One time in Banff, as I passed by a construction crew excavating for a new building, I noticed immediately that the site had once been a lake, which meant it would probably contain fossils or minerals. The workmen understandably couldn't allow me down there, so I bribed one to bring me up a bucket of debris. How pleased I was to find trilobites and ammonites, as well as some unusual minerals in it.

Once the rocks are mine, I shape, curve and polish them into jewellery including pendants, rings, brooches, and earrings, as well as home accessories such as paper-weights and table coasters of polished agate slices. I wear the jewellery I have created at the slightest provocation. I've even shaped samples containing fossils such as ammonite, trilobite and seahorses into useful forms.

Lapidary work is fascinating because it combines detective work with geology – the outer appearance of the rock gives clues to what life or mineral vein may be frozen within. It's the same process as a sculptor taking a block of marble and studying it before carving into it. If you can find the right way to cut the sample open without harming it, you may find an insect frozen in amber, a vein of valuable mineral, or an attractive shape that used to be some living thing. I have a stunningly beautiful coral sample that grew like a weeping willow.

Rocks will never cease fascinating me. I can imagine the power of nature and the struggle for existence in every sample. Why did that insect or leaf fragment get into that rock? How did it retain its own design and colour? It's a mystery, a story no one will ever know. It truly excites the imagination.

Working with minerals and fossils brings geological history to life. In one fossilized prehistoric mammoth tusk from Alaska, you can actually see the creature's hair. You can hold in your hand a plant or snail that was caught in a volcanic explosion billions of years ago, or a fossil that bears the embedded tooth-mark of a dinosaur. I've entered caves, where what nature has done with 4000 years of dampness, is so beautiful it's a miracle. Rocks and fossils represent the wonders of the world.

I've realized that my interest in minerals, in tropical fish, art and in music has a common theme. Their form and design, their colours and their beauty astound and intrigue me.

For a long time before I took up these interests, the only fun I ever really had was my music, the creative side of life. I had neither the time nor the inclination for sports. But Lotte was quite athletic, so this began to change. Even on our honeymoon, she had me up on cross-country skis.

Once we could afford it, we rented various small cottages near Fourteen Island Lake, in the Laurentian Hills, for a few weeks each summer while the symphony and McGill were on vacation. There we could enjoy our growing family and the beauty of Canada, in particular Quebec, which after all our travels, we considered the most beautiful place on earth.

In 1955, knowing we were going away on our musical tour of Europe, we wanted a holiday with our boys first, so we searched the papers for a cottage to rent. Mr. Frank Lewen wrote us with a better idea, "You are not new to us – we see you from a rear point of view when we attend your concerts," and offered to sell us a plot of land on a private lake he owned in the Laurentians. It made sense to us. We could enjoy time as a family, I could have a quiet, beautiful place to compose, and it was close enough to commute to Montreal when business called.

Looking at the site entailed a certain drama in the way that our lives often seem to have. Lewen drove us to a landing where we boarded his motor launch. He had some difficulty starting the outboard motor, which fascinated Boris, who got his head just a bit too close. When the motor suddenly burst into power, the recoil action of Lewen's elbow knocked little Boris in the head.

When he recovered, we crossed the lake in drizzling rain, then left Lotte and Boris in the boat, covered with raincoats, while Lewen and I climbed up the hill to the highest point of land. The view was breathtaking! Miles of trees and two beautiful lakes below us. We bought a site overlooking Lac des Chats and Lac des Becscies. The land went right down to the beach on Lac des Chats where we built a stone wall, a barbeque pit and a wharf.

We designed our chalet with great fantasy. The architect Spencer Lewen wanted to create a corner of Switzerland in the Laurentians, which very much appealed to Lotte. The exterior is built of half round logs, and red shutters adorn the windows. Inside is a central great room with a cathedral ceiling and field-stone fireplace. We called it Fiddlesticks because all the shutters and even the well cover, had violin shaped cutouts.

The boys were fascinated by the construction, which served as a good training ground for them in the practical aspects of being handy around the house, something I never was all that interested in or was expected to do. Eleven-year-old Boris built a detailed scale model of the chalet in balsa wood and took so much pleasure in overseeing the construction that the not too pleased workmen referred to him as "L'inspecteur Boris."

My parents shared in the purchase of a granny flat of two rooms. They liked this arrangement as they loved being with the boys and taking a role in their care and general education. I think the extended family was valuable as it provided the perspective of two sets of loving adults of different generations, and from a prac-tical perspective, they could look after our children when we were in town for concerts, or away on tour in Europe. As family, they loved the boys in a more personal way than a housekeeper. And they made sure the boys practised their musical instruments every day.

But mainly, our stays at Lac de Chats enabled us to retreat with our children and relax from the pressures of our public music careers. It was at our cottage that I began to conquer my fear of the water and learned to wade fearlessly. I spent hundreds of utterly useless but pleasant hours clearing brush with a scythe and clip-pers, and joining Lotte and the boys as spectator in their sports. It was a wonderful time of family bonding.

Actually, even at St. Sauveur we didn't leave our musical en-terprises behind. We built huge doors for the garage, which when fully opened revealed a stage complete with piano, from which we gave trio concerts of chamber music. The trio consisted of Lotte, Carl Larsen, one of our neighbours who was an aeronautics engineer and gifted pianist, and me. It was a happy re-creation of the McGill String Quartet's barn origins. This time around though, we had town criers – Boris and Denis. Our young entrepreneurs hired a local farmer, Mr. Foisy, to tour the township with horse and wagon, while they perched on the hay, announcing our concerts. Our audience enjoyed the music from their cars or in their own folding chairs on the grass.

While Lotte was alive our chalet became the focal point for family gatherings. Our children and grandchildren travelled from their homes in Toronto and Hamilton to join in the merriment. The main cottage was extended with a garage and a private chalet for Lotte and me. Later I purchased adjoining lands and we even entertained a dream to build a summer school there. Eventually when it became clear that both boys' lives and career were being built away from Montreal, we sold the added acreage but kept the cottage.

In retrospect perhaps the sale of the properties was a hasty decision, since over the last decade Denis has returned to Montreal and makes extensive use of the property summer and winter and Boris also visits more often. I still derive great pleasure walking that mountain top and observing the towering pines my boys planted there forty years ago.

I have described mainly Lotte's and my achievements in this autobiography, and written little about our sons Boris and Denis. Both are at the top of their profession as performers and educators.

Boris began as a violinist and is now a conductor and music director, who runs his own festival in Muskoka and in Toronto and Hamilton where he founded the National Academy Orchestra, a unique mentor apprentice training ensemble for professional musicians. He is also artistic director of the New West Symphony in Los Angeles, our McGill Chamber Orchestra, frequently guest conducts orchestras in Europe and Israel, and has an award winning young people's concert series at Ottawa's National Arts Centre, where he has recently been appointed principal youth and family conductor. Lately he has developed an active international career as a motivational speaker.

Denis plays as chamber musician and soloist, and as principal cellist of the Quebec Symphony Orchestra. He conducts, teaches, and is founding artistic director of the Montreal Chamber Music Festival. Both of them have tremendous energy and resourcefulness.

Of course Lotte and I felt it only natural to expose our boys to music from day one. Boris's first words having been "oso bolo," we decided he should take up his father's instrument, the violin, as early as practically possible. I told him, "Boris, it's easy to listen to music; it's more challenging to play." I had an eighth-size violin made for him, and when he was three we began to practise, or rather Lotte began with him. She organized his schedule in true German fashion. He rehearsed each day and on Sundays she dressed up his teddy bears in bow ties and aligned them on the chesterfield, where he would play for them to show off his progress. Boris thinks this may be the reason he always wears bow ties today.

At some point, Wilfrid Pelletier heard Boris, and immediately invited him to play at one of his Youth Concerts. I wrote a simple composition for the occasion and after the performance, Pelletier interviewed Boris onstage. Asked if he had any difficulties with the piece his father wrote, my son replied that every time he played it to me, I would change it, so he had to learn it all over again. Boris also performed solos with the Montreal Symphony as a small child. In order not to exploit our son or ourselves, we thought it wise that he continue with teachers outside of his home, so we sent him to Joseph Berljawsky and later to Yaëla Hertz. It was evident that Boris loved the stage – he was playing for a live audience and they adored him. But he was not destined to remain with the violin for long. He studied the French horn at the *Conservatoire du Québec*, he learned solfège at McGill Conservatory and with Ria Lenssens, he studied theory. By the time he was twelve he had realized that long hours devoted to lonely practice were not what he, very much a people person, wanted.

Boris was a born leader. He organized the children on our

street to give theatrical presentations in the park opposite our house during the summer months. He tried selling lemonade in the park, but didn't have a permit, and some foolish person called the police. We didn't interfere. Boris handled the situation himself and gave us the first taste of his skill at problem-solving.

We were more fortunate than many parents and students are now, because the high schools treated music as an important curriculum subject. The school that Boris attended had an orchestra, but when he returned exhilarated from the Markevitch competition in Mexico, he declared, "I've got to start my own orchestra, and we're going to compete at the Ottawa Festival." He founded and conducted the Philharmonic Youth Orchestra while at West Hill High School, and they won the Ottawa Music Festival Award and the National Festival Chamber Orchestra Award in Montreal. For these projects, he acted as conductor, manager, publicist and fundraiser.

Having witnessed all the goings-on in our household, it was natural for him to be an extrovert, a success kid, so he approached CKGM, our local Montreal pops radio station, about his orchestra. He prepared his brief perfectly because he had seen how his Mum did it. The station owner, Geoff Stirling, was thrilled with Boris's proposal, and agreed, "If you win the competition, we'll carry it for you." CKGM subsequently became the fledgling orchestra's sponsor. From then on, conducting was pretty much Boris's direction.

We watched all this happen without offering advice unless it was asked for. We did, however, ask him to pursue his conducting studies with Pierre Monteux. We believed it would teach him discipline to be exposed to an orchestral situation with rehearsals from morning to night and he would see how conductors work. So Boris travelled to Maine, where Monteux gave classes throughout the summer, performing concerts in a huge barn converted into a concert hall. Even that was a lesson – the students could see how conductors like Monteux made up for whatever acoustical shortcomings the barn may have had.

Later Monteux took Boris as his assistant with the London Symphony and on his tours. Our oldest also spent a year as assistant to Leonard Bernstein, whose determined flashy approach he has adopted. Now Boris is successful around the world. He has performed for youngsters, for kings and queens, for steelworkers, and for the Pope.

My sons were born seven years apart, so Denis was basically alone with us from age seven or so, since Boris was away often from the time he was fourteen. Denis also began music lessons early. He started on the piano. He practised it regularly and studied under George M. Brewer, organist of a well-known Unitarian church on Sherbrooke Street, and the Montreal pianist Rose Goldblatt, with whom I had worked. Denis competed as a pianist in his age class, and won first prize in a Kiwanis festival.

During that period, Lotte was giving cello lessons at home, and Denis would listen in through the door. One day a little girl was taking a cello lesson, accompanied by her mother. Lotte suggested that the instrument was too large for the child, and let her try her personal half-size instrument which was much easier to play. The girl's mother agreed to purchase the instrument, and was actually taking it to her car, when Denis burst into tears and cried, "She's taking *my* cello! Don't let her! I want to play the cello like Mummy."

Lotte apologized to her student's mother, and the cello remained at our home. From then on, Denis became a model cellist, practising regularly and with a will. He proved not only very gifted on the cello, but for music generally. Every work he played had meaning and character. We believed he had done the right thing, moreover, it was his choice. Denis had many select teachers, such as Walter Joachim, Zara Nelsova, Leonard Rose and later Janos Starker and finally Gregor Piatigorsky. He left Montreal and home when he was about twelve, to study with Zara in Toronto. Because she had been Lotte's teacher in Canada, he absolutely insisted we get him to Zara by one means or another. Like his older brother, he was quite independent and determined.

Denis attended my conducting classes at McGill and, on one occasion, I entrusted him to conduct a concert where he featured my *Violin Concerto* played by another student of mine, Blair Milton. Denis too formed his own orchestra, Philomusica. At age thirteen, he conducted his first concert, an all-Mozart program, from memory. (Normally I didn't interfere with my boys' performances, but

I recall pulling the score for the *G Minor Symphony* from Denis' hand, as he coped with momentary pre-concert jitters). Denis is now known internationally as a fine soloist and chamber musician. He teaches at the *Conservatoire de Musique de Montréal*, and spent many summers teaching at the Music Academy of the West in Santa Barbara, California. He runs his own annual Montreal Chamber Music Festival with resounding success.

Our sons have gleaned much from their distinguished teachers and, I hope, something from their parents.

Since they were seven years apart in age, and away from home a lot, they really did not have much in the way of a shared childhood. Each one developed a distinct personality in his profession, as well as in his personal life. Their competitive spirits began early – they competed over everything – and did not abate. On one point they thought alike – they fell in love with charming young ladies from the same city, Hamilton, and were married in August 1976, in a double wedding ceremony at Montreal's Temple Emanu-el, with a reception at McGill. Thus Julie Fraser McKay and Ardyth Webster became the daughters we never had.

Boris and Ardyth have three children – Alexandra, David and Benjamin. Denis and Julie have four – Talia, Aleta, Vanessa and Joshua. My grandchildren are all distinguished in their own way – not one of them is a musician.

One last avenue of the Brott family experience remains to be explored. It is our penchant for writing poetry, especially using rhyme. Lotte and I, our sons, my brother Steve and other family members years ago established a family tradition of writing poems to one another for special occasions such as birthdays and anniversaries. It's been good family fun. (It's been professionally useful, too, when I wrote lyrics such as those for *Centennial Cerebration*, the text of which follows.) We have kept many of these family poems, as they make a much more personalized souvenir than the oh-so-ordinary commercial greeting card.

Here's my offering for you who have troubled to read thus far:

> *I submit my words from other times,*
> *So to close this epistle of verbal crimes*
> *Brother, brother, have you got a dime?*

Centennial Cerebration
Music and Words by Alexander Brott

SPEAKER:
Man, oh Man, you chronicler of time
One moment ridiculous, the other sublime
Professing innocence, while planning deceit
Toying with passions, when suffering defeat.

CHOIR:
One hundred years ago, men of will, willed a Nation,
Little dreaming of perpetual irritation
Strife was rife, rife was strife
But men of will, willed a Nation.

British bombast, frenetic French
Both with the blessing of the Royal Bench
Busily engaged in quenching each wench
For men of will, willed to quench.

A shot-gun marriage, the inevitable carriage
With squalling infants to perpetuate the barrage
Napoleonic laws and Vatican power
Vying with pompous Victorian Tower
Decreed – no divorce shall flower!

Founding Fathers and all that lot
Welcomed each migrant sot
To join in this hallowed plot
And benefit from naught to fraught
For fraught to naught was all they bought

Now, men of will still will this Nation
Despite continued irritation –
American domination, contrived elation –
From Brigitte Bardot and Benedictine brandy
To Bilingual Biculturalism and anything handy
Yes, Men of will, will still this Nation

Shall we join in their volatile cerebration?
My invitation!

SPEAKER:
Mesdames, Messieurs, le temps est venu,
Français est partout et nous sommes chez nous,
Les sages qui montent leurs drapeaux sans honte
Tiennent leurs propres comptes.

CHOIR:
Le destin proclame avec tonnerre et voix,
"Québec aux Québecois" pour la centième fois
Arrêtez remplace "stop" et populaire "pop"
Mais monnaie reste "money" et "cash" caisse sonnez.

"L'Homme et son Monde" – idée profonde
"Les Nations Unies" un grand défi
"Défence de la Paix" – contradiction assez
"Notre cause est juste" – indulgence illustre.

Feuille d'érable – fleur de lis
Que chacun fasse son propre nid
Car l'homme et son monde, tourne toujours en ronde,
Sans raison, sans cause, plus ça change, plus c'est la même
chose.

Man in his World chronicles time
One moment ridiculous, the other sublime
Professing innocence, when planning deceit,
Toying with passion, while suffering defeat.

SPEAKER:
Still, men of will do will our Nation,
Little caring about constant irritation
The struggle itself prompts oration,
But, will it help build a stronger nation?

O! Canada!

To the McGill Chamber Orchestra on its 45th Anniversary

by Alexander Brott

October 15, 1984

A year of anniversaries, 300th for Bach and Handel
Scarlatti couldn't even hold a candle.
Yaëla's 25th with the MCO,
How she survived it, I'll never know.
A man with a stick, demanding results
With every flick
May make even angels thoroughly sick.
My 70th birthday, three score ten
The mere thought quivers my pen.
But joy of joys, music is my ploy
It serves the nation and deserves ovation.
Modesty is a known fault, and the proverbial conductor has
no faults!
Hence my conviction and courage
I herald a mirage
That we all be together
Regardless of weather
From the orchestra's 45th to the orchestra's 50th.
To Yaëla I present this token
For many a word unspoken.
Its anniversary is about three million
Which (mere mortals say) might as well be a billion
A timeless symbol – that we share our worth
Since of mutual respect there is no dearth.
May the spirits continue to embrace and hover
Music is such a platonic lover;
And now I run for cover.

Lotte's Story

When Lotte first brought me home to meet her parents, they were appalled that their beloved daughter's prospective husband was both a Jew and a violinist.

The Goetzels were enlightened people. They had ensured a good education for their daughters and had expected them to pursue a business profession. Music was fine only as a hobby. Intent on steering his daughter away from a music career – and from musicians – Walter Goetzel enrolled Lotte in a business school. She smuggled her cello to her friend Mildred Goodman's home and practised there after school. Lotte was determined to become a musician and to marry the one she loved.

During one argument, Walter demanded that his daughter prove that she could make a better living as a musician than in business. She responded to his challenge by answering a newspaper advertisement for a cellist to play Saint-Saëns' *The Swan*. The locale turned out to be a night-club. Undaunted, Lotte played the piece wearing a long white taffeta gown, while seven half-dressed beauties danced around her. The act was advertised in the *Montreal Gazette* as "Lotte and the Seven Loveliest", and when her father saw it, he threw a fit. Lotte resigned from the club but she had proven her point. She had earned an impressive $300 for that week, a fortune in 1941. In the end, both music and business turned out to be her dual métiers and her parents' wishes were, at least, partially fulfilled.

Together we enjoyed 56 happy years of marriage and the MCO's 60 years of success is largely due to Lotte Brott's outstanding management skills. It's easy for audiences and even musicians to assume that an orchestra's success rests on the shoulders of the music director who stands front and centre at every rehearsal, concert and reception. To a certain degree that's true, but to survive and thrive, an orchestra needs someone else even more, a skilful business manager. Lotte was manager extraordinaire, public relations officer, tour organizer, fund-raiser, respected cellist, sought-after teacher and society hostess, all rolled into one. The concept of three lives in music pales in comparison. It's also true that our sons' successes are traceable directly to their mother's encouragement and talent.

Lotte was a survivor. She grew stronger with each personal and professional hurdle, religious persecution in Europe, marriage to an impoverished musician, the explosion in the CBC studio, life-threatening health problems and career challenges. She coped with comfort and adversity, talent and prejudice, success and ill health, with equal energy and intelligence. And she always kept her sense of fun.

Lotte Goetzel was born in Mannheim, Germany on February 8, 1922, into a comfortably well-off family. She first studied the cello as a social amenity, not intending it to be her career. Her mother, Else, was an amateur violinist and her father, Walter played piano. They encouraged Lotte to study music so they could play trios and entertain their guests in their luxurious four-storey home on Colinestrasse. Her parents loved the arts as much as they loved Germany. Her father had been decorated by the Kaiser in World War I. They were cultured successful business people, respectable products of the German business intelligentsia of the nineteenth century.

Like my family, the Goetzels were Jewish, though not outwardly practicing Jews, and Lotte had little occasion to encounter religious prejudice. But as she grew up, Germany became an unfriendly place for Jews. In 1936, fourteen-year-old Lotte was all set to perform in a school concert. She had practised for days and her mother had sewn her a pretty new dress for the occasion. Suddenly the school principal came backstage. He informed her that she was not permitted to play her solo because, "The Gauleiter, a high-ranking Nazi political official, is here, so I cannot allow Jews on the stage." Lotte ran home in her new dress, crying, "I'm not going back to that school!" She remembered that taste of discrimination for the rest of her days.

Although Lotte's parents were loyal Germans, they sensed that their girls would be better off somewhere else. They sent Lotte and her older sister, Lena, to school in Neuchatel, Switzerland while the family waited to see what would happen in Germany.

In Switzerland, Lotte studied with the famous cellist Emanuel Feuermann, who encouraged her musical abilities and kindled her desire to make music her life. Meanwhile her parents fled Germany in 1939, just before the outbreak of war. They travelled the world searching for a new home, despite the fact that their family roots in Mannheim dated from two years before Bach and Handel's birth in 1685. The displaced family finally settled in Montreal. When Lotte graduated from the Zurich Conservatory, both girls joined them. There Lotte became a close friend of my student and friend Mildred Goodman, who was around the same age and lived in the same neighbourhood. The girls played together in a piano trio and at the McGill Conservatory where I taught. Later we often laughed over the fact that Mildred, who was like a younger sister to me, advised Lotte to steer clear of me because she thought I was a ladies' man!

My first attraction to Lotte, apart from the obvious, was her sound. When she auditioned for the McGill String Quartet in 1942, we were all struck with her musical energy and talent. She played with a warm rich sonority. If she had devoted more time to it, she could have easily been a soloist of the first rank of international distinction. Her choice, however, as she reassured me many times, was to be an orchestra manager and principal cellist. She always said she never wanted to become a great soloist. Instead she told interviewers, "I couldn't have imagined a happier life."

Nevertheless, she had a distinguished career as a cellist. Lotte studied on scholarships with both Jean Belland and Zara Nelsova here in Canada, then played with the McGill String Quartet for most of the first decade of its existence. When she joined the Montreal Symphony Orchestra, she became its youngest member. Although her choice of career and of husband remained a sore point with her parents, Lotte forged ahead, with my complete support. She went on to serve as first cellist of the McGill Chamber Orchestra until her commitments as manager dictated that she play alongside Walter Joachim, whom she greatly admired. We were acutely aware that the Montreal Symphony and the McGill Chamber Orchestra were lucky to get her because she had turned down a scholarship to Juilliard to play with us.

Lotte and I were different in many ways, but our association was one of respect and appreciation and we complemented each other. She was positive and outgoing while I tended to be searching and retiring. She exuded a sense of courage and adventure while I was more of an observer by nature. An adept sportswoman, Lotte loved swimming, hiking, skiing, canoeing. In fact, when a car wasn't available, she simply wheeled around Montreal on her bike, going from rehearsal to rehearsal with her cello strapped to her back. She glowed with health and exuberance, while I was fearful of hurting my hands and being unable to play the violin. But my wife inspired me to try new and different things – she breathed a sense of adventure and courage into me.

The original independent woman, Lotte was one of the early working mothers and she set the bar high. In addition to playing in both orchestras, she taught the cello at home and at McGill University and from 1946 to 1952, she performed with the Little Symphony of Montreal, as well as freelancing for the CBC, on occasion.

We were fortunate that for the first seven years of our married life, we lived in my mother and step-father's apartment on Maplewood Avenue. It wasn't easy. Lotte had to make compromises. Two strong women sharing one kitchen is a challenge, particularly for one raised in much more comfortable financial circumstances. When she and Mother didn't agree, I tried to be the peacemaker. I would say, "Lotte, never mind the small things. So he'll wear the blue sweater. Find comfort in your music. Practise." We were an extended family of both Old World and New World influences and, I believe, our sons benefited by exposure to both ways of life. Too few people in our time grow up with several generations living under one roof. There is much to be said for it.

In the 1940s, when professional working mothers were rare, Lotte forged an eventful, fulfilling life, juggling career and homemaking. To her, the combination was only natural. Her view was that any woman who truly had something to contribute could find a way to leave her mark. And Lotte certainly left her mark.

She once tried to explain her philosophy to an interviewer, "You just have to believe. I was certain of my husband's immense talent and of the importance of his work. A small musical group can't afford to hire a manager and my husband was too taken up with his work to look after the day-to-day details. I was glad to do it."

Saying, "You just have to believe," didn't do justice to the skills she employed to bring about our successes. As my manager, Lotte felt no task was too hard, no person too exalted to be given an opportunity to perform one of my compositions or to offer me a conducting engagement. I held the less forward view that if the product was excellent, someone would find the way to my door. Of course, there are many roads that lead to Rome – but hers was faster.

Perhaps the best-known and notable of her achievements was her ground-breaking establishment of corporate sponsorships for concerts, which were completely unknown in Canada until 1940.

Thanks to Lotte, our summer concerts on Mount Royal, which had begun under the patronage of Mayor Drapeau, were later sponsored by the Dominion Stores grocery chain and became known for several successive and successful years as the "Dominion Concerts Under the Stars." Every summer thousands of Montrealers and tourists, plus the sponsor corporations themselves, enjoyed the fruits of my wife's innovative ideas and her persuasive charm. What Lotte began is now taken for granted – witness the number of corporations that sponsor jazz festivals, the ballet and symphony concerts.

When Lotte was invested as a Chevalier in the Order of Quebec in 1996, the citation read in part:

> Lotte Brott was the first to find sponsors to aid in defraying the always high costs incurred in the organization of concerts. She was the instigator of summer concerts on Mount Royal and the Pops Concerts at Maurice Richard Arena, with the collaboration of the City of Montreal and for which she obtained

the sponsorship of Kraft Food. She also took the initiative of presenting several gala concerts at Notre Dame Cathedral and Marie Reine du Monde Cathedral with the McGill Chamber Orchestra, a choir and soloists of international reputation.

Lotte was the driving business force throughout our professional lives. She used her charm, her flashing blue eyes, her persuasive and motivational talent to propel us personally and professionally. Her skills allowed me to concentrate on my creativity, to devote myself to my art.

Lotte was in top physical form until age thirty-four, when we discovered a small lump in her breast. A succession of diagnoses by Montreal's best doctors revealed that she needed to be operated on immediately. It was to be an exploratory procedure at first, so I was unprepared when the doctors emerged after three hours to say the lump was malignant. Could they have permission to do a radical mastectomy? Since Lotte was under anaesthetic, I had to make this crucial life-changing decision for her.

As a subscriber to our McGill Chamber Orchestra, Dr. Eric McNaughton was aware of her need to be able to play the cello again, so he spared the muscles under her arm. When she returned from the recovery room, Lotte said sadly, "I guess they had to go ahead." I reassured her she could still play her music. Then she asked for make-up, comb, mirror and a frilly nightgown and quickly planned a recital for ten weeks to the day following her surgery. She had her cello brought to the hospital as soon as possible and ignoring the pain, she began an exercise regimen including a strengthening exercise in which she inched her left hand slowly up the wall, so she could play at that recital. She performed at the recital and went on to play professionally for another 38 years.

Eight years later, without the slightest warning, her doctor broke the devastating news to her that he had detected cancer in her other breast and that she again required immediate surgery. She was stunned, as was I. We had considered her home-free. Because we couldn't believe it, we got a second opinion and a third, after which she had the operation. Although the surgeon told her that this second operation was as successful as the first, not surprisingly, the sparkle of élan and self-confidence went out of her for a while, but not for long. Even as she was healing, she started resuming her usual activities, despite all the pain and discomfort. Within a few months she was back to her usual speed.

The disease however, proved stubborn. Twenty years later Lotte underwent cancer surgery again and from then on, she experienced a slow, agonizing descent caused by other related conditions. What had started out in her late thirties as a slight difficulty in walking and a problem with eyesight and distinguishing temperatures was finally diagnosed as the early stages of multiple sclerosis. She handled this challenge with her usual grace and courage.

Over 32 years, the multiple sclerosis gradually stole her physical mobility. At first she ignored it, much to her harm, since she sometimes fell and injured herself. But she didn't seem to care. Eventually she used a cane and only after two falls and two hip replacements did she use a second one. Finally she required a wheelchair in which she not only performed her concerts, but also travelled on tours. Today society recognizes disabilities and provides special parking places, ramps and elevators but Lotte faced her problems while general care for the disabled was in its infancy.

Lotte was very proud, perhaps even vain. She had herself wheeled into position on the stage before the symphony audience was admitted so they would not see her entering the stage on a wheelchair. She left the stage only after the last patron had gone. No one could ever photograph her in the chair or holding a cane. She would have people get her into position, support her weight on someone's arm and only then allow her picture to be taken.

Eventually her list of operations became so long that it took hours to get her medical history. But my Lotte was still Lotte – the setbacks only made her try harder. If anything, the MS increased her determination to accomplish ever-greater feats. One of my wife's favourite sayings, even when she was ill, was, "There's nothing worse than doing nothing." She looked after the orchestra's business and raised funds even from her hospital bed. Right to the sudden end, she got up early and was working at her "desk" on our dining room table by 8:00 am every day.

From a professional standpoint, Lotte forced the MSO to

recognize that her physical walking problems had nothing to do with her ability to play the cello. Several times she had to prove she could still do the job by re-auditioning for her position. Each time the administration could not deny the strength and quality of her performance. Lotte kept her principal position on the first stand of the Montreal Symphony Orchestra for forty-two years, in the last decade using a wheelchair to get to rehearsals to which she had once ridden by bicycle. Of course, her disability created problems for the orchestra on tour, but today our laws would not allow the discrimination she endured. In the end, she was forced to leave the orchestra by mandatory retirement rules alone but not without challenging them. She didn't want to give in to illness, nor age.

Lotte loved to cook and had the kitchen redesigned so she could prepare meals from her chair. Later, she refused to acknowledge any weakness by getting help at home and she put on such a brave face, that to suggest we needed it was almost an insult to her courage. This meant I became her helper around the house as well as with the orchestra. I assisted her with cooking, getting into and out of bed, in and out of wheelchairs and in and out of cars. As I too was getting older, this became increasingly hard for me. Our duplex required climbing up and down stairs to get to our first floor residence. Even after making the steps smaller they became impossible for her to negotiate and I couldn't lift the wheelchair any longer. Denis insisted until we finally agreed to install a lift in our house.

In 1988, Lotte was named Dame of Grace in the Order of Malta. She was selected a Member of the Order of Canada in 1990 and, in 1996, she received the Order of Quebec. That was the year we jointly achieved the Vital Lifetime Award from the Lifetime Association of Quebec. Lotte was honoured with the Commemorative Medal for the 125th anniversary of the Confederation of Canada in 1992 and was named International Woman of the Year 1997-8. Of course, she always won the "Order of Alexander Brott."

Lotte died on January 6, 1998 at age 75.

Con Fuoco Sin' Al Fine:
With Spirit to the End

Today, I have only slowed down, somewhat, my own form of "rallentando". I did take official retirement from my position at McGill University in 1985, after forty-six years as a teacher at that great institution. Even this was not the end of my academic life, as I continued to teach at *Ecole Normal* and *Ecole Pierre Laporte*, and my work with Les Jeunes Virtuoses also involves a kind of teaching. For that matter, so is conducting – the Italian word mae-stro means teacher. I continue some conducting with the McGill Chamber Orchestra, which still proudly bears the name of the university which aided in its birth. It is my fervent wish that the orchestra will continue its activities under this noteworthy and historic name.

Our work has not gone unnoticed. In 1985, my seventieth birthday was acknowledged in several forums. Radio Canada International issued a recorded collection of my music, *Anthology of Canadian Music: Alexander Brott*, on seven albums, one for each decade of my life. Retrospective articles on my career appeared in the newspapers, and the CBC broadcast a concert I conducted from Christ Church Cathedral on its Arts National program, in-cluding my arrangement for string orchestra of Bach's *Sonata No. 1 in G minor* for violin.

Just the month prior to that concert, we had warmed up with a grand concert featuring the luscious soprano Victoria de los Angeles and the Elmer Iseler Singers at Salle Wilfrid Pelletier. De los Angeles flew from Spain specifically for the engagement, an effort typical of the loyalty so many artists have shown us over the years, devotion which always paid great dividends for our audi-ences.

The year 1989 saw many celebrations, since it was fifty years since I had formed the McGill String Quartet. We've always calculated the McGill Chamber Music Society's dates from 1939, since the McGill Chamber Orchestra continued under the same aegis, as a natural progression from the string quartet. Of all the compliments we received for the milestone, one of my favourites came from the reporter who described the orchestra as, "a cultural institution as integral to our city as Montreal smoked meat."

In September, 1989, we held a gala concert at Salle Wilfrid Pelletier, for which our favorite flutist Jean-Pierre Rampal joined us, as did guitarist Alexandre Lagoya, violinists Corey Cerovsek and Franco Gulli, bass soloist Gary Karr, and harpist Marisa Robles. The audience included not only our loyal regulars but Quebec's Lieutenant Governor Gilles Lamontagne, Mila Mulroney, and Lise Bacon, Quebec Minister of Culture. It was a beautiful, memorable evening.

We had lasted for half a century, no mean feat in a competitive and funds-starved business. For me, it's been an honour to have lived through, and influenced, so much of Montreal's musical history.

We were well aware, however, that to continue to thrive as we had, we needed to keep our programs fresh and alive. But it was time for Lotte and I to take things a little easier. We had worked almost nonstop since the early 1940s. So Boris agreed to become the McGill Chamber Orchestra's co-conductor. From there, it was a gradual and natural transition to him taking over in 2000.

Boris began a series of multi-media educational concerts sponsored by the *Montreal Gazette*. As before, each concert was devoted to a different composer, but this time the *Gazette* published full-page articles prior to each of the five weekly concerts, with stories about that week's featured composer and his influence on society. Special teachers' manuals were provided to help in lesson preparation. At the concerts, images of period paintings, drawings of the circumstances of the composers, and clips from recent films about them, were projected on a large screen behind the orchestra. The composers themselves were brought to life onstage by actors who portrayed them and Boris wrote dialogues in which he interviewed each composer about himself, his times and his music. In the same manner that young New York audiences had been captivated by Bernstein, our Montreal children and their parents were totally enthralled. In this way between 9,000 and 12,000 new listeners each year were introduced to great music and the McGill Chamber Orchestra.

Boris found sponsorship from Hoechst Celanese for a new series of multimedia concerts called *Stained Glass*. His wife Ardyth did world-wide research for examples of stained glass relative to the music. The concerts took place in the ballroom of the old Windsor Hotel, where the McGill String Quartet had once inaugurated a series in the former Prince of Wales Salon.

We were happy to see Boris boost the orchestra's popularity with new ideas and new sponsors. Meanwhile, unable to stay still ourselves, Lotte and I promoted an eight-concert *Connoisseur Series*. For some of these we ventured away from our usual Maisonneuve Theatre in Place des Arts. In 1993, we used Salle Wilfrid Pelletier for a concert with Itzhak Perlman playing Mozart, for an evening of singing by Canada's "Mr. Rigoletto," Louis Quilico, and for the fund-raising event where Denis and his former classmate Yo-Yo Ma played the Vivaldi *Concerto for Two Cellos* together. Boris conducted and Lotte played in the cello section. It was gratifying to have our whole family involved that night.

In 1990, Denis, who had been a frequent guest artist with the Chamber Orchestra over the years, returned to Montreal to become a cello professor at the *Conservatoire* and to join the McGill Chamber Orchestra as principal cellist.

Three years later, Boris, Denis and I joined forces to make a compact disc in Analekta's *Canadian Composers* series. Ours was the first instalment of this collection. The disc contains my *Paraphrase in Polyphony* and the *Seven Minuets and Six Canons*, plus Angèle Dubeau playing my *Violin Concerto*, and Denis in my *Arabesque*, with Boris and I sharing conducting duties.

For the next season, 1994-1995, we celebrated my eightieth birthday on March 14, with a gala concert at the awe-inspiring Notre Dame Basilica. And I got the day off! It was scheduled to feature cellist Mstislav Rostropovich, a longtime favourite with the MSO. Then at the eleventh hour, we got more excitement than we planned. Three days before the concert, Slava told us he was too ill to come. Lotte once again saved the situation, when she convinced Itzhak Perlman to fly in especially for the event, despite having a rehearsal in the Midwest the next morning. We made a small change of program to the Mendelssohn *Violin Concerto* for him. Boris conducted that evening, although it was his birthday too, and Denis played principal cello, with Lotte right behind him. Pierre Trudeau and his sons sat at our table, and my entire family of daughters-in-law and grandchildren were there. What a joyful and wonderful celebration it was.

Following the concert, Mayor Pierre Bourque hosted a reception at Montreal's City Hall. It was not only pleasant, but also fortuitous for Denis, who was introduced to Mayor Bourque. Denis subsequently presented to him the ideas which emerged as the annual and very successful Montreal Chamber Music Festival, over which Denis presides as founder and artistic director.

During those later years, I was pleased and humbled by recognitions from the nation, province, and city, as well as international honours. For a lifetime dedicated to performing and promoting classical music in Montreal and Canada, it was especially rewarding to have my efforts recognized both by peers and those outside the music world. For the orchestra's thirty-fifth anniversary in 1974, my friend Harry Pollack, a former violinist with the Montreal Symphony, and therefore a fitting choice to create this artwork, sculpted a bronze bust of me. It stands in the foyer of Place des Arts' Theatre Maisonneuve.

To add to my honorary doctorate from the Chicago Conservatory College in 1960, and the degree from Queen's in 1973, I was invested with the Order of Canada, in October 1979. The citation for it acknowledged me as, "Montreal musician, teacher, composer and conductor, who has brought hitherto unknown Canadian music and musicians to international audiences."

Boris became an Officer of the Order in 1986 for his role in building professional orchestras in Hamilton, the Maritimes, Regina, and Kitchener and with the CBC Winnipeg Orchestra. Lotte was honoured in 1990. It is of great significance to me that three of us have been so decorated by our country. All four of us were awarded knighthoods by the Order of St. John of Jerusalem, Knights of Malta.

Probably the most significant tribute for me took place in1980, when McGill conferred an honorary Doctor of Music degree upon me. I value it especially as it is a recognition not only from my alma mater but also from my colleagues of over forty years standing. As part of the convocation ceremony, Boris conducted my composition *World Sophisticate* and Paul Pederson, Dean of the Faculty of Music, read a lengthy and flattering biographical précis, ending with the following words:

> However without doubt, Dr. Brott's greatest renown as a conductor rests with the extraordinary success of the McGill Chamber Orchestra. Under his leadership, this ensemble has acquired a national and international reputation through its concerts, broadcasts, international tours and recordings. The orchestra has commissioned many new works and has given over fifty Canadian compositions their first performances. On occasion these performances have been of new works by Alexander Brott, the composer. Dr. Brott's compositions number in excess of one hundred, and include works for all media, from such special combinations as the brass and soprano work we are privileged to hear today, to works for large orchestra. It is undoubtedly his orchestral works, which have been performed by orchestras throughout the world, that have brought him his international reputation as a composer. Throughout all of this performing, conducting and composing activity, there exists another Alexander Brott – the teacher who for 41 years at McGill has nurtured the talent of many students who have gone on to important musical careers of their own.

In 1993, the city of Montreal declared me a "Grand Montréalais." And in 2000, on my 85th birthday, Mayor Pierre Bourque sent me a letter of congratulations filled with praise. That same year I received the Queen's Fiftieth Anniversary Jubilee Medal. Of my many prestigious awards, these are the most meaningful to me because they recognize not just one composition, but my entire life's work.

Throughout the 1990s and into the 2000s, the McGill Chamber Orchestra has continued to thrive. Our make-up has changed over the decades, personnel have necessarily come and gone. We take on free-lance musicians as needed, even from concert to concert if appropriate, because we enjoy the flexibility this arrangement gives us. The orchestra has not become a permanent, full-time, year-round ensemble. Indeed, this was never our plan. Other orchestras have come and some have gone and still the McGill Chamber Orchestra continues to enjoy a respectable audience share and support. The players, the volunteer committee, and Boris and I, are steadfastly loyal to the orchestra. It is, and always will be, a team effort. It is a *Ritual*.

Revitalizing the orchestra is also a team effort, and an idea I have always believed in. Conductors and orchestras can't afford to rest too long on their laurels. Audiences expect and deserve new ideas and terrific value for money – something out of the ordinary, something memorable.

There have been many changes over our sixty-five year history, but the quality of the product has never differed. We established a successful formula early on, by providing a potent combination of internationally-known soloists backed by Montreal's best chamber musicians. This formula still works.

Recently I re-read an encyclopedia article on my career saying that I pursued a conducting career over one as a composer or violinist. I disagree. I aimed to be the total musician, because I knew men who were. I worked with the great violinist, pianist, composer and conductor Georges Enesco. I met Sergei Prokofiev, another brilliant pianist who composed. When I say the total musician, I really mean the total person. My work as violinist, conductor and composer belongs together – each skill is an integral part of who I am.

My life changed radically and permanently the day Lotte died. Her initial cancer surgery took place at a time when little was known about treatment for breast cancer. The radical mastectomy had left her with the lymph ducts in her right arm tied off. These often became infected and swollen. One of the infections travelled through her bloodstream and affected her heart muscle and valves. It was this problem which eventually took her from us.

The last concert Lotte attended was a Christmas concert in Quebec's Eastern Townships on December 20, 1997. The Jeunes Virtuosos performed and I conducted. We were returning to Montreal in my car, when Lotte complained of severe pain in her right arm, going up all the way to her back. We phoned from the car to the doctor, asking him to be at our house when we arrived. After examining her, he called an ambulance and ordered immediate attention.

After five days in hospital, Lotte seemed to be improving, but she had trouble breathing. On Christmas morning, she briefly succumbed but was revived. They performed an angioplasty and she was placed in intensive care, where she battled with all her strength. She could not speak – machines had to breathe for her. The staff tried to get her to breathe on her own, but to no avail. I held her hand. I kissed her. She could not respond. She could not utter a single sound. After suffering for more than two weeks, she passed away in the early morning of January 6, 1998, during the worst ice storm Montreal has ever known.

When Lotte's body was interred at Mount Royal Cemetery, it must have been one of the most horrible days in this city's history. The sky seemed to split open to receive her spirit. Torrents of freezing rain fell. Huge trees waved in the raging wind as if they were stalks of corn. Ice-laden massive branches crashed to the earth. Rabbi Lerner could barely complete the burial eulogy, as the cemetery officials ordered people out of the grounds for safety reasons. I did not feel my legs. It seemed as though I was being moved involuntarily. Both Boris and Denis were my pillars of strength.

I was numb for days. It had been too sudden. The very foundation of my life had collapsed. My sons' families were so supportive. My house had no electricity or heat – Montreal was under a state of emergency, and Boris had to fly to Los Angeles to conduct his orchestra, so Ardyth took me to their home in Hamilton. But how could my family know the degree of my anguish? Lotte was more than my mate – she was my inspiration. Yet, lonely and devastated as I was, I knew I had to go on for her sake.

With Lotte gone, so were my dreams. It seemed senseless to keep our dream house on the lakeshore in Kingston. It was too full of unfulfilled plans and I felt alone there. I sold it and brought our collectables back to our Montreal residence, the upper storey of which became the office of the McGill Chamber Orchestra. This move marked my permanent return to Montreal, where I hid my sorrow in work, work, work. One of the results of this period was an extended composition I wrote on a commission, to mark the millennium. We performed *Millennium Sinfonia* on my birthday in 2000, at Place des Arts, but there was someone missing in the audience.

We commemorated Lotte in several ways, including a memorial concert which set up a trust fund to establish scholarships and concerts in her name. Most significantly, we vowed to continue the McGill Chamber Orchestra which had been inextricably linked with her. The orchestra has been perhaps my wife's greatest achievement – its every performance and each corporate sponsorship pays tribute to her talent.

As a permanent physical memorial to Lotte, I had a unique tombstone specially designed for her. It is a full-sized cello, lying on its side, made of blue-speckled granite the colour of her eyes in the sunlight. It stands at the top of Mount Royal, with a view of the St. Lawrence River, right in the middle of a forest glen and the natural setting she so loved. There is a place for me beside her, for when my work is done. The inscription on the cello memorial reads:

TOGETHER WE HAVE MOUNTED THE SUMMIT SUBLIME
TO WHAT PURPOSE IS TO WEEP AND WHINE
TOGETHER OUR VOYAGE DIVERSE AND DIVINE
WITH YOU FOREVER MINE, I FOREVER THINE!
– Mount Royal, January 6, 1998

After Lotte's death, I had to muster all my strength to deal with responsibilities we used to handle together. At home, I realized I had to learn to tend for myself without my wife to consult. Luckily, my sons were most helpful and I felt that I could count on their wisdom, both professionally and personally.

Boris had for the better part of a decade shared Lotte's and my duties with the orchestra. Now, he immediately put his law studies in abeyance to tend to the orchestra's administrative needs and inject renewed vigour to the programs. Looking back from my position of sixty-plus years of professional experience, I recall my composition teacher Douglas Clarke's words, "There is room for only one lion in the cage." His wisdom holds true for most fathers and sons in any circumstances, but it is especially true for conductors. So I stepped out of the cage, leaving Boris as the new head of the musical pride.

At the same time, our concertmistress, Yaëla Hertz, announced she was retiring from the position she had held since 1959. We're still trying to discover whether any other concertmistress – or concertmaster – has ever served such a long term – and under the same conductor. Yaëla accepted the title of concertmistress emeritus, and Martin Foster, a violin professor at the University of Quebec at Montreal who had been associated with the McGill Chamber Orchestra for some time, became our first new concertmaster in over forty years. Our talented and resourceful Tania Plaw resigned as board president after (only!) thirty-four years of service. Boris convinced Canadian astronaut Marc Garneau, a staunch supporter of the orchestra, to accept the chairmanship in her place. The old guard thus made way for the new.

With Boris at the helm as music director and conductor, I conduct only when requested. This is normally one work per concert, and the rehearsal for that work as well. We have both vowed to continue with the McGill Chamber Orchestra concert series, where great music and great artists reign supreme, in tribute to Lotte's memory. I'm available when he needs me to fill in.

As a show of independence, Denis has established a highly successful series of chamber music concerts on the Chalet atop Mount Royal, under a new society called the Montreal Chamber Music Festival. My repertoire and my music library are available to both sons as required.

I live quietly in the care of my housekeeper, Luisa Mignogna, who used to attend to Lotte's needs. Luisa is an excellent cook, has a wonderful memory, and can locate anything in the house I ask for.

For now, I live in part to help commemorate what my wife accomplished and stood for. She was an irreplaceable original. I am eternally grateful that she came my way. She shed so much light and laughter – she epitomized the challenge of intellectual and musical argument. Throughout my adult life, Lotte supported every creative effort I engaged in, and I appreciated it. Most importantly, our children and grandchildren are her physical legacy. Her voice continues in Denis's gifted cello playing. She was a role model for her daughters-in-law to aim for. I sometimes feel guilty that she sacrificed much for our life in music. She only had a true home of our own when it was almost too late to enjoy it.

* * *

I find myself writing what should be a retirement section. I'm not sure what to say. I've never believed in full retirement. There's always something to do – put my library in order, write intelligent program notes, adjudicate, conduct my own works. I do all of these. My advice to others, if I may be so bold as to take on the role of Polonius lecturing Laertes, is to surround yourself with youth, however fickle. Have springs in your heels. I would suggest from personal experience to exercise and keep fit. Don't overeat – it becomes difficult to part with the poundage. Don't envy the impossible. Don't be enthralled by a vacuum; master your resources. See the ridiculousness of it all. Enjoy your achievements, and thank the people who helped you on your journey.

Survivors my age must contend with accusations that we have outlived our era. But music is not politics – the leaders need not be dethroned for newcomers to share the glory. Experience, interpretation, talent, and musical values are not the sole prerogative of youth. We are all "of our time," and can and should enjoy the diversity of each generation's interpretation. Music should be more than a clique playing for another clique. I believe that older musicians should relax a little, make room for younger people, yet remain active. There's plenty of room on the stage for both experience and youth.

I have been asked many times by well-meaning individuals trying to justify retirement, "Don't you get tired of playing the same works over so many years?"

Really, I don't. I'm never bored. Just the opposite. Every time I come to music such as Mozart's *Violin Concerto*, Vivaldi's *Four Seasons*, the Beethoven symphonies, I find a new dimension. Summer becomes warmer, winter becomes colder, Mozart gains more depth, and semi-precious stones remain eternal. No, I am never bored.

Our children have taken over the struggle – I wish them success. May they appreciate and enjoy the fruits of our labours, bearing in mind my favourite adage, "The more you own, the more owns you." But more than that, I wish them the joy of achievement. There is no greater satisfaction than living in the hearts and minds of the giants of music. My mother knew it instinctively – my wife knew it by choice.

I have been prompted and prodded by colleagues and my family to record my experiences on paper. This requires introspection, and at age 89, I feel as if I'm watching my life in replay form. Could I have done better? Would I have been happier? I think not. Lotte is beside me still in inspiration – she would have wanted me to tell our story. She had the foresight to preserve clippings which have given me proof of our presence and helped me stay accurate.

If I have not expressed the nitty-gritty of my sentiments, it is not because I didn't feel them. I wrote my feelings into my music. Nothing is ever achieved without love, sweat and tears. Not even death. I watched my mother die. I watched my wife die. These two women meant everything to me. Yes, I am a survivor, but they were my lifejackets.

One of my motivations in writing these memoirs has been to show our grandchildren, the next generation of musicians, and all those who face diversity, how Lotte and I fought the battle of circumstance and existence, on our terms. We experienced most of the hardships, sacrifices, jealousies, ethical dilemmas, joys and rewards our profession can offer. We lived with more than our share of adversity and illnesses and fought to realize our dreams despite them. As we aged we discovered that the golden years are not quite so golden. As Sir Walter Scott wrote, "Breathes there a man who at the halfway mark, has not felt the frost of time?"

Yet we should exit gracefully and with gratitude.

May time be kind to us. May our story inspire anyone with similar aspirations. And so, to quote from Leoncavallo's *I Pagliacci*, "La comedia e finita."

I cannot resist leaving you with my final offering:

> *And now that nature's had its way*
> *I thank her for another day.*
> *The truths unfold, my story's been told.*
> *So let posterity praise or scold.*
> *Now you must add to, or take from the sum,*
> *Of all the work that I have done.*
> *Praise to you all.*

Appendix A – History of Professional Orchestras in Montreal

MONTREAL PHILHARMONIC SOCIETY 1877-1930
1877-1899 Montreal Philharmonic Society Guillaume Couture
1898-1919 Joseph-Jean Goulet
1927-1929 Jean-Josaphat Gagnier (Directeur musical Radio-Canada)
Pioneers J.J. Gagnier, J.J. Goulet and Guillaume Couture from ad hoc ensembles to play on Sundays when film theatres are dark. 1897 All nine symphonies of Beethoven given their Canadian premiere.

THE MONTREAL ORCHESTRA 1930-1941
Musicians from theatre orchestras put out of work by the end of the silent film ear band together under the initiative of Julio Romano. They engage Douglas Clarke, Dean of the McGill Conservatorium of Music to conduct.

LES CONCERTS SYMPHONIQUE DE MONTREAL 1934-1953
Mme Athanase David resigns from the Board of Montreal Orchestra and forms this new group to promote francophone musical interests. Both CSM and MO exist in competition but with many of the same player playing in both orchestras until 1941. Clarke's illness and the political influence exerted by Mme David finally caused the Montreal Orchestra to close its doors after the 1940-41 Season

McGILL CHAMBER ORCHESTRA 1939-
An outgrowth of the McGill String Quartet founded by Alexander Brott gives its first regular season of Chamber Orchestra concerts in 1953. The orchestra has toured extensively to 17 countries on four continents. It pioneered the commissioning of compositions by Canadians through the Lapitsky Foundation and later the Canada Council. Boris Brott became the orchestras Artistic Director in 1999. Alexander Brott remains Founding Conductor and at age 89 continues to conduct the orchestra regularly.

Montreal Women's Symphony 1940-1969
Founded and conducted by Ethel Stark the MWS was the first Canadian symphony composed exclusively of women.

Little Symphony of Montreal 1942-1952
Conducted initially by Bernard Naylor. Performed at L'Hermitage. Followed by Carl Bamberger and George Schick. Many concerts broadcast on CBC radio.

Les Concerts Symphonique de Montreal becomes Montreal Symphony Orchestra/*Orchestre Symphonique de Montreal* 1953
Continues to perform in 1300 seat High School Auditorium Le Plateau. Many great European conductors encouraged by Managing Director Pierre Beique to guest conduct including Sir Thomas Beecham, Eugene Goosens, Leonard Bernstein, Charles Mûnch, Pierre Monteux, Victor de Sabata, Erich Leinsdorf. Paul Paray, Georg Solti, Leopold Stokowski, Bruno Walter and George Szell. Longer periods by Desire Defau (1940-1952) Otto Klemperer (1951-58) Igor Markevitch (1958-1961) Zubin Mehta (1961-1967) Franz-Paul Decker (1967-1975) Raphael Frubeck de Burgos (1975-1978) Charles Dutoit (1978 – 2002).

In 1963 the orchestra moved into its newly built home Place des Arts.

Orchestre des Grands Ballets Canadiens, 1957-
Full symphony orchestra founded in 1957 by Ludmilla Chiriaeff, *Les Grands Ballets Canadiens de Montréal*, 4 productions per year.

Concerts Under the Stars 1960-1968
A series of popular concerts presented at the chalet atop Mount Royal established by Lotte and Alexander Brott. These concerts were also the introduction of commercial sponsorship to Canada. Over 5,000 attended each performance. The concerts also supplemented the income of the MSO musicians as their season at that time was in the winter only.

Montreal Pops Orchestra 1965-1969

An additional entrepreneurial venture by Lotte and Alexander Brott these concerts started at the Montreal Forum were over 10,000 people could attend for only $1.00 each. Eventually the series moved to the Maurice Richard Arena and took on the Boston Pops flavour with the audience seated at tables and wine and cheese available for purchase. The series was operated collaboratively with the MSO in 1969 and then taken over by the MSO. The concerts continue to this day with various orchestras performing.

Montreal Chamber Orchestra, 1974-

Founded by conductor Wanda Kaluzny this orchestra gives a series free concerts each season.

Orchestre Métropolitain du Grand Montreal, 1981-

A full symphony orchestra founded in 1981 by graduates of faculties and conservatories of Music in Quebec and Montreal has been led by Agnes Grossman and is now led by Yannick Neges Seguin gives a regular series or concerts throughout the island of Montreal and has just begun to record.

I Musici de Montreal, 1983-

Founded by cellist Yuli Turofsky formerly first cellist of the McGill Chamber Orchestra, this chamber orchestra of 14 permanent members has a regular season of concerts in Montreal and region, tours extensively and records.

Ensemble Contemporain de Montréal, 1987

The Ensemble is dedicated to the creation of new Canadian music, commissioning and performing new works as well as providing composers with a forum to explore and refine their art. Since its inception, the ECM has premiered 125 compositions; more than 100 of them have been written by Canadian composers. Artistic Director: Véronique Lacroix, 12 concerts/year

Nouvel Ensemble Moderne, 1989-

Established in 1989 by the pianist and conductor Lorraine Vaillancourt, the Nouvel Ensemble Moderne became the first permanent chamber orchestra featuring an exclusively contemporary repertoire in Canada. It is composed of 15 of Montreal's most accomplished musicians. The NEM's "raison d'être" is to present and promote the most remarkable musical pieces of the 20th century. 9 concerts/year + frequent tours

Ensemble Appassionata, 2000–
Artistic Director: Daniel Myssyk 4 concerts per year A core of 14 strings occasionally augmented by winds and percussion, the Ensemble Instrumental Appassionata came together in July of 2000 with the mission of bringing orchestral music to new audiences in the Montreal area.

Appendix B – Original Compositions

Accent, L'   Ref: 31
1971
For narrator and string orchestra or string orchestra
Timing: 00:15:00

Analogy in anagram   Ref: 1
1955
*3*3*3*3, 4441 (or euphonium), timp, 1 perc. strings, harp
Timing: 00:11:00

Arabesque   Ref: 2
1957
Solo cello 1111 1110 1 perc, harp also for solo cello and piano
Timing: 00:12:00

Aurora borealis (Laurentian Idyll)   Ref: 33a
1973
*1111 2000 timp, strings
Timing: 00:11:00

Aurora Borealis (Laurentian Idyll for Symphonic Band)   Ref: 33b
1973
*3*3*52 4331, 4 cornets, 1 euphonium, string bass
Timing: 00:11:00

B-22 An orchestral fantasy (Celebration 2000)   Ref: 70
1969
*2*222 4231 timp, 3 perc, strings
Première in Québec city
Timing: 00:12:30

Badinage   Ref: 99
1968
For choir and piano
Timing: 00:04:30

Berceuse (see also *Lullaby* and *Procession of the Toys*)   Ref: 69
1947
For piano or piano and voice
Timing: 00:04:00

Canada, a Case History (part of *Sept for Seven*)   Ref: 40, 25
1945
For high voice and string orchestra
Timing: 00:04:30

Canadian trilogy (see *Canada, a Case History*)   Ref: 40
1945
SSMM, piano, 1 male reciter
For Boris and the Whales
Timing: 07:12:30

Canadiana   Ref: 98
1955
For choir
Timing: 08:12:30

Centennial cerebration   Ref: 32
1967
For narrator, SSA chorus, and string orchestra.
Timing: 00:22:00

Centennial colloquy   Ref: 35
1965
*22*3,1basset horn,*3   4000   1 perc
Timing: 00:23:00

Characteristic dance (see also *Invocation and Dance*)   Ref: 41
1939
String orchestra
Timing: 00:11:00

Chassidic Dance   Ref: 41
1939
For harp and violin
Timing: 00:05:00

Circle, Triangle, 4 Squares   Ref: 28
1963
For string orchestra
Timing: 00:11:00

Concertino for violin and orchestra   Ref: 4
1950
Violin solo, string orchestra
Timing: 00:21:00

Concordia   Ref: 5
1946
*3*3*3*3 4231 timp, 1 perc, strings
Timing: 00:21:00

Corriveau, (La)   Ref: 7
1967
*3*3*3*3 4231 timp, 3 perc, piano, strings
Timing: 00:27:00

Critic's corner   Ref: 8
1950
For string quartet and percussion
Timing: 00:15:00

Cupid's quandary   Ref: 72
1975
For solo violin, string orchestra, and percussion
Timing: 00:22:00

Curioso furioso   Ref: 88
1965
For string orchestra
Timing: 00:06:30

David's Genie (Hymn to her)   Ref: 82
1978
Sketches for Hymn II Her
Timing: 00:15:00

Delightful delusions   Ref: 9
1950
*3*3*3*3 4431 timp, 2 perc, harp,strings
Timing: 00:06:00

Double entente for a double marriage   Ref: 87
1976
For string quartet
Timing: 00:05:30

E dai p milo   Ref: 77
1976
For string orchestra
Timing: 00:16:00

Elie, elie lama sabach tani   Ref: 10
1964
For contralto, SSAA chorus, and piano or organ
Timing: 00:04:30

Emperor's new clothes, The   Ref: 52
1970
For narrator or singers and orchestra: 1111/2110/timpani, percussion, strings
Timing: 00:20:00

Espoiranto, (L')   Ref: 80
1966
For SSAA or SATB chorus and keyboard
Timing: 00:04:00

Evocative provocations   Ref: 73
1975
2222 2210 1 perc strings (or gamba,sax, basset horn, guitar, luth,
flute de pan)
Timing: 00:15:45

Fancy and folly   Ref: 11
1946
*3*3*3*3 4331 timp, 2 perc, strings
Timing: 00:07:30

Fanfare   Ref: 12
1965
*3222 4221 timp, 2 perc
Timing: 00:03:00

Fantasy in Bb   Ref: 46
1939
String orchestra
Timing: 00:06:20

Five Miniatures for Eight Players   Ref: 13
1950
0011-1000-2vl-1vla-1cello
Timing: 00:08:30

For Talia's 13th Birthday   Ref: 106
1993
Solo voice and organ or strings
Timing: 00:02:30

From Sea to Sea   Ref: 15
1947
*3*3*3*3 4431 timp, 2 perc, strings
Timing: 00:34:15

From the Hazel Bough   Ref: 36
1959
For medium voice and string orchestra
Timing: 00:02:00

Fun-ethic-s   Ref: 43
1968
For SA chorus and piano
Timing: 00:07:00

H. B. Sauce   Ref: 71
1975
*2222 3211 timp, 1 perc, piano and celeste, strings
Boris' 10th year as conductor in Halmilton
Timing: 00:07:00

How Thunder and Lightning Came to Be   Ref: 68
1973
*2222 2210 timp, 1 perc, soprano, bass, speaker,chorus
of children also for piano,bass, perc, chorus of children
Timing: 00:20:00

Hymn II her   Ref: 82
1978
Solo flute, solo bassoon, or solo cello and solo bass and strings
Timing: 00:15:00

Indian legends   Ref: 64
1972
For soprano and bass, both playing percussion
Timing: 00:05:00

Invocation and dance for solo violin and orchestra   Ref: 55
1939
*2*222 2220 1 perc, harp, strings also for violin and piano
Timing: 00:10:54

Israel   Ref: 54
1952
For SATB chorus
Timing: 00:06:30

Kaleidoscopic imagery   Ref: 102
1994
For piano, 4 hands
Timing: 00:09:00

Lament   Ref: 16
1940
For string orchestra or string quartet
Timing: 00:05:00

Lullaby and procession of ladies   Ref: 56
1949
For strings, guitar, harmonica
Timing: 00:04:30

Lullaby and procession of toys   Ref: 17
1939
For string orchestra or string quartet
Timing: 00:08:00

Lysistrata   Ref: 103
1975
Sketches for a play
Greek play

Martlett's muse   Ref: 18
1962
*3*3*3*3 4331 timp, 1 perc, strings
Timing: 00:08:00

Millennium Prelude "Computer Sage"   Ref: 112
1999
*100*1 strings
Part of Millenium Sinfonietta
Timing: 00:05:00

Millennium Sinfonietta in 3 movements   Ref: 113
1999
Timp, 4 perc, piano, strings
Timing: 00:10:00

Mini-minus for chamber orchestra   Ref: 37
1968
For violin, clarinet, trumpet, trombone, bassoon,
double bass, and percussion
Timing: 00:16:00

Mutual Salvation Orgy for brass quintet   Ref: 19
1962
For 2 trumpets, horn, trombone, and tuba
Timing: 00:12:00

My Mother, My Memorial   Ref: 83
1978
*2222 4221 timp, 2 perc, harp, strings
Timing: 00:08:00

Nursery Suite   Ref: 48
1940
For 2 recorders, violin, viola, cello
Timing: 00:09:00

Oracle symphonic poem   Ref: 20
1938
*3222 4331 timpani, percussion, piano, strings
Timing: 00:08:30

Overture (Sombre Vigil)   Ref: 111
1999
String orchestra
Timing: 00:06:00

Papageno revisited   Ref: 90
1989
2222 2200 timp, strings
Timing: 00:11:00

Paraphrase in polyphony (Centennial Paraphrase)   Ref: 34
1967
Solo piano *3*3*3*3 4331 timp, 2 perc, strings
Timing: 00:23:00

Prelude to oblivion atomie style   Ref: 21
1951
1111 0320 timp, percussion, harp, piano, strings
Timing: 00:04:15

Prisms   Ref: 74
1984
For flute and guitar
Timing: 00:07:30

Pristine prisms in polychrome   Ref: 22
1966
For solo violin
Timing: 00:10:00

Profundum praedictum   Ref: 38
1964
For double bass and string orchestra also for solo viola
Timing: 00:22:00

Prophet, (The)   *Cantata for soprano and tenor*   Ref: 23
1960
Soprano, tenor solo   1111 1000   1perc, harp, strings,
also piano reduction
Timing: 00:14:00

Psalmody for Denis   Ref: 75
1973
For unaccompanied violoncello
Timing: 00:07:15

Quintet for recorder and strings   Ref: 96
1940
Recorder (alternatively sopranino, soprano, alto,
tenor and bass recorder) and strings
Written for Mario Duchesne
Timing: 00:13:00

Rakocki March (Hungarian March) (Berlioz/Brott)   Ref: 89
1955
For strings (no contra-bass)
Concert under the stars
Timing: 00:04:30

Rhapsody for cello   Ref: 97
1958
Cello and piano
Timing: 00:12:00

Ritual   Ref: 58
1942
For string quartet and string orchestra
Timing: 00:09:00

Royal tribute to Queen Elizabeth II   Ref: 24
1953
*3*3*3*3 4431 2perc, harp, strings
Timing: 00:12:00

Satie's Faction   Ref: 93
1965
see also Trivial Persuit or E dai p milo
String orchestra
Timing: 00:06:00

Saxi-foni-saties   Ref: 60
1972
For 4 saxophones
Timing: 00:16:00

Sept for seven   Ref: 25
1954
For narrator, clarinet, saxophone, violin, viola,
violoncello, and piano
Timing: 00:14:25

Shofar   Ref: 76
1976
For solo cello
Timing: 00:06:30

Songs (Lullaby, Park Bench, Legacy)   Ref: 65
1949
For voice and piano
Timing: 00:12:30

Songs of contemplation   Ref: 6
1945
For high voice and string orchestra
Timing: 00:13:00

Songs of the Central Eskimo   Ref: 64
1972
For voice and piano
Timing: 00:10:15

Songs of the Totem Pole   Ref: 64
1972
For voice and piano
Timing: 00:05:00

Spasm for six   Ref: 67
1971
For six percussionists
Timing: 00:10:00

Spheres in orbit   Ref: 26
1960
*3*3*3*3 4431 timp, 1perc, celeste
Timing: 00:17:15

Strangers yet (part of *Songs of contemplation*)   Ref: 6
1945
For unspecified voice and piano
Timing: 00:03:30

String Quartet   Ref: 45
1940
String quartet
Timing: 00:30:00

Suite for piano no.1   Ref: 61
1941
For piano
Timing: 00:14:00

Symphony in two movements "Veritas"   Ref: 57
1936
*32*3*3 4331 timp, 3 perc, strings
This piece won an award at Juilliard
Timing: 00:16:00

Tempo di Marcia   Ref: 39
1948
String quartet
Timing: 00:03:30

Three acts for four sinners   Ref: 42
1961
For 4 saxophones
Timing: 00:10:00

Three astral visions   Ref: 3
1959
For string orchestra
Timing: 00:29:00

Three on a spree   Ref: 49
1963
For flute, oboe and harp, or 2 violins and piano or flute, violin,
and harpsichord, or violin, oboe and piano
Timing: 00:12:00

Time's Trials Triumph   Ref: 79
1977
For solo voices, unaccompanied SATB chorus (S divisi), and
strings
Timing: 00:15:00

Tout de Suite   Ref: 66
1971
For solo cello
Written for Gregor Piatigorsky. Dennis' cello teacher
Timing: 00:08:30

Trivial Trifles (Trivial Pursuit)   Ref: 93
1965
Satie's Faction Version for 2 oboes and 2 bassoons
Timing: 00:06:00

True Blue, Blew Thru   Ref: 120
1996
String orchestra
Timing: 00:14:29

Vignettes en caricature   Ref: 14
1972
5 pianists
Timing: 00:05:45

Vision of the dry bones   Ref: 27
1960
For baritone, string orchestra, and piano obbligato or harp
Timing: 00:12:00

War and peace   Ref: 29
1944
*3*3*4(includes Eb clar)*3 44,4 cornets,31   timp, 3 perc, harp,
piano, strings
Timing: 00:22:00

World sophisticate   Ref: 30
1962
For soprano, 2 trumpets, horn, trombone, tuba, and percussion
Timing: 00:07:00

Young Prometheus, (The)   Ref: 50
1969
2222 2220 timp, strings
12 complete preludes and fugues
Timing: 00:50:00

Arrangements

Bachianas Brasileiras (Villa-Lobos / Brott)   Ref: 86
1980
0000 1211 strings
For the Canadiian Brass
Timing: 00:11:00

Bachianas for Boris   Ref: 78
1976
2222 2110 timp, strings
Written in Fort Lauterdale
Timing: 00:10:00

Concerto for 4 violins (Vivaldi/Brott)   Ref: 84
1994
0000 1211 4 violins, 2 violas, cello and organ (arranged for the
Canadian Brass)
Timing: 00:12:30

Concerto for Two Cellos (Handel / Brott)   Ref: 108
1996
2 solo cellos, strings, cembalo
Work for two cellos in the style of Handel op.2 no.8 in g min
Timing: 00:12:00

Für Elise (Beethoven / Brott).   Ref: 92
1982
For string quartet. Comic arrangement for the Orford Quartet.
Theme for radio program Amsterdam, Netherlands.
Timing: 00:02:30

Gaspard de la Nuit (Ravel / Brott)   Ref: 51
1971
3*3*3*3 4331 timp,2 perc, celeste and piano, harp, strings
Timing: 00:21:00

Genesis (Corelli)   Ref: 91
1984
String orchestra
Performed in Everett Point
Timing: 00:03:30

Kinderscenen (Schumann / Brott)   Ref: 100
1972
2222 2210 timp, 1perc, strings, harp
Timing: 00:15:00

O Canada/God Save the Queen   Ref: 104
1954
2322 4220 timp, strings
Timing: 00:03:00

O McDonald   Ref: 101
1954
String quartet
Children's concert
Timing: 00:04:00

Partita in E Major no.6 (Bach / Schumann / Brott)   Ref: 94a
1985
For solo violin, strings and continuo
For the Bach anniversary, CBC commission
Timing: 00:26:00

Peter Wuff (Prokofiev / Brott)   Ref: 44
1978
For strings
Educationnal concert
Timing: 00:06:30

Scherzo-Caprice #18 (Rode / Brott)   Ref: 47
1936
*1120 0000 00 strings
Timing: 00:03:10

Seven Minuets and Six Canons (Beethoven / Brott)   Ref: 63
1970
*1202 2000 strings
Timing: 00:19:30

Seven Sonatas (Scarlatti / Brott)   Ref: 95
1985
For strings or piano
Timing: 00:24:00

Sonata in g min. (Bach / Schumann / Brott)   Ref: 94b
1985
For solo violin, strings, harpsichord
Timing: 00:18:00

Suite for two cellos and piano (Menotti/Brott)   Ref: 105
1981
Two cello and string orchestra
Arranged with composer's approval
Timing: 00:23:00

Tchaikovsky Songs (arrangement for strings)   Ref: 107
1981
For soprano and strings
Timing: 00:17:00

Three Intermezzi (Brahms / Brott)   Ref: 53
1972
For strings
Timing: 00:11:00

Three Preludes and Fugues (Beethoven/Brott)   Ref: 50c
1970
String orchestra
Timing: 00:25:00

Toccata (Frescobaldi / Cassado / Brott)   Ref: 59
1974
Solo cello, 2222 2000, strings
Timing: 00:06:15

Trauer Musik (Beethoven / Brott)   Ref: 62
1970
For 4 trombones and strings with men's choir
Timing: 00:12:30

Various Pré-Revolution French Music (Edited by AB)   Ref: 121
1962
String orchestra
9 suites
Timing: 00:11:00

Index

Czerny, Carl 69

~~

Dachau 127
D'Albert, Francois 124
Damrosch, Walter 24
David, Antonia 33, 83
David, Mme Athanase 37, 85, 141, 199
David, Senator Athanase 3
Davies, Michael 151, 159
Davis, Barbara (Babs) 67
Dawson, David 125
De Lay, Dorothy 167
De los Angeles, Victoria 187
De Ville, Claude 50
Defauw, Désiré 29, 59, 76, 84, 85
Deslauriers, Jean 44, 48
Della Pergola, Edith 147
Della Pergola, Maestro Luciano 147
DeSève, Alfred 15, 18
Desy, Jean 114
Devonshire Public School 13, 16
Di Sabata, Victor 141, 200
Diamant, Bernard 50, 146
Dorati, Antal 45
Dounis, Dr. Charles 55
Downes, Olin 62
Drake, Miss 25
Drapeau, Jean 91-94, 96, 149, 183
Dubeau, Angéle 101, 129-131, 162, 189
Dumbarton Oaks Estate 24-25
Dunlop, Evaleen 86
Dupire, Jean 93
Dupuy, Pierre 61, 114
Duschenes, Mario 42, 146, 147
Dvorak 5, 92, 121, 126

~~

Eckhardt-Gramatté, Sonia 48
Edelweis Hotel 30
Eglise Saint Laurent 139
Elgar, Edward 19, 108
Eligh, Gordon 160
Elman, Mischa 84
Elmer Iseler Singers 187

Enesco, Georges 19-21, 49, 84, 144, 192
Entrement, Philippe 39
Erenworth, Gisella 25
Ernst 25, 46
Expo '67 41, 66, 67, 91, 94, 152

~~

Farrant, Edward 68
Father see Lenson, Abraham
Fay, John 160
Fay, Lorreta 160
Feuermann, Emanuel 29, 84, 181
Fiedler, Arthur 88, 89, 91, 92, 162, 163
Fixman, Annie see Brott, Annie
Florman, Gûnile 111
Ford, Robert 121
Forrester, Maureen 50, 74, 145, 146
Fort Henry (Kingston) 154, 162, 163
Freedman, Harry 48, 90, 92, 97, 122
Friedberg, Professor Carl 24

~~

Gabora, Gaelyne 122, 125
Gagné, Roland 11
Gagnier, J.J. 48, 99
Gagnon, Andre 125, 145, 155, 161
Garami, Arthur 34, 41, 42
Garbo, Greta 136, 145
Gardner, Samuel 17, 44
Garneau, Marc 162, 195
Glazounov, Alexander 22, 25, 46
Glick, Srul Irving 97
Glinka 122, 164
Glyndebourne Festival 109, 115
Goetzel, Lotte see Brott, Lotte
Goldblatt, Rose 71, 74, 146, 174
Goldschmidt, Nicholas 100
Golschmann, Vladimir 76, 79, 137, 138, 146
Goodman, Hyman 86
Goodman, Mildred 9, 21, 25, 103, 146, 179, 181
Goossens, Eugene 146
Gould, Glenn 145
Grieg, Edvard 112, 140